TOMORROW NEVER COMES...

By Derek S. Lupson

First Published in 2015 by Derek S. Lupson.

Written by Derek S. Lupson. Photographs courtesy of Derek S. Lupson.

Editing by Anne Grange at Wild Rosemary Writing Services

© Copyright Derek S. Lupson 2015

All rights reserved.

No part of this publication may be reproduced, stored in a retrieval system, or transmitted in any form without the prior permission of the author by any means. This includes electronic, mechanical, photocopying, recording, or otherwise.

Acknowledgements:

Thanks to Anne Grange of Wild Rosemary Writing Services for helping me to complete this devastating task that's travelled the world with me for over forty years.
Many thanks to my good lady wife Nesta for her unfailing support.

CONTENTS

Map of Ethiopia	Page 1
Dedication	Page 2
Introduction	Page 4
Chapter 1 Deep in the Heart of South Yorkshire	Page 5
Chapter 2 Kenya: Sleaze and Safari	Page 14
Chapter 3 Ethiopia: A Hell of a Challenge	Page 27
Chapter 4 Good Old Asgers!	Page 42
Chapter 5 The Ex-Pats	Page 52
Chapter 6 The Stallion	Page 66
Chapter 7 Assab: Customs and Corruption	Page 77
Chapter 8 Geeta	Page 93
Chapter 9 The Goods Arrive	Page 101
Chapter 10 A House of my Own!	Page 109
Chapter 11 The Great Day Dawns	Page 113
Chapter 12 Grand Opening – and a Lucky Escape	Page 127
Chapter 13 "Mr Lupson! What happened to you?"	Page 147
Chapter 14 Madam Mocambo	Page 157
Chapter 15 A Change from Egg and Chips	Page 161

Chapter 16 Haile Selassie	Page 172
Chapter 17 Lavender	Page 180
Chapter 18 A Night of Passion	Page 200
Chapter 19 Lupson in Love	Page 210
Chapter 20 The Officers' Mess	Page 224
Chapter 21 My Last Night with Lavender	Page 235
Chapter 22 The Rebellion	Page 241
Chapter 23 A Dangerous Encounter	Page 248
Chapter 24 Back to Assab	Page 259
Chapter 25 The Danakil Tribes	Page 265
Chapter 26 The Burning Cross Ceremony	Page 272
Chapter 27 Death of a Great Fighter Pilot	Page 274
Chapter 28 Lupson Leaves	Page 287
Chapter 29 Lavender in London	Page299
Epilogue: A Beginners' Guide to Ethiopia	Page 304
Further reading and information	Page 313

Map of Africa showing Ethiopia

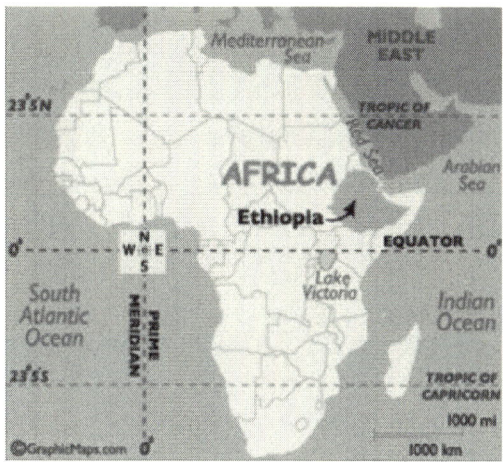

Map of Ethiopia

Map of Ethiopia, showing Addis Ababa and Debre Zeit. Assab and Massawa are now part of Eritrea.

Dedication

This book is dedicated to Madam Mocambo, who ran the local bar and brothel. She took in any woman or girl who was in trouble and gave them food and shelter until such times as their problems had been resolved. She protected the girls and allowed them to ply their trade, but only if they wished. Often the girls were very young. She treated them like a mother and was an amazing person. Sadly, she died of a liver problem some two years after I left Ethiopia.

> In this land where babies cry
> And mothers weep as they watch them die.
> As every day may be their last
> No hope for future, only the past.
>
> In mudded huts they huddle there
> Hoping for their unanswered prayer
> The sun does rise and then the moon
> Bringing some light to their darkest gloom.
>
> This wise old World does pass them by
> With little food and little pride.
> They sleep upon their precious ground
> Which soon will be their burial mound.

Dedicated to the wonderful nation of Ethiopia which the world has soon forgotten.

Mother and child: victims of the Ethiopian Famine in 1974.

Introduction

It took me a considerable time to understand that the African people are very proud, and that they did not wish to seem rude or lose face, especially to a foreigner and a white man also.

Rather than refuse to do something or reject a request for help, they would say "yes" to whatever I needed and when asked when it would happen, whatever it was that was required, they would pretend to think and then say: "Tomorrow".

It took me months before I learned that "Tomorrow never comes…"

A true story of adventure, love, lust and danger…

***

When I arrived in Ethiopia, King Haile Selassie was on the throne, and the country was ruled and reasonably stable. But it was very poor, and about to enter its most difficult period of famine and death.

When I left, the Kingdom was no more, the country was divided, millions were dead or dying, and the world was beginning to hear about Ethiopia and its famine.

A sad period in this beautiful, harsh country with its beautiful people, with a history second to none, of which Mussolini once wrote: "give me Ethiopia and I will feed the World". It could have, with proper management, at least have fed its own.

Now, through bad management, civil war, corruption, and greed, millions were about to die.

Chapter 1
Deep in the Heart of South Yorkshire

Me as a young supermarket manager, with no idea of my impending African adventure.

The Armalite rifle was forced through the window of my beaten-up old Renault Four car and rammed up my nose, forcing my head back at a very painful angle.

My car was surrounded by the rebels, all dressed in their Ethiopian Air Force Uniforms, all shouting, and very excited.

Two of their leaders were arguing whether to shoot me or not...

Here I was: a youngish retail executive, outside the rebel-held Air Force Base of Debre Zeit, deep in the heart of Ethiopia, while two rebels argued about killing me. It is at times like this that one wonders how the bloody hell one got into such a situation.

***

It all began some 4,000 miles away, deep in the heart of South Yorkshire. I was expecting a visit from our District Manager to the supermarket that I was running for the NAAFI organization. It was a special visit, as the Managing Director was with him, doing a routine inspection of the District Manager's patch, or so I thought.

My staff and I had worked hard to ensure that all was to the highest standard, and I felt proud of what we had achieved. I was in my best suit, and stood outside the shops dutifully waiting for the VIP visitors to arrive.

It was then that I noticed a small Fiat 850 car, belching black smoke and labouring under its heavy load, heading towards me. I moved forward and was about to ask the driver to move it out of the way, as I was expecting a VIP, when I realised that the District Manager was driving and our Managing Director was cramped in beside him.

They both were grinning from ear to ear, obviously at the look of disbelief on my face. Here was our MD and District Manager arriving for a VIP visit in a very old small Fiat 850.

The District Manager, Mike Gannon, introduced me to our Managing Director, Edward McGowan, and explained that his usual staff car would not start as he was about to set out to collect the MD from Doncaster train station, and, as time was short, and the only car available was his wife's shopping run-about, he had been forced to use it.

Fortunately, our MD had a good sense of humour and appreciated the funny side of it, and even though Mike had offered to get a hire car, he had insisted that the Fiat would do.

This was a strange start to a day that was about to change my life for ever.

***

Edward McGowan proved to be one of nature's gentlemen and a really nice person. He toured the premises, talking to both staff and customers, and seemed to be really enjoying the visit.

We went through to my office for coffee and to discuss the establishment's performance. The MD seemed very interested in my experience in the retail trade, and as he was about to leave, he said he thought I was the ideal person for a little job he had in mind.

He had an evil glint in his eye as we shook hands, and he said that he would be in touch in the near future.

It was all very intriguing, and in spite of questioning the District Manager the following day to try and find out what the MD had meant, Mike was also none the wiser.

***

Two days later a white envelope arrived marked Personal and Private. It was a letter from the MD, thanking me for an excellent visit, and stating that I would be invited to attend the HQ in London in the near future.

There was still no hint of what he had in mind for my future: a job that was about to change my life forever.

A further two days past and another white envelope arrived, addressed Personal and Private. I opened the letter to find the originator was a Mr Hudman, Manager Overseas Service, NAAFI HQ, London.

I was invited to attend his office for interview the following week.

Still no hint of what for.

I was interested, as the letter had come from our Overseas Division, and I had not worked for that department before.

I knew that the British Forces had bases throughout the world, and thought that perhaps I was required for Hong Kong, Cyprus, Belize, etc. etc. But still there was no hint or even rumour of what I was required for. I just had to be patient, until all was revealed.

My girlfriend was obviously also intrigued by it all, and agreed to drive me to the train station, providing that I phoned her as soon as I knew what our HQ had in mind. I was soon aboard the London express, heading for the NAAFI HQ and whatever the MD had planned for me.

***

NAAFI HQ was an impressive building with tight security. I arrived safely, still wondering what it was that the MD had in mind. "A little job", he had said.

I asked the porter to take me to the Overseas Service Department and I duly arrived outside the office of Mr Hudman, Manager of the Overseas Service, which had a very impressive door.

I knocked, and a young lady, who was his secretary, opened the door, I entered a very imposing office, with maps of the world covering the walls. This was after all, the Manager of the Overseas Service.

Hudman's secretary very kindly offered me a cup of tea, and explained that the boss was at a meeting and would be back in five minutes.

I settled down with my cup of tea and some thirty minutes later, a large well-dressed man entered and introduced himself as Mr Hudman. I did not take to the man. He was abrupt, and obviously thought himself very important.

We exchanged the usual pleasantries. It was a nice day, I had had a pleasant journey down from Doncaster, I had enjoyed the MD's visit etc. etc. All I really wanted to know was why I was sitting here.

The pleasantries finally came to an abrupt end, when Hudman said: 'I suppose you want to know what we want you to do.'

I managed a weak 'Yes please.'

Hudman stood up, and walked towards the map of Africa.

'We want you to go to Ethiopia,' he said.

He might just have well have said 'we want you to go to Mars', as the year was 1973 and most of the world had not yet heard of Ethiopia. A decade later, it would and the world's conscience would be stirred.

***

Here I was, a 31-year-old retail executive, reasonably fit, who played the usual sports, escorting a young lady from the local riding school, enjoying a good social life, and now this man wanted to change all that, and send me to darkest Africa.

Having recovered from the shock, I asked the obvious question: 'Where is Ethiopia?'

Hudman did not seem surprised at the question, but was clearly impatient to get on. He pointed to the top right-hand corner of the map of Africa, above and slightly to the left of Kenya.

Hudman brought out a more detailed map of Ethiopia, and started to explain that I was to be seconded to the Ethiopian Air Force, and would be based at their station at Debre Zeit. He had not bothered to ask if I minded going to Africa, or being seconded to a strange Air Force in a strange country.

My mouth had gone dry, and I began to get excited at the thought of the proposed adventure in darkest Africa. If only I had known what was ahead of me I should really have declined his kind offer and got back to the safety of my friends in Doncaster.

I was younger then and still held the spirit of adventure close to my heart.

Hudman continued with his briefing.

'We want you to go to Ethiopia and train the Imperial Ethiopian Air Force to run their own organisation based on the NAAFI concepts.'

I could not believe my ears, I was to go to this strange land and train an Air Force. Did he really mean me?

They must have made a mistake.

The Manager of the NAAFI Overseas Service saw that I was a little shocked and surprised by the thought of going off to a country that I had never heard of, and asked his secretary to bring me another cup of tea.

It was obvious that I was not going to be given the chance to say no. It had been automatically assumed that I would welcome the opportunity of serving on the African Continent.

Mr Hudman indicated that I should sit, and he began to brief me about the project in hand. Some two years previously, Iskinder (known as Scinda) Desta, the grandson of the King of Ethiopia Haile Selassie had attended the Royal Naval College at Devonport to train in naval tactics etc. During his training, he had made use of the NAAFI facilities and thought it was an excellent organisation. So he wanted the Royal Ethiopian Navy to have its own canteens and shops based on the NAAFI concept.

Scinda Desta did not actually pass the Devonport training course, but the fact that he had attended the English Royal Naval College ensured that on his return to Ethiopia, he was made Admiral of the Fleet by King Haile Selassie, his grandfather.

Little did I realise that within the next year, I would have the dubious pleasure of meeting Scinda Desta and being a guest at sumptuous dinner at his residence at the Port of Massawa, surrounded by beautiful ladies.

On the Admiral's return to Ethiopia, he had explained the role of the NAAFI to his Grandfather, and they both thought it would be a good idea to improve the welfare of his Forces. NAAFI was contacted and invited to run an organisation for the Ethiopian Navy.

NAAFI initially declined the offer, as it was outside their normal remit.

The Admiral would not take no for an answer, and the Chairman of NAAFI was invited to attend the Foreign Office to explain what was going on.

The Foreign Office had received a stern letter from the Ethiopian authorities demanding to know why NAAFI had not accepted their request for help in setting up the Ethiopian Forces Trading organisation.

It was made quite clear to our Chairman that the Foreign Office held Ethiopia in great esteem, and they would not wish us to upset them in any way. The Chairman was invited to rethink NAAFI's refusal to help. It would be a very good idea if the NAAFI did as the Admiral requested.

So the job of setting up the first Ethiopian aspect of its trading organisation was given to Norman Lee, an ageing Supervisor of NAAFI.

A suitable relation to the Royal Family was found to act as manager and a small Naval Shop was established at the Ethiopian Naval base at Massawa. The staff members were trained by NAAFI, and NAAFI also arranged for supplies to be transported from their warehouse in Kenya to the Ethiopian Naval shop.

Although it was a very small initial operation, it became quite successful and soon became firmly established and appreciated by the naval personnel.

It was due to the success of the Ethiopian Naval operation that I was now being invited to go to Ethiopia to set up a full trading organisation for King Haile Selassie's much loved Royal Air Force.

I was to go to the Ethiopian Air Force HQ at Debre Zeit and establish a Supermarket, and once this was operational, I was to take over their canteens and provide a full refreshment service at two locations within the Air Force base.

I could not believe my ears: Hudman was still talking, assuming that I knew all about setting up a business in darkest Africa.

The job should not be too hard for a man of my experience, Hudman continued. All I had to do was to establish a thriving business for the King of Ethiopia's military forces, deep in the heart of Ethiopia. Just like that!

I was offered another much needed cup of tea before I departed our NAAFI HQ, still in a state of shock.

I had not a clue of what I was being led into, or how the experience would change my life forever.

When I returned to Doncaster after the initial interview, my girlfriend thought that I should go to Ethiopia, as it was a chance that should not be missed. After all, I had been selected personally by the Managing Director and it was a chance to enhance my career.

Two weeks later, I was again summoned to NAAFI HQ in London. This time I was to have a full medical, and have both arms pumped full of various injections to protect my body against the various ills of Africa.

Our medical people had not sent anyone to Ethiopia for many years, and after discussions with the foreign office, it was decided that I should have every type of inoculation known to man to protect me from every possible African disease.

I do not remember travelling back to Doncaster, as the injections had a very powerful effect. Two days later, I managed to get out of bed, having suffered a minor dose of a number of ills that are associated with hotter climes. I later discovered that I should not have had so many types of inoculations on the same day.

It took a further five days to feel better, but I still wondered at the wisdom of accepting the job.

There were hundreds of questions that remained unanswered, questions that our HQ should have been able to answer, but all they would say was that I was not to worry, as I would be fully briefed by Norman Lee, the supervisor of NAAFI East Africa. I would also have the full support and backing from the NAAFI organisation. They would be behind me. They would be 3,000 miles behind me!

My posting orders finally arrived, together with my new passport and visa for entry into Ethiopia. I was to fly to Kenya the following week and spend ten days getting acclimatized and receiving briefings and training from Norman Lee and his staff.

***

One week later I set off on the train to London and eventually to Heathrow Airport. Having bid a tearful farewell to my girlfriend and my friends from the local Riding Club, I was finally on my way to Africa.

Although I was upset at the thought of not seeing my friends for a while, I felt excited at the prospect of visiting a new land.

I had not travelled on a Jumbo Jet before, and I could not believe its size as I gazed from the airport lounge at the engineers making the final fuel drop and getting the plane ready for our flight. We were eventually called forward and I was even more impressed as I entered the aircraft. It was huge.

The service was excellent, and I was soon tucking into a nice meal, followed by a bottle of wine, a large brandy, and lots of coffee. I then settle down to watch the movie.

I awoke to the Tannoy announcing that we would be landing in Kenya in one hour, and breakfast was about to be served. I made a dash for the loo, had a quick wash, and began to feel better. Breakfast was served, and I felt ready to face whatever Africa had to offer, or so I thought.

The aircraft made a perfect landing and here I was. Lupson had arrived in the land of real Jumbos. My adventure was about to begin. There would be no turning back now. Lupson was in Africa.

Chapter 2
Kenya: Sleaze and Safari

Mayfair Hotel, Nairobi: My first taste of Africa.

The doors of the superb jumbo jet were flung open and I was immediately struck by the heat. It was hot, bloody hot and I had not come dressed for a hot climate.

Typically, our NAAFI HQ had failed to mention what type of clothing I should have brought. The Overseas Department had been sending staff all over the world for years and seldom got their briefings right.

I was later to discover that they had got quite a lot of points wrong. What a shower they were! I was assured by our personnel officer that they had not lost anyone yet. But there was always a first time, wasn't there?

I staggered from the plane, found my luggage, and fought my way through the customs and immigration. As I staggered towards the exit, I was immediately set upon by dozens of would-be taxi drivers, all wanting to take me to wherever I wanted to go at a very cheap price. They were arguing amongst themselves and all trying to get my attention. It was hot and very noisy and smelly.

Thank god a friendly face suddenly appeared. It was John Singleton, our local auditor, who had been sent to pick me up and take me to Norman Lee. He had been delayed by a road accident and apologized for the delay. The Taxi drivers were still fighting over my trade. John helped to drag me and my luggage through the crowd to his car, and the Taxi drivers finally got the message that I did not need their services.

I had not seen John for many years and he welcomed me to Kenya. Norman Lee had asked him to take me to the NAAFI HQ at East Camp, where he was waiting to meet me. As John drove from the Airport at Nairobi, I could not help but notice how soon the roads began to deteriorate, as did the surrounding buildings. We headed towards East Camp and the surroundings got worse. Concrete buildings were replaced by wooden shacks, and as we got closer to East Camp, these shacks were replaced by cardboard and scrap metal. The whole area approaching East Camp was an appalling mess. (Or so I thought at the time. I did not realise that much worse was to come when I would eventually arrive in Ethiopia.)

I had been around a bit, but I had never seen such poverty, and the smell was awful. This had to be the end of the world. How could people live like this? Hundreds of people lived in this shanty town, with only the odd stand-pipe for their water supply. Adults, children of all ages, dogs, goats, and fowl all seemed to exist in this awful cess pit with no sanitation.

Although there was rubbish and filth everywhere, there was no sign of malnutrition, and the children seemed happy playing amongst the filth. There was even the odd drunk lying around, proving that they must have had some form of income, if only to purchase the booze.

John noticed the look on my face as we passed through the slum. He said that the situation appeared to be getting worse. Even in his short time in Kenya, he had noticed that the cardboard city was growing, with more and more young people joining it.

It had only been a few short years since Kenya had achieved its independence from Great Britain, but there were increasing signs that all was not well, and the infrastructure had deteriorated alarmingly.

The roads were not being repaired or cleaned, and even the government buildings were crumbling fast, even though Kenya was receiving vast sums of money from the O.A.U. and Great Britain.

This money was obviously not being used to support the people of Kenya, and nobody seemed to care.

It was no longer safe to walk the streets of Nairobi alone. Even in daylight, you risked being mugged, or worse.

At night, it was sensible to drive as close as possible to your destination, ensuring that your car doors were locked, the windows were closed, and that you had company. A large dog would also help as a deterrent.

Crime in Kenya was on the increase and even the law enforcers were corrupt.

It was sad to hear this from John. Not too long ago, Kenya was considered the "Jewel in the Crown" of Africa, but that was when it was under the rule of the British, and they had long gone.

The old and wise would have preferred the good days when Britain maintained the country but now they had freedom, freedom to what? Die?

As we approached the main gate of East Camp, I noticed how suddenly the environment changed. It was clean and tidy. There was a smartly dressed guard at the gate, who stood to attention as we approached. He was very polite, and he checked our identity cards and raised the barrier. As we passed, he saluted.

It was obviously very British here, and it was good to see that some of the standards were being maintained.

The whole camp was the same: very neat, clean, and tidy, and in stark contrast to the scene we had just passed.

John escorted me to the office of the East African NAAFI Supervisor, Norman Lee. We still had an organisation in Kenya. Even though the majority of the British Forces had left, there was still some remaining, training the Kenyan Forces.

In addition, NAAFI supplied the Kenyan NAAFI equivalent and also trained their managers and staff. They also operated a large warehouse in the barracks.

We took advantage of the situation to supply the neighbouring Ugandan Forces.

Idi Amin had also trained in England, and when he conducted the coup, took over the country, and elected himself president, he immediately promoted himself from Corporal to General and also awarded himself some medals, which upset the British.

He became a tyrant and ruled the country with the backing of the Ugandan military. He kept the military happy by supplying them with luxury items and lots of free booze and fags, most of which were supplied by NAAFI through its Kenyan Warehouse.

Every month NAAFI dispatched a train load of supplies to Uganda.

They even supplied Amin with bicycles, which were used by his troops to travel around the country, raping and murdering anyone who got in the way or stood up against Amin and his thugs.

The matter of supply eventually came to light and questions were asked in the British parliament. It was an embarrassing time for NAAFI and they were soon forced to stop supplying the Ugandan military.

Some years later, Idi Amin was forced out of the country having lost the backing of his military. NAAFI had stopped supplying his troops with the luxuries which kept them happy, and this may have contributed to his downfall.

As we entered Norman Lee's office, he arose from behind his desk and greeted me. He was every part a small man, but with an arrogance that I was to cross sometime later. He was the "Lord White Man", showing the blacks how it should be done. I was starting to make a habit of not liking some of the NAAFI senior managers.

Norman handed me an itinerary which his admin official had prepared. I was to remain in Kenya for ten days, during which time I would be trained in the ways of Africa. I would also be allowed to see a bit of Kenya at the weekend.

The effects of the journey were beginning to catch up with me, and it obviously showed. Norman took me outside and introduced me to his admin official, who would take care of my training needs.

John Cholerton was the admin official for East Africa. He was a nice bloke. We hadn't met before, but soon became good friends. We both had friends in the midlands, as he was from Nottingham, not too far from Doncaster. It transpired that neither of us liked his boss Norman Lee.

After checking my various documents, John also noticed that I was beginning to flag and said he would take me to my hotel to allow me to rest. I really was feeling tired and the heat was getting to me. John brought his car around to the front of the office. I climbed in and we set off through the city. This time we headed for the tourist area, a very smart part of Nairobi.

We arrived at a superb hotel surrounded by exotic gardens. It was owned by a Kenyan Indian business man and was kept to a very high standard. I later discovered that most of the successful businesses in Kenya were run by the Indian community. They seemed to have taken over where the British had left off, including most of the rackets and underworld exploits. Drugs, prostitution, protection and vast property deals were all controlled by the Indian communities, a form of Mafia.

We entered the smart hotel entrance and were met by a chap who appeared to be six foot tall and six foot across, a tough looking sly bastard. He was the receptionist and obviously also took care of the security of the front desk and entrance.

He welcomed us both with a large grin that was not reflected in his eyes.

The man had my booking and I signed the register. John Cholerton said that he would pick me up at nine o'clock the following morning, ensured that all was well with my hotel, and departed.

I went to my room, had a quick wash, and then returned to the reception to check on meal times etc. The big man was still there, with his gold-plated teeth and menacing smile. I mentally christened him "The Big One". He told me the times of meals, but as I was about to return to my room, The Big One asked me if I required any other services. He said it in a leering way and I was unsure as to what he meant. He drew back a curtain behind the reception, and there stood five scantily dressed girls, all smiling, and offering their wares.

'They will take care of your every need,' The Big One said. 'You can have them one at a time or all at once, at a price of course.'

All of the girls were quite ugly, although most had very big boobs and good bodies.

It was a bit of a shock, being confronted like this by the as the Big One had done and I was a bit taken aback.

'It's very kind of you and your girls,' I said. 'But I've been travelling for a long time now, and I'm far too tired to take advantage of your combined offer.'

The last thing I felt like, having travelled for the past twenty four hours or so was to get my leg over! I needed a shower and sleep.

'When I feel rested I may take them up on their offer,' I made my excuses and left the lobby.

The Big One seemed a little upset at my declining his girls, but when I explained how tired I was, this seemed to placate him.

But this was a big mistake, as I had to try and avoid him for the next ten days, making excuses whenever our paths crossed as to why I did not have time to screw his girls – neither one at a time or all at once! I did not fancy either option, as they were no more attractive on later occasions than the first time I saw them.

Having escaped from the reception, I returned to my room, had a long hot shower and lay on my bed.

I awoke some time later, not knowing where I was but feeling a lot better. I took another shower, and shaved and dressed for dinner.

I walked through to the garden area and watched the guests enjoying a late swim in the hotel pool. The gardens were superb and full of beautifully coloured birds (of the feathered type). I ordered a gin and tonic and settled down to study the dinner menu.

The pool had a sauna adjacent to it and as I sipped my Gin and Tonic, the door opened and out stepped a beautiful Indian lady. She was tall and elegant and walked in a lithe, sensual way that drew the attention of all males in the area. She noticed me admiring her and smiled, obviously enjoying the moment.

'Don't even think about it, Sir,' a voice whispered in my ear. The waiter had reappeared and noticed my admiration of this beautiful creature. 'She is the woman of the owner and he is a very dangerous man. May I suggest you stay away from her, Sir?'

In view of the size of the receptionist, I didn't want to cross the owner! I decided to heed the waiter's advice and thanked him. But she really was beautiful.

She passed very close to me with a sly smile on her face. She exaggerated her walk as she passed. As she approached the hotel, a good-looking playboy type appeared on the steps and it was obvious that she was his. He was clearly filthy rich, very fit, and they deserved one another. I would be wise to stay far away. Even in this harsh, beautiful country, where animals hunted for suitable partners, it was sometimes wise not to try your luck.

I ordered the largest steak on the menu with full trimmings. I was suddenly very hungry. The meal was excellent and this was followed by a large brandy and coffee.

Darkness had fallen and it was a lovely warm night. The smell of the gardens and the atmosphere was fantastic. I felt content with the world and decided to go to bed. It had been a long hot day and I was very tired.

***

I slept the sleep of the godly and when I woke again, I didn't know where I was or what time of day it was. The journey had taken its toll and jet lag was certainly affecting me.

I remembered that I was in darkest Africa, alone, and missing my friends in the UK. I had yet another shower and went through to breakfast.

The fresh fruit, hot coffee and eggs and bacon revived my spirits. I began to enjoy the thought of the adventure that lay before me.

My car arrived, driven by one of our local staff, a happy chappie, who did not stop talking for the whole journey to the office.

We sped through the awakening city of Nairobi and I saw some odd sights. It was certainly different and I had not got used to the heat and the smell of abject poverty. It was a strange smell that seemed to cling to your hair and clothing.

I still did not realise that I would experience far worse in the coming months.

I spent the hot day being briefed by all concerned on how the NAAFI Overseas operation worked: supplies, staffing, customs, importation, etc. etc. and the day flew by.

At the end of the day, my new colleagues and friends suggested that we explore the city of Nairobi that very night. It was agreed that they would collect me from my hotel at eight o'clock.

I returned to my hotel, and made the usual excuses for not wanting to screw the receptionist's girls, set the alarm clock, laid on the bed, and fell asleep.

I awoke to the sound of my alarm clock, had a quick hot shower, and prepared myself for a night out on the town with the lads.

The lads arrived and all seemed in good spirits: watch out Nairobi, the lads were about to paint the town red!

It was a hot night and we decided to go on a club crawl. The beer was cool and good, and we consumed vast quantities, as lads do.

We eventually ended up at the notorious Star Light Club. It was very rough, very loud, and very full, mainly with local prostitutes of all shapes and sizes and looks.

It was a sleazy place, to say the least, full of people determined to have a good time, no matter what the cost in health or money.

We met a British businessman who was well pissed, and being held up by two local girls.

He was a hell of a character and known by my colleagues. He regularly visited the clubs of Nairobi during his business trips to Kenya and enjoyed the company of the girls. He actually bragged that he had caught VD on a number of occasions, but he was not bothered, as penicillin had soon cleared it up. This was before the world was to learn the curse of AIDS.

I doubt if he is still alive. If he has not succumbed to disease, he would have been destroyed by the drink.

He really was a stupid prat and the last we saw of him, he was being dragged outside by the two prostitutes to a waiting taxi. He was determined to screw them both but I doubt if he ever made it. It was a classic case of a Brit trying to keep his end up.

The girls in the nightclub were not a pretty sight. Even though it was quite dark and we were well pissed, we could not fancy any of them. They all wore blonde wigs and lots of make-up. Their African features did not go with their blonde wigs and they would have looked much better without them.

They were a determined bunch, all out to earn a shilling or two. We spent a considerable amount of time pushing the girls away, but they would not take no for an answer and were becoming a pest.

Two of them started fighting over poor old John Cholerton, who just stood there, totally pissed, and bemused at the scene surrounding him. Both were trying to pull him away from the other, and it was then that they began to fight. While they fought, we decided that we'd had enough for one night and it was time to escape.

I don't remember travelling back to the hotel, but I awoke the next day, hung over and, thank god, alone.

The next few days zoomed by, with lots of studying and briefings, and the weekend was soon upon us.

My new work colleagues had become my friends, and we all decided to experience a mini safari over the weekend. We would all go down to Tsavo Game Park and spend a weekend at the Water Hole Hotel.

In view of the heat, we decided that we should set off early in the morning, and the lads picked me up at 0700hrs on Saturday morning. John Singleton was driving, and he seemed adept at missing the potholes and the local inhabitants.

Our car sped out of Nairobi on the main and only road towards Mombasa. I was still fascinated by the sights of Africa, and early in the morning, it had a fantastic feel. Even with all its poverty, it was a beautiful, yet harsh country.

We were all in good spirits and enjoying the start of our adventure. As we drove out of

Nairobi we soon entered the scrubland and saw many wrecked cars and trucks.

John explained that there was little or no control over the state of the vehicles in Kenya and that most of drivers had not been trained or indeed had a license or insurance. So when a truck was badly damaged, they just abandoned it in the scrub.

There were often fatalities and quite often, people were buried by the side of their vehicles. No one seemed to care very much.

It was a beautiful day, hot with clear skies. We passed many local people, and it was an amazing sight to see the Maasai warriors in their red robes, carrying their spears. They were magnificent.

After an hour of bumping over very rough roads, we came to the entrance to the National Park and turned off the road onto a dirt track, which thankfully, had a sign directing us to our hotel.

The park was fantastic and we soon saw all types of wildlife. Antelope, hyenas, lions, and at last the fantastic sight of elephants. In their natural homeland, they were a beautiful sight. We were also impressed by the wide variety of birds: all shapes and sizes, from scavengers to graceful heron types. It was magnificent to see so much wildlife in its natural habitat. We were impressed by the giraffe, and surprised how fast and gracefully it travelled.

We were like a bunch of excited kids, and why not? We were in Africa, and it was great to be alive. If you have never been to Africa, you must go and experience it.

We turned down yet another track and there stood our hotel. It was a good hotel and its balconies overlooked a large watering hole. The Manager welcomed us, and invited us to have some cool drinks, which we did with much pleasure.

It was very hot and dusty, and so we all took advantage of the showers in our rooms.

Having showered and been refreshed, we went through for lunch. We really enjoyed the barbecued meat and fresh salads, followed by a few beers.

We decided to drive and explore a bit more, into the heart of this magnificent park, while it was still light, and as we travelled, we saw more African sights: herds of elephants, deer, and the odd lion. Some lions were still asleep, obviously letting their lunches digest until it was time to hunt again. Once the lions were full, they appeared to be of no threat to other wildlife, which came quite close to them without showing any fear.

They must have known that the lions had eaten and did not wish to chase after them for the kill. We travelled on through the bush, fascinated by all that we saw. We then turned back towards our hotel.

We had been told that as soon as it got dark, most of the types of animals would come to the water hole in front of our hotel, and that we should not miss this spectacular event.

We arrived safely back at the hotel as it was getting dusk. We all went through to our respective rooms, showered, and changed for dinner.

The dining room overlooked the veranda, which in turn overlooked the watering hole. The atmosphere was great and we were fascinated by watching the arrivals of the animals, all trying to quench their thirst and stay safe.

The meal was superb, and we all had many beers before moving out to the veranda. The other hotel guests were also sitting around the veranda, awaiting the arrival of Africa's fantastic array of wildlife.

There appeared to be a strict pecking order, as each variety of animal came cautiously out of the bush and into the floodlit area, to quench the thirst of the African heat. It was a fantastic experience and one that I shall never forget. The evening was superb and the sounds and smells of the jungle were a welcome interlude, prior to my departure to the strain of what lay ahead of me in Ethiopia.

We all sat spellbound as Africa performed in front of us.

Elephants in front of Mount Kenya

I awoke to a banging on my door. All the lads were up and ready for breakfast. It was an excellent cooked breakfast, with fresh fruit.

We packed our belongings and went to pay our bills. It was then than one of our party discovered that his wallet was missing.

In spite of a search and much argument with the management, who assured us that nothing like this had ever happened before, and that all of his staff were honest and trustworthy, the wallet was never found. We had a whip-around and paid the bill, and set off back to Nairobi.

Apart from the missing wallet, it had been a superb weekend, and the memories of the Kenyan Bush will remain with me forever.

Chapter 3
Ethiopia: A Hell of a Challenge

A postcard showing Addis Ababa in 1973

Departure day finally arrived and I set off for the airport, accompanied by Norman Lee, the NAAFI Command Supervisor for East Africa. His driver loaded my cases into the car, and we set off at a hell of a pace through the suburbs of Nairobi.

I had bid a fond farewell to my new found friends and set off my adventure as adviser to the Ethiopian Air Force. I was still young and naïve.

The Ethiopian Airline 737 roared down the runway and climbed into the bright blue skies of Africa.

The aircraft banked suddenly and headed north. Mount Kenya soon came into view, and its sight was breathtaking. It was beautiful with its contrasting colours, basking in the early morning sunshine. There were extremes of colours, from the grassy planes to the dark rock, to the snow-clad peak. It was magnificent, and I was very excited at the thought of the adventure that lay before me.

The plane headed west towards Ethiopia, and we were soon flying over the northern hills of Kenya which were, in contrast to the burnt planes of central and Southern Kenya, green and lush.

Lunch was served by the beautiful Ethiopian air stewardesses. I was immediately impressed by their beauty. They did not have the Negroid features of most Western African Nations. The Italian influence over the centuries had given them much more refined features, and they were tall and very elegant, and moved through the aircraft with a graceful air.

Norman Lee was his usual arrogant self, but we did manage to exchange a few pleasantries. He was obviously in a good mood, and was about to show young Lupson how things should be done.

The pilot announced that we were approaching Addis Ababa International airport, and would we kindly ensure that our safety belts were fastened? The aircraft came down to a smooth landing, and we were soon bouncing along the runway.

Lupson had landed in Ethiopia.

The aircraft came to a halt adjacent to the terminal, and the doors opened. Heat gushed in. The air hostesses were very pleasant and welcomed us to Ethiopia. They hoped that we would enjoy our visit, and thanked us for travelling on Ethiopian Airways.

We strolled across the tarmac, and my first impressions were that the surrounding countryside was quite green. I didn't realise that Addis Ababa was quite high in the hills, and that it was the middle of the rainy season.

But little rain had fallen, certainly not enough to overcome the impending disaster of failed crops, famine, disease and the death of millions.

As we entered the terminal building, a larger than life, lumbering Ethiopian Major rushed forward to greet us. His face was split from ear to ear with a genuine grin of welcome.

This was my trainee, Major Asgedom Teshome, and I liked him from the first moment we met. He was obviously very nervous and excited, and could not stop talking.

'Welcome to Ethiopia, Mr Lupson!'

This was punctuated by many salutes.

'How are you, Mr Lee? How are you, Mr Lupson?'

The poor chap was very, very excited.

'Welcome on behalf of His Majesty's Imperial Ethiopian Air Force.'

We thanked him for his warm welcomes, and at last, he started to calm down.

By this time, our baggage had arrived, and Asgedom had gathered it up, put it on a cart and started to direct us towards the exit. We felt like royalty, with no customs or immigration formalities. Asgedom was leading us through it all – a right Royal Welcome!

We were about to go through the exit, when all hell broke loose, and we were suddenly set upon by the Airport Security, Customs and Immigration, all shouting at us, and demanding to know what the hell we thought we were doing, as the whole airport came to a standstill. Asgedom had got us into real trouble, as was to be the case on numerous cases in the future. We were, to say the least, embarrassed.

Asgedom was explaining in his native tongue that we were guests of the King, etc. but the officials didn't seem too impressed, and led Asgedom away, and took me and Norman Lee back to the end of the Immigration queue.

Norman Lee was red-faced and obviously troubled by it all. But I couldn't stop laughing. It was a hilarious situation. I appreciated it all the more, as it had upset Norman Lee. He needed bringing down to size, and the airport officials had done it. Our fellow passengers all stared at us, and this added to our embarrassment. Dear old Asgers, as I came to call him, had made my arrival a truly unforgettable one.

We started clearing Immigration, and were carefully questioned by the Immigration Officer. The Immigration Officer then discovered that, although I was supposed to work in Ethiopia, I only had a tourist visa. I had only been in the country for half an hour or so, and we had caused disruption throughout the airport, and to crown it all, I had the wrong visa. They were really pissed off with Lupson already.

They all spoke very good English and expressed their feelings very well.

Thank god Asgers was then released from custody, having explained our mission in detail. He was backing out of the office of the senior Immigration Officer, bowing, and thanking him, still explaining that we were guests of His Majesty, and here to support the Imperial Ethiopian Air Force.

The officials had accepted Asgers' explanation, and we were finally released into his care, after assuring them that the visa problem would be sorted out within the next few days, possibly tomorrow!

This was the first time that Asgers had got me into trouble, but, as already mentioned, it would not be the last.

Asgers was clearly very embarrassed and kept apologising, saying that it had all been a misunderstanding, and that he was truly sorry that we had been embarrassed.

Asgers led the way to our transport. He had kindly brought his own car, as it would be more comfortable. The car was a mid-fifties Opel, which had seen much better days.

The suspension had obviously gone and there were signs of rust throughout. But it was the thought that counted.

We soon discovered that the seats had also broken and had no springs left.

It was in this vehicle that we set off for my new home in Debre Zeit.

Asgers set off from the airport, and I was very impressed with the area surrounding the airport. There was a wide, double-laned road heading for the city centre, and it was well cared for.

The car headed towards the western side of Addis Ababa, and we came upon the palace of His Imperial Majesty, King Haile Selassie. It was a beautiful building and had marvellous gardens, surrounded by a large spiked iron fence, decorated with a spear motif.

The spikes came in very useful for the King, as some twelve years earlier, he had ordered that the leaders of the student revolt should have their heads cut off, and displayed on the spikes as a deterrent for any other would-be trouble makers. I was to learn the whole story at a later date, and I will reveal all later. It did show that the King and his government were quite ruthless – and in such a primitive country, I suppose they felt they had to be, to maintain some form of control.

We rumbled on, past the palace, and turned west, towards Debre Zeit. As we left the surroundings of the King's sumptuous palace, we headed for the outskirts of the city. Everything started to deteriorate. The roads were not repaired, shanty huts made of rusting metal and wood replaced the city's stone building, and the local population looked in poor health, living in a different world to the area surrounding the King's palace.

It was a sad sight, with the local population living in slums, with no sanitation, little food, and that awful stench that is peculiar to this type of environment.

Norman Lee was deep in conversation with Asgers, questioning him on how the project was progressing since his last visit. Asgers looked very uncomfortable, and I started to get worried.

Norman Lee was asking detailed questions but was not getting any straight answer. Asgers was saying that we would see Tomorrow. That word came up too often. Asgers was looking even more sheepish, and I worried more.

We left the outskirts of Addis, and came out into the open countryside. It was quite flat, and looked very dry.

Asgers' car was making a difficult job of negotiating the roads, and we were being thrown around. We were very hot and uncomfortable.

We passed through numerous shanty towns and they all appeared to be in a very poor state. Chickens, goats and people all lived in the same run-down makeshift shacks. It was a sad sight.

We left the plains surrounding Addis, and began to climb to higher ground, and eventually arrived on the outskirts of Debre Zeit.

After the usual shanty huts, we came upon stone-built accommodation that was a vast improvement on the makeshift shacks.

'You must be very tired after your journey,' Asgers said. 'I'll take you directly to your hotel.'

Norman Lee was still pressing him for details of progress, but Asgers would not be put off. All would be revealed tomorrow.

We arrived at the smartest hotel in the whole area, and it was pretty awful. A half-naked guard, armed with a spear, guarded the entrance, and he looked quite menacing.

The hotel was of Italian design, and very run-down, it was run by a half-Italian Ethiopian, who did his best to achieve a reasonable standard. It was still very bad in comparison to Nairobi though.

The hotel had a strange musty smell and its furnishings were old and stained. The whole place was in need of decoration.

The owner carried our luggage to our rooms, with Asgers close by, helping, and still chatting nervously. He still evaded Norman Lee's questions and insisted that all would be revealed tomorrow, at our meeting with the Colonel of the Debre Zeit Base. Asgedom was very nervous and backed out of the hotel, trying to escape from Norman Lee. Norman was not happy.

We agreed to meet for supper, and I returned to my room. I felt in need of a bath. Although there was water, it was cold, and the bath was stained through old age. This was to be my home for the next two months, and it was pretty grotty, to say the least.

I felt a bit better after my cold bath and wash, and went out onto the balcony to survey the village of Debre Zeit. My new home had a harsh magic that I fell in love with – a place that I shall never forget.

At the appointed hour, I joined Norman Lee in the hotel lounge for a gin and tonic, and we went through to the dining room for supper. The menu was very basic and had an Italian flavour, but it was edible, and I was very hungry.

We passed the evening chatting about the day's events, and Norman could still not appreciate the funny side of our arrival at Addis Airport. He was very worried about the lack of information forthcoming from Asgers, and the following day, his fears were to prove correct. We were both tired and went off to bed.

I awoke during the night, being attacked by mosquitos, and I decided to leave the light on in a vain attempt to distract them away from me. In the morning, I surveyed the damage to my body. The mosquitos had really enjoyed themselves and I was covered in bites. I had a lukewarm bath, shaved and staggered down for breakfast. Hot coffee, two boiled eggs and toast revived my spirits, and even Norman seemed in a better mood.

Asgedom duly arrived, and brought a ray of sunshine as he appeared though the hotel entrance, with his inevitable grin spread from ear to ear. He was still nervous, and enquired if we had slept well. I explained that I had been attacked by the mosquitos, and he went through to the hotel owner to sort it out. It was agreed that my room would be sprayed, and a net provided for me.

Asgers said that the project officer was waiting to meet us, and it had also been arranged for us to meet the Base Commander.

We left the hotel and got into Asgers' old jalopy, and set off for the Air Force base. Asgers' car bumped over the pot holes of the road through Debre Zeit. The town was like something out of the Wild West, with wooden shacks on stilts, and the occasional brick-built building. I was fascinated by it all. There were all sorts of people, dressed in all sorts of clothes, from loin cloths to jeans, and some of the women bared their breasts. There were all sorts of animals wandering freely, scavenging for food. Chickens, goats, even the odd cow – and dogs roamed everywhere. Debre Zeit was the main market town for the area, and it was very busy. I was fascinated by it all.

Our car left the village and headed north, some two miles up the road. On the right hand side was the entrance to the Imperial Ethiopian Air Force base, and it looked very smart, in comparison to the surrounding area. Asgers' car was obviously recognised, and the guard came to a smart attention, and saluted and waved us through.

The King had obviously decided to invest in his Air Force, and the whole area was kept to a very good standard.

We drove past storage areas and into the admin area, with its imposing HQ. Asgers ushered us into the HQ building, looking even more nervous. He knocked on the door of the project officers, and we were invited in by an orderly. The Colonel rose from his desk to greet us. This was Colonel Mengistu Woldameron, and he was totally different to Asgers. He smiled, but there was no warmth in this greeting. His eyes were cold and steely, and he evaded looking at me directly. I did not take to this man on my first meeting, or at any time in the future. He was not a man whom I could trust.

Mengistu was obviously a bit of a player. He had spent a considerable time in the USA. He was very slim, very smart, and obviously very sure of himself.

Norman Lee and the Colonel obviously didn't get on too well with one another. We were formally introduced and offered refreshment. The orderly served some very strong coffee, and we were invited to sit around the conference table. There followed an embarrassing session, during which I thought Asgers would pass out. Every question that Norman raised was met by a polite smile, as the Colonel evaded giving a direct answer. There had been little progress since Norman Lee had last visited. Everything was in-hand and would commence Tomorrow.

Norman was getting more and more hot under the collar, and I could not understand why. The colonel had, after all, promised that all would be sorted out the following day. I was naïve and blissfully unaware of the fact that tomorrow never comes in Ethiopia.

I would eventually learn that the Ethiopians were a very proud race, and that rather than lose face or embarrass foreigners, they would promise that it would happen tomorrow. It was the eternal hope of Ethiopia that things would happen and improve tomorrow. Sadly Tomorrow has still not come for Ethiopia.

More coffee arrived, and the conference continued. Norman was doing his best to remain calm and polite, but was finding it increasingly difficult.

The Colonel was obviously well trained, and maintained a calm attitude towards Norman, which seemed to upset him even more.

There was a knock at the door and a smart aide appeared to say that the General was now ready to meet us, and would we all follow him to the General's office?

As we were ushered into the office, the General arose from his desk. He was shorter than Norman and appeared to have the same style and arrogance of small men who have power. He greeted us, showing slight distain for Norman, and ordered coffee for us all.

There followed a similar meeting to that held with the Colonel. Little progress had been made, but tomorrow, work would commence, staff would be provided, etc. etc. Poor old Asgers looked more and more embarrassed by it all, but managed the odd sheepish grin.

Norman was finding it difficult to maintain his temper, realising that all of the promises made to him during his last visit had failed to materialise.

He gave me a look of despair and I must confess that I had no sympathy for him. He was obviously not liked in Ethiopia, and I could understand their feelings.

We were obviously wasting our time, and thank god the meeting came to an end, as the General had to fly off to another base in the North. He was very polite and thanked us for our visit.

As we left his office, Norman was very quiet, obviously biting his tongue. He looked furious.

We returned to the Colonel's office and it was decided that we should have some lunch. We visited the HQ's café area, and had some sandwiches and more coffee. Our conversation was restrained but polite.

Norman then asked to visit the site of the first project that I was due to commence work on, a supermarket for the Imperial Ethiopian Air Force. I thought that Asgers would die: he choked on his sandwich and looked even more worried.

The Colonel agreed that we should visit the site of the supermarket. He explained that there was obviously a lot to be done, but that Asgers would escort us there straight away.

We thanked the Colonel for lunch and set off again in Asgers' old car.

We headed back towards the village of Debre Zeit, and headed slightly south. On the outskirts of the village, there was a large accommodation area, which was fenced and patrolled by the Air Force guards. We turned into the area, and once again, Asgers was recognised and the guard stood to attention, opened the barrier, and rushed us through. We climbed slightly uphill, and the car bumped over the poorly maintained road, and came to a halt outside a large run-down building. This was the old Ethiopian Air Force Officer's Mess, and had not been used for a couple of years since the King had provided his Air Force with a very smart facility, half a mile down the road.

Asgers was looking sheepish. It was obvious that he had not been near the place in weeks.

He unlocked the door and ushered us into a large building which had obviously seen better days. Not a good start.

We wandered through the old building and it really was in a poor state. Obviously, since the building had been abandoned, nature had taken over, and dampness and mildew were evident.

The walls had holes and the windows had been broken.

This was to be the pride and joy of the Ethiopian Trading Organisation, and it required a miracle. I thought that Norman Lee was about to blow a fuse – his face was as dark as thunder, and I really felt sorry for poor old Asgers. I was beginning to feel sorry for myself.

It was after all, my project, and it was I who had to sort it out.

We now realised why our Ethiopian friend had been so evasive to Norman's questions. If anything, the situation had deteriorated since Norman's last visit. He had been promised everything would be started tomorrow, but nothing had been done.

Tomorrow had seemed a long way off, but I was here in Ethiopia, I was here to show the Ethiopian Air Force how to run their own trading organisation based on the NAAFI concept of welfare for service personnel.

I had not realised that I would have to build their shop, supply the fittings, supply the decoration, arrange bank credits, arrange the supply of cash registers, find and train the staff, source local stock items, and arrange the clearance and transportation of NAAFI stock through the Ethiopian port of Assab, establish an accounting system etc. etc…

I had been misinformed by my HQ and had been truly dropped in the muck.

It was a hell of a challenge, but I was young and had a sense of humour. I would really need it in the coming months.

I should have told Norman what to do with the project, packed my bags, and gone home to sanity.

Looking back, that would have been the most sensible thing to do.

Asgers squirmed and tried to evade old Norman, as he ranted and raved around the building. He was in danger of having a heart attack as he highlighted the points that had not been actioned since his last visit.

As this point, I decided that enough was enough, and stood between Asgers and Norman. I told Norman that it was obviously not Asgers' fault, and that now I was here, things would get moving. I felt the need to defend Asgers. He was a great bloke, and just didn't have a clue on where to start.

I had begun to defend Asgers as I would have to on numerous occasions from now on.

I managed to calm Norman and we agreed to call it a day. Tomorrow was another day, and we would get the project started.

The day had zoomed by as did the next two, but I had begun to fall in love with the harsh magic of Africa. Ethiopia was beautiful, but extremely hard. Its people had nothing, not even fresh water. Millions were dying of starvation. The two-year drought had made a difficult situation impossible.

And Norman Lee was getting upset because he had lost face.

Norman Lee's bloody shop took on a different importance, when you looked outside the wire fence perimeter and saw women and children close to death through starvation.

There followed meeting after meeting between Norman and myself and the Ethiopian Air Force authorities, and it became obvious that we did not even have a formal agreement on how the project should be run or financed. It had all been done on the whim of the King's grandson, Admiral Scinda Desta. No one had signed any contract or documentation, yet, here I was, the advisor to the Imperial Ethiopian Air Force, here in Ethiopia.

Following lengthy negotiations, it was agreed that the project should proceed, and Norman managed to persuade them that I needed my own car.

It was agreed that one should be purchased by the Ethiopian Air Force, but debited to NAAFI.

It just so happened that the Colonel had a brother-in-law who sold cars in Addis Ababa, and he agreed to escort us to the showrooms.

We arrived in a very smart set-up, with gleaming new cars, suitable for the new advisor to the Imperial Ethiopian Air Force.

At the very back of the showrooms stood a broken-down Renault 4, a bit bashed, and very second-hand.

The Colonel introduced us to his brother-in-law, and there followed lengthy negotiations, as I wandered through the display of beautiful new cars.

It was, of course, agreed that the Renault 4 would be the ideal car for me. I couldn't believe it, but I had no say in the matter. The car was robust and just what the new organisation needed.

Obviously we had been set up, and the Colonel and his brother-in-law had made a few bob on the deal. My new/old car would require some work on it, but it would be ready tomorrow. So much for my new exulted position. My car was at least ten years old and had cost a fortune, but the Colonel had assured Norman that all cars cost a fortune in Ethiopia.

We returned to Debre Zeit, and began the negotiation for my accommodation. It was agreed that I should have my own house, with a maid and a guard. It would be arranged as soon as possible. Things were looking up – I would soon have a car, a house, a maid, and a guard (I was a little naïve).

At last, it was time for Norman to return to Kenya, and his last duty on the night before he left was to introduce me to the expatriate community. Transport was arranged by the Air Force, and we left the left the hotel after supper and drove toward the outskirts of the town, down yet another dusty track.

The expatriate community had a social club within its own guarded compound, and it would help to maintain my sanity over the coming months.

We entered the building and we were impressed by the standard of the accommodation. It was comfortable, clean, and had a bar. Things were looking up.

There were about fifty members of the Club, from all parts of the world: French, Russian, German, British, Indian and American, and all of them were involved in various projects in Ethiopia. Thank god I had found a bolt-hole of sanity.

Norman had met one or two of them during his previous visit, and introduced me to them. It was a great evening, and we had quite a bit to drink. All of the members were keen to meet me and to discover what I was up to. They were also interested in our retail outlet and hoped that it would be up and running soon. They hoped that it would enable them to purchase some decent British food.

It was quite late by the time our driver returned to take us back to our hotel.

We bade a drunken farewell to my new found friends, and staggered off to the car.

The following morning, Norman and I both had hangovers, and a very quiet breakfast.

Asgers suddenly appeared, and with his usual broad grin, the world seemed better.

We paid Norman's hotel bill, and once again, set off in Asgers' old car. At least my new car would have better suspension.

Norman was obviously pleased to be escaping Ethiopia, and was in a good mood. It was agreed that he would return within six weeks, by which time, I should be firmly established, and the project would be on its way.

We managed to get Norman through the departure formalities without any major incidents, and had a last cup of coffee before saying our goodbyes.

Asgers and I stood and watched the Ethiopian Airlines plane speed down the runway, and at last, I was on my own in this strange land.

My adventure was about to really begin.

Chapter 4
Good Old Asgers!

It was after I saw Norman Lee off at the airport, and Asgedom left me at my hotel, that I suddenly felt very alone. I surveyed my dilapidated hotel. Here I was, a white man, alone in a strange, hostile country, thousands of miles from my friends and family.

I went to bed and fell into a fitful sleep, hoping that the new day would soon dawn, and things would look better.

I awoke, had breakfast, and cheered myself with the thought that I would get my new/old car today. I would be independent and mobile.

Then Asgers arrived and soon disillusioned me. There had been a phone call. The car was not ready yet, but it would be Tomorrow.

We set off for the site of the new supermarket, with Asgers still nervous, but in good spirits.

We walked the building and I gave instructions to Asgers. I needed builders, today. I needed electricians, today. I needed decorators, today. I was getting angry and I let it show. I demanded to see the General, but had to put up with the Colonel. I let the Colonel know my feelings, and it worked. I actually got a builder on site. One out of three was good progress for Ethiopia.

It would not be the last time that I was to lose my temper with Asgers and the Colonel, but I was determined to show Norman Lee that I could make it work.

In the next few weeks, I managed to get the roof repaired, windows replaced, holes in walls repaired, and the decoration commenced.

Poor old Asgers didn't know what had hit him. I had him running around like a blue-arsed fly!

My car, needless to say, took another two days to be ready for collection, and I was quite excited at the thought.

Asgers agreed to take me to the dealers to collect it, and we set off in good spirits.

Asgers was determined to please me and was getting used to me giving him a hard time if things did not go to plan. It was difficult to stay mad at Asgers for long. He was such a pleasant, easy-going guy.

We arrived at the garage and were met by the slimy brother-in-law of the Colonel, who apologised for the delay in having my car ready.

There it stood in all its glory. It had character, and would never let me down. But it had a very strange gear change stick that could easily be mistaken for a brake handle, as I would later discover.

The Colonel's brother-in-law explained the various controls and Asgers beamed, as he was happy that something appeared to be going right at last.

We agreed that I would follow Asgers back to Debre Zeit and we set off in my new/old car. It felt good and I felt that I had independence at last.

The car ran smoothly and we arrived back at my hotel. I thanked Asgers for taking me to collect the car and I invited him in for a coffee.

I had parked my new car at the top of the car park, which was on a hill, safe and away from the locals.

We had just sat down and ordered coffee, when there was much shouting and confusion outside. We took no notice, as there was quite often confusion in Ethiopia. The door suddenly burst open, and in came the hotel guard with the manager.

'Your car, Sir, your car!' shouted the manager, and pointed outside.

Asgers and I dashed outside, and we immediately saw my new/old car, rammed into the wall at the bottom of the hill.

Another guard had two youths pinned against the wall and all were shouting.

My beautiful car, which I'd had for some two hours, now had a very dented front wing.

I surveyed the damage, unlocked the car, and then noticed that the handbrake was off and the gear change lever was in the wrong place. It became obvious that I had not used the handbrake and that my car had run down the hill on its own.

I managed to pull the guard off the two youths and explained to Asgers what had happened, who in turn explained to the manager and his two guards. I apologised to all concerned and gave the youths a couple of dollars for their trouble and also rewarded the guards and thanked everyone for their help. We managed to straighten the wing to enable the car to be able to move, and it would be alright until I found the time to have it repaired properly.

Asgedom started to laugh. He was very happy that I could also make mistakes. We both fell about laughing and returned to our coffee.

The following day, we again returned to survey the progress of the shop. I was now able to get to work under my own steam, and I got there at least half an hour before Asgers. By the time he arrived, I had made a list of the next things that had to be done.

The fabric of the building was coming on, and I was pleased with our progress. Even Norman would be pleased.

I had learned how to get things moving. The secret was to shame them into action. To the Ethiopians, I was this strange white man, who insisted that things happened and when they did not, he took off his coat and started doing the job himself. The ploy worked, and poor old Asgers spent much time running backwards and forwards to the Colonel and the General, begging for assistance.

I was a guest in their country and I was actually getting my hands dirty doing tasks that should only be done by the lower members of society. This was not acceptable to Asgers and his superiors.

As long as it made things happen, I carried on, in spite of protest from all concerned. It was amazing how things progressed. More and more workmen appeared and the shopping complex began to take shape. The office was built, electrical sockets and new lights were installed, and toilets were repaired. It was great to see, and I was enjoying myself.

It was then that I informed Asgers that we were ready for the shop fittings to be installed. It was at this point that Asgers became nervous again. He made some excuse and dashed off.

Asgers appeared the following morning and still looked nervous. I began to get a bit worried. We had a cup of coffee, and then I decided to broach the subject of the shop fittings again. Asgers choked on his coffee and began to babble on that it was in-hand etc. I decided not to believe him and suggested that we go and see the Colonel. After all, he was supposed to be the project officer and I had seen little of him over the last two weeks.

We duly arrived at the Colonel's office and entered into lengthy discussions, during which the Colonel and Asgers became even more evasive, until they realised that I was not giving up. I would not accept that it would be sorted out "Tomorrow".

After much coaxing, they finally admitted that the shop fitting had not been ordered, as the supplier, an English company based in Addis Ababa by the name of Mitchell Cotts, were refusing to give the Imperial Air Force credit, and would not supply the fittings unless they paid cash up front. Mitchell Cotts had dealt with the Air Force on a number of occasions, and had always had problems being paid. They were refusing to deal, unless the Air Force paid for all of the fittings in advance, and with cash.

After much discussion, it was decided that I should visit the company and arrange the supply. After all, I was British, and it was a British company. Both the Colonel and Asgers appeared happy at their decision. I should have been more worried than I felt.

An appointment was made to meet the MD of Mitchell Cotts the following day. Asgers and I set off for Addis. Asgers was in his best No.1 uniform, and this should have made me feel even more worried.

We arrived in Addis and found the Mitchell Cotts building. It was very impressive, and as we entered, I noticed that Asgers was holding back and letting me take the lead. I realised that he was very nervous.

We went to the reception desk and explained our mission, and that we had an appointment with the MD. Asgers was fading into the distance.

The receptionist arranged for someone to take us through to the person who would deal with us. We were eventually ushered into a very smart office, where we were introduced to the man I thought was the Managing Director. He seemed very polite and very helpful. He ordered coffee for us all, and I began to explain my mission. I had been sent here by the NAAFI organisation and I'd been appointed as advisor to the Ethiopian Air Force, etc. etc.

Asgedom had doffed his cap and he squirmed in the seat beside me. I could not understand what his problem was. My discussions were going very well, but the Mitchell Cotts man was adamant that he would not give the Air Force credit.

He had the fittings, and would supply them the following week, once he had received payment. I then explained that I represented the NAAFI organisation which had a multi-million pound turnover, and assured him that the bill would be paid.

To my amazement, the chap agreed to give me personal credit, on my word that the bill would be paid within two months of the fittings being delivered. I could have fallen off my chair. The company was not prepared to give the Imperial Ethiopian Air Force credit, but they would give me credit.

An Englishman's word still counted in some parts of the world.

The chap explained to Asgers in his native tongue, and even Asgers looked impressed. Lupson had done it. We would get the fittings delivered the following week and receive two months in which to pay for them.

Next week sounded plausible. If he had said Tomorrow, I would have been worried. Actually, I should have been worried in any case. I was still naïve.

We thanked the chap most profusely and Asgers and I strode out of Mitchell Cotts with a new air of confidence. We had climbed a mountain, and all of a sudden, Asgers was back by my side. We had done it!

Asgers was very proud of our achievement and we decided to go to the most expensive restaurant in town to have a celebration lunch. The food was excellent, and we really enjoyed our hard-earned reward.

In high spirits, we returned to Debre Zeit.

The chap had promised us delivery the following week, and this was what we needed. Our first consignment of NAAFI goods from the UK was due in the port of Assab in the next couple of weeks, and we needed to get the shop completed and up and running as soon as we could. We needed some money to start flowing.

There was a hell of a lot to do and time flew by. I worked all hours, swore, cussed, cajoled, and made myself a general pain in the arse to everyone, but my tail was up, and things were really moving.

Asgers was getting more action and support from the Colonel as he appreciated what we had achieved. He obviously thought that it may earn him extra Brownie points with the General, now that the project appeared to be succeeding. Even the General was realising that we meant business and would not take no for an answer.

The week zoomed by and we eagerly awaited the delivery of the fittings. Nothing arrived, our phone calls were not returned, and we were getting nowhere.

Asgers was indignant.

'The MD promised you, Mr Lupson. We'll have to go into town and sort them out. You must tell them that you will report them to the NAAFI HQ in London. They are a British company, and must not let the Imperial Ethiopian Air Force down. Sort them out, Mr Lupson,' he said.

We decided to return to Addis the following day and demand to see the MD, and let him know of our displeasure.

The following day, we set off again. Asgers, in his best uniform, and me in my suit.

We arrived at the Mitchell Cotts office and were ushered through to the MD's office. The office was larger than I remembered it to be and it certainly looked more impressive.

I was full of confidence as I strolled arrogantly into the Managing Director's office.

He looked a bit different to what I remembered, but at that stage, most of the Ethiopians looked the same. At least, the educated, smart ones did.

I shook his hand, and without giving him chance to say much, I demanded to know what he thought he was playing at. Why had he not supplied our fittings? I would report him to our NAAFI HQ. I reminded him that I was after all, the advisor to the Imperial Ethiopian Air Force. We would ensure that his Head Office would hear of this poor standard of service.

I was showing them! And I turned to Asgers, to show him that I was really sorting them out. To my amazement, Asgers was in a terrible state. He was fumbling with his hat, his eyes bulged and he looked as though he were about to pass out.

And the chap behind the desk reacted totally differently to the way he had done on our previous visit. He arose from his desk, his face as dark as thunder and started ranting and raving at Asgedom. It became obvious that this was not the man we had first met, but a totally different character.

He ranted and raved and looked as though he was about to have us executed. Poor old Asgers was distraught and began grovelling and begging forgiveness. It had all been a dreadful misunderstanding.

It was then that the Managing Director turned on me and began to bellow.

'Who are you? Who do you think you are? Do you realise who I am?' he demanded. By this time, I was totally confused and also a bit worried. The MD continued to shout.

'I will have you thrown out of the country! How dare you threaten a cousin of His Imperial Majesty?'

I could not believe my ears. I had been in the country some five weeks, and I was about to be banished for life. I had insulted a relation of His Imperial Majesty. Obviously the chap I had met before was a different person and was much more junior than this chap. This really was the Managing Director of Mitchell Cotts Africa, and was also directly related to the King.

It was now my turn to start grovelling. I apologised dozens of times and explained that it had all been a terrible misunderstanding. As I was asking his forgiveness, I was also trying to fight off one of the MD's aides, who had entered the office upon hearing the commotion. The aid was trying to drag me out of the MD's office, but I was having none of it.

Asgedom was nearly in tears. His face had drained and he was begging for forgiveness.

'It's a terrible mistake – a misunderstanding,' he said. 'This Englishman is here on the orders of your uncle His Imperial Majesty.'

He saw his career as an Ethiopian Air Force Major going up in smoke. It seemed an age, but I was still in the office, dodging the aide, and the MD slowly cooled down. I was now able to apologise again and explain my mission and the frustrations I was having in trying to commence a very difficult project. The MD listened as I explained all, and then agreed with Asgers that I was obviously an honourable man. A bit stupid, but honourable.

He ordered his aide to bring coffee, and the situation improved. Asgers was still very upset and continued to apologise.

The coffee arrived, delivered by his secretary, who looked a little bemused at the ranting and raving she had obviously overheard.

The MD listened carefully to us, and made a phone call and gave whoever was on the other end a dressing-down.

The MD and I appeared to be getting on well, and to my amazement, he agreed to arrange for the fittings to be delivered the following week. I would personally be held responsible for payment and the letters of credit were drawn up for me to sign.

I signed the letters of credit and thanked the MD for his understanding. We shook hands and apologised once more and slowly backed out of the MD's office. His aide gave us a strange look as we made a quick exit out of the building. The MD's secretary gave us a smile of amusement. It had been an interesting encounter, and she had witnessed it all. We thanked her for the coffee, and got the hell out of there!

Thank god I had been spared from being thrown out of the country – and we had also been promised the fittings. It was a result!

Both Asgers and I were shaking from our experience. The MD could have had us thrown in jail as well as having me deported. He really was a powerful man, and I had insulted him. Partly due to Asgers' prompting.

We returned to the restaurant, had a light snack, and lots of coffee, and we began to feel better.

I looked at Asgers and we began to laugh. We laughed and laughed, and tears ran down our faces. The locals looked at us as if we were mad. But we had both come through an extremely difficult situation, and we were now brothers in arms. He had dropped me in the cart again, but we had got out of it as firm friends. Good old Asgers!

We returned to Debre Zeit and looked forward to the arrival of the fittings. On the way back, I decided to take my personal life into account. I had the car but I was still living at the hotel, and all work and no play was no good.

I arranged to meet the Colonel the following day to show him the progress we had made, and also to hasten the allocation of my house and staff.

Chapter 5
The Ex-Pats

An Ethiopian market: unchanged since Biblical times

That night, I decided to go out to the ex-pats club, and took a shower, had an early supper and set off in my car for the club.

As I approached the gates, I saw sets of evil eyes reflecting my headlights. It was a pack of hyenas on the scrounge and they really did look awful. I drove at them and they scattered into the night. Hyenas are basically cowards but are quite brave in numbers.

I drove up to the club and headed for the bar.

It was good to meet some of my own kind again and have a drink and relax. At the bar was a tall, bronzed guy in his early fifties, every part the ex-pat bushman.

'I'm Alfred,' he said, and also introduced me to his trusty dog. We sat and chatted over a very nice cold beer or two. Alfred had escaped over the border from Kenya when Kenya received its independence. Jomo Kenyatta, the first president of Kenya, had decided that he did not want the foreigners to remain in Kenya, and wanted them to leave, but to leave behind all of their wealth. Alfred had decided that this was not fair and had managed to sell his farm and extract his money from the bank. Under cover of darkness, he had driven north to Ethiopia with his dog, his Land Rover, and all of his possessions.

Alfred was one hell of a character – a tall, rugged man, and he still managed to attract the young ladies.

We became friends, and I enjoyed listening to his stories of Kenya, and how it was in the days of the British Empire.

Many more members of our club drifted in and we all sat around, enjoying each other's company.

There was a French ex-pat called Pierre, who had a wife and two children. Pierre had a doctorate in something and was heavily involved in experimenting with farming in Ethiopian. He and his wife kept themselves to themselves and appeared to be unfriendly. But his kids were nice, and full of fun.

There was John Murray the Third. Ex-Texas, USA, a professor in Animal Studies, he was in Ethiopia to try to improve their cattle breeding programme. He was a typical warm and friendly American, larger than life, a bit loud, but a very nice guy. He was in his early sixties, but had a much younger wife and three children.

His wife Angie was slim and fun-loving. Born in India, she was a beautiful girl with long black hair and dark smouldering eyes. She enjoyed the good life and was often escorted out on the town by the young Ethiopian Air Force Officers. John, her husband, did not seem to mind, as long as she got home before dawn and took care of the home and children. She was a very caring mother, and as they had local servants, her home tasks were not too hard on her. She obviously needed to enjoy her youth. She was obviously potential trouble, and I decided to keep her at a distance. I would be friendly, but not too friendly, but between me and you, I wouldn't have minded giving her one, if I could have got away with it!

There were numerous British ex-pats, all involved in various projects in Ethiopia. I was introduced to Peter and his wife June. Peter was a very interesting character and was contracted to the Royal Ethiopian Air Force by British Air Corporation, to try to keep the Phantom bombers in the air. BAC had sold a number of ageing Phantom bombers to the Royal Ethiopian Air Force, and it was Peter's task to try to maintain them. A near impossible task.

Peter was a quiet person. His wife June was a large, motherly type with a bubbly personality to match her size.

Dave and Nicky Johnson were also Brits. Dave had a doctorate in Maths and Science, and was in Ethiopia to teach maths to the Senior NCOs of the Ethiopian Air Force. They were both in their late twenties and were very nice people. As they were nearer my age, we soon became firm friends. Nicky was a real character and seemed to have no fear of the local surroundings. I'm sure that Dave thought I fancied his wife, and he was right to suspect me, although I respected them both too much to make a pass at her. I'm sure she would have been very upset if I had done so.

Then there was Robert, a teacher in General Studies to the Ethiopian Air Force. It transpired that he was into young boys, and I disliked him from the start.

And the unforgettable Professor Jan Ruschin, a massive twenty-stone freak, born in Russia, who drank like a fish and ate like a pig. He was fat, ugly and had bad breath. He had an excellent brain though: a real boffin. He was married to a slim, very pleasant American girl called Elizabeth. They had met at University in the US, and Elizabeth had then fallen for the then slimmish Russian with a brain.

They had two young children and it amazed us all that this fat freak had managed to produce such good kids. Jan was a thoroughly nasty piece of work. He always carried a small .22 pistol, and had a passion for the local prostitutes. He was also into beating them up, when in one of his off-moods. He was not liked by anyone, but he had a brilliant brain and was an excellent teacher, and therefore was tolerated by the Ethiopians. He was always on edge, sweaty and was always eating and drinking to excess.

There was another British couple, called John and Ruth Cummings, a nice couple, middle aged and quite normal. They had a splendid home and kept up a high standard of living. Ruth was the proud owner of an Arab stallion, and it turned out to be a really superb beast. We seemed to get on well right from the start, and once I mentioned that I was into horses, Ruth asked me if I would be kind enough to help exercise her horse. I could not believe my luck. Although the Stallion was on the small side for me, he was apparently very strong and full of fire. I looked forward to the challenge of mastering this magnificent horse.

It transpired that John was a research professor and was in Ethiopia to study tsetse fly. The fly caused the disease of sleeping sickness, which was prevalent throughout the whole of Africa. There were lots of strange illnesses in Africa and in particular, Ethiopia. The sad fact was that most of the ills were caused through lack of sanitation and clean water. Poor diet and starvation also contributed to the high death rate of the Ethiopian nation, but the situation was about to get worse as the rainy season had once again failed.

The crowd that I had just met would be my friends and family for the duration of my tour, and we would undergo many trials and tribulations before we parted company. A strange bunch thrown together by fate.

We sat on the veranda of the ex-pat club. It was a single storied house that had been allocated to us by the Ethiopian Air Force for our recreation.

Although I had nothing against Africans or the Ethiopians, it felt great to be among people who, however strange, were similar to me. They had the same sense of humour, and understood how strange it was for me to be in a land totally different to anything I had ever experienced before. It was really good, and for the first time in months, I did not feel alone in the world.

The beer flowed freely, and was obviously having an effect on us all. A party atmosphere ensued.

The noise of the bush interrupted our conversations from time to time. Strange grunting noises, animal screams, and the laugh of the hyenas.

The night was very dark, and had a strange foreboding beauty. The evening flew by and it was soon time to depart. As I was about to leave, someone mentioned that the Ethiopian Air Force base had a good film showing, and we all agreed to meet the following night. I was delighted at the thought of meeting them all again soon, as my hotel was not the best of places to spend an evening. We all said our farewells and I set off in my beaten-up Renault car for the hotel.

As I drove away, strange shapes began to appear in front of my headlights. Very large dog type creatures, with evil red eyes – very ugly looking beasts. A pack of hyenas, on the prowl for the odd poor dog, or other animals and occasional humans. They hunted in packs. An awful sight to behold. I drove at them with full headlights and they scattered into the darkness.

I later found out that although hyenas were cowards, they would "have a go" if they thought they could win. Otherwise, they were scavengers and did the work of the local council, by cleaning the streets of any dead animals.

I arrived back at my hotel, a little pissed but happy, and safe and sound. I only had the mosquitos to fight off during the night.

I had a quick wash in cold water, and fell into my bed. I was soon fast asleep. It was good to have made some friends in this god-forsaken land.

***

Dawn broke, and I awoke with a bit of a hangover, and feeling very tired. It was Saturday, and I was about to take off one of the few days that I had managed since my arrival in Ethiopia.

I staggered down to a late breakfast and decided that it was an ideal day to explore the local village of Debre Zeit. My two boiled eggs and lots of coffee made me feel much better.

I donned my bush jacket and bush hat, and felt quite the part. I decided to walk, and set off towards the town centre. The village was like something out of the Wild West, with shanty type huts and shops. The odd concrete building stood out, but the majority of buildings were constructions of mud or wood.

The village was situated some forty kilometres from Addis, and was a support village to the HQ of the Imperial Ethiopian Air Force.

There was a modern bank, a post office and plenty of bars. The main road ran from my hotel, through the heart of the village, and there was a throng of locals, all busy doing whatever locals do. There was an odd drunk lying on the side of the road, trying to get over the night before. There was a mixture of dogs, goats, chickens and people, and lots of donkeys, all heavily laden, on their way to the main market square.

I obviously stood out like a sore thumb, being white and well clothed, and the beggars surrounded me wherever I went. I had learned not to give to beggars, or you would never escape them. It was best to ignore their pleadings and continue as though they were not there.

There were some pretty awful sights: starving people with rotting teeth, and many had open sores all over their bodies. They were, in the main, dressed in rags and a lot only had a loin cloth. All the men carried sticks, spears or the odd rifle. Most carried machetes.

It was a very strange sight, but what hit me most of all was the smell. There was no sanitation, and men and women alike did whatever they needed to do, wherever they felt like it. It was a strange smell of sewerage, human sweat, and general filth.

Flies were everywhere, and it looked as though God had allocated each person a quantity of them, which followed them wherever they went. Flies attacked me, but at least I tried to get them off me. The locals seemed to accept them, and the flies were up their nose, in their eyes, and all over them. In addition, the mosquitos were biting, and it was quite uncomfortable just being there.

Africa looks romantic on film, but when you experience the smell and the pain, it's a bit different.

The Ethiopians are a good looking race, with fine features: tall, slim, and those who were reasonably fit were quite athletic looking. But most of the children I saw had pot bellies, a sign of malnutrition.

There were a few mixed race people, who were obviously part Italian. There were some really beautiful women with very fine features and bodies. These contrasted with those who were not so fortunate.

The main street of the village was an amazing sight, but it was difficult not to let it affect you. Here was a mass of humanity with less than nothing and no job prospects. Most would be lucky to survive into their late twenties. The world did not seem to care and no one was aware that the situation was going to get worse. It was hard to imagine how it could get much worse than it already was, but it would.

I continued my walk with a heavy heart. The situation was hopeless.

I wanted to help. I wanted to give, but I dared not. Otherwise I would not survive. I walked faster to try to rid myself of the beggars. I would have to harden myself to it all, or go mad.

I tried to get rid of the beggars with the few words that Asgers had taught me, but it did not work. I suppose if I was in the same state as they were, I would also persist in trying to get help.

Turning off the main street, I headed towards the market square. It was bedlam, with thousands of locals trying to sell me anything from chickens to jam jars. The market had a smell of its own, and mingled with the aroma of herbs and spicy cooking that was well under way, for their one and only meal of the day – that's if people had the odd cent to purchase it. It was a fascinating sight and one that I had not experienced before. It was strange, but even with the mass of destitute locals, I never felt unsafe. I don't know why that was, as I obviously looked well-fed and well-heeled and could have been a target for robbers.

In the centre of the market stood the hanging trees. I had learned that they had only been used some six months prior to my arrival in Ethiopia. I was told that some time earlier, three locals had raided one of the local shops. They were apparently very drunk and out of their minds. They had murdered the owner, having slashed his throat with their machetes. The owner's daughter had arrived and witnessed her father dying. And then the three had turned on her and raped her. They had stolen more alcohol, and finally passed out, but the owner's daughter managed to escape and got help from the neighbours. The police arrived and found the three criminals still dead to the world. They were dragged off to the local jail and received a beating from the police.

The three were found guilty of theft, murder, and rape, and sentenced to death by hanging. The following day, they were dragged out to the hanging tree, and in front of vast crowds, the police proceeded to hang them. They decided to hang them one at a time, to teach a lesson to those who would follow a life of crime. The first man was dragged forwards. He was made to stand on a makeshift stool, and a rope was placed around his neck. The stool was kicked away and the prisoner was left hanging, his body twitching and fighting to stay alive. It apparently took a considerable time for him to die and some of the crowd cried as they watched the poor wretch die.

His fellow accomplices in crime were made to watch their friend die, and now they were about to share the same fate.

They were screaming and begging for mercy, but it never came. The next was brought forward and dealt the same fate. As the bodies swung by their necks, body fluids burst out from all parts, and it was a horrible sight to see.

The third and youngest had been forced to watch and was beside himself. By this time, parts of the crowd felt sorry for the young lad and were also shouting for mercy. Their pleas were ignored by the police, and any local who got out of line received a whack on his head from the police batons. It was very rough justice. But considered necessary to maintain some form of law and order in this harsh land of Ethiopia.

The third and youngest criminal was dragged forward, and hanged. Part of the crowd jeered and laughed. Some of the crowd were in danger of getting out of hand, having felt that it was not necessary to hang them one at a time, and that the youngest one was put through such an awful ordeal before he met his Maker.

Police reinforcements arrived and dealt very firmly with those who protested. They were made to disperse without any mercy, and the police wielded their batons with great ferocity. The bodies of the three murderers were left hanging on the tree for several days as a deterrent, pecked by birds and decomposing in the African heat. It must have been an awful sight, but this was Ethiopia, a very harsh, yet beautiful country, where life was very hard and very cheap.

I stood there, imagining what it must have been like on the day of the hanging: the bursting eyes, the excrement and urine and the screams of those who were about to die an awful death.

There was a voice at my side, and there stood Nicky. She had read my thoughts, as it had been in her company that the fat Russian freak, Ruschin, had taken great delight in telling us the dreadful story, not missing any part of the detail of the death of the three robbers, murderers, and rapists. It was difficult not to feel sorry for at least the last two to die. They surely deserved to die, but it could have been done more humanely.

I looked down into the sanity of the smiling, blue, and comforting eyes of Nicky. Dave was right: I did fancy his wife. She was an amazing girl. Here she stood alone, in the midst of thousands of Ethiopian natives, not speaking their language, but out shopping for fresh fruit and vegetables without a care in the world.

She stood with her rucksack on her back, a young, thin English girl, in a seething mass of humanity. She smiled, and we decided to get away from the tree, and find a local tea seller. We sat on the rough benches and ordered tea. It was great to find a bit of sanity in this less than real world I now found myself in.

The tea arrived, and we sat and chatted. The thick, sweet liquid quenched my thirst and made life feel good. Nicky was on good form. I must confess I had great difficulty in concentrating on what she was saying. I had not talked to a woman for a considerable time, and she was a really attractive person.

At last, it was time for her to move on, and she assured me that she would be perfectly safe and would walk home, having purchased all she needed.

We bade farewell and said that we would meet with the rest of the gang at the picture that evening. The day had improved.

I returned to my hotel, having experienced at first-hand some awful sights and smells. The local population was in a very poor state of health and malnutrition was evident everywhere.

It was a sad state of affairs, but the situation was slowly getting worse, as the rains had failed again, and the poor subsistence farmers were not even able to satisfy their own family's needs. People were starting to die.

This potentially beautiful country was being brought to its knees, and the world was just about to realise just how bad the situation was. Something should have been done. But it was already too late.

I had a late lunch snack, a snooze on the bed, and then got up and started to prepare for the night out at the cinema.

I set off to meet my new friends/family. It felt as though I was going out to something special, as it was a long time since I had been to a cinema. I arrived at the airbase's cinema and noticed the large crowd of smartly dressed, well-fed people from a mixture of cultures, all waiting outside. They were a strong contrast to the local population I had seen earlier. It was all very strange and unreal. Less than half a mile away, people were dying and in an awful state, and here we were, going to the cinema.

The crowd of ex-pats were gathered on the far side of the cinema forecourt, and as I approached them, they all turned to greet me. It felt great to belong to a crowd who were "my own".

It was then that I noticed a group of Indian people also amongst the crowd waiting to go into the cinema. They turned out to be Raj and his wife Janine, a couple who were both teachers, and a small, petite, beautiful girl, whom they seemed keen to protect as though she was their daughter. She was not, but had arrived in Debre Zeit at the same time as the married pair, and they had become almost like her parents. She was very good looking, with long black hair, and sparkling eyes which lit up her whole face when she smiled.

I was introduced to her and we seemed to have a rapport from the moment our eyes met. Her name was Geeta, and she had run away from her husband, who had beaten her and abused her in an awful way. It became very obvious that her protectors didn't want me anywhere near their adopted daughter. Our mutual attraction had been noticed by Raj and Janine, and they were having none of it.

We all entered the cinema, and although the film was quite good, I lost interest in it and only had eyes for Geeta. Our eyes met on a number of occasions, and we exchanged secret grins when no one appeared to be looking. I don't remember much about the film, but it became increasingly obvious that Raj and Janine were determined that we should not get close that night or for a number of months to come.

I was obviously trouble and they had to protect Geeta at all costs.

I was determined to find out more about this lovely young lady. She was obviously single, as I was, but it was the strict conditions of the Indian culture that were trying to keep us apart. They succeeded tonight, but they would not keep us apart forever. We obviously liked one another, and the day would come when we would get together.

The next day, I returned to work. I had to devise an accounting system that was simple to use, and was not going to be fiddled by the Colonel. I would trust Asgers with my life, and probably did, but the Colonel was a different kettle of fish.

It was Sunday, and I was alone in the building that would one day soon become a very smart supermarket. I spent the next three hours working hard and came up with a double accounting system that even Asgers could operate.

It entailed entering an opening stock figure; a goods received figure at cost price, and a retail price, goods purchased locally and their retail selling price on one side. And on the other side, columns for goods sold at our full retail price, goods reduced to clear, and goods used for cleaning etc. and a column that if one deduced one from the other, it would give the estimated value of the stock on hand. It would only need a physical stock check to balance the account. It sounds complicated, but it did actually work.

Well satisfied with my morning's work, I broke off and went to the ex-pats' Club. Alfred and his trusty dog were there, and we sat with a beer and chatted again. Alfred related tales of his time in Kenya. His heart was in Kenya, but he dared not return there unless the political climate changed, and I suspected that he would be dead before that happened.

He related tales about being a farmer in Kenya. Once the country had received its independence, life had become impossible for the ex-pat community. They were being forced to leave their farms, which were being taken over by the locals, with little or no compensation. If they were asked to leave Kenya, they had to leave most of their possessions behind. As was the case with a number of the ex-pat farmers, Alfred decided to gather as much of his fortune as he could, and make a dash for the Ethiopian border. It was a risky business, and had he been caught, he would have spent considerable time in jail, or even worse. As it was, he had managed to get over the border in his four-wheel drive, with a lot of cash, his rifle, and his dog. He had eventually arrived in Debre Zeit and was now managing a cattle farm for the American research team. Alfred really was a character and a very tough cookie!

It was a lovely day and the sound of the Bush carried though to our little part of civilisation. Birds were singing and some strange grunts were also heard. Even the hyenas got into the act with their strange laughing sound.

I had intended to return to my accounting project, but after another beer, decided against it. It was Sunday, after all, and a lot more of the ex-pats were beginning to arrive.

Ruth arrived with her husband, and the subject changed to horses. She once again invited me to exercise her horse, and I agreed that I would, the following afternoon. I had fortunately brought my jodhpurs and boots, so I was reasonably well prepared. I had no safety hat, but I would have to chance it.

We all had a snack barbecue lunch, and the day soon passed by. I returned to my hotel, and after supper, turned in for an early night.

Chapter 6
The Stallion

Ruth's stallion.

Monday soon dawned, and I had a quick shower, changed and went off to work. It was time to chase up the project and ensure that we were on schedule.

Asgers arrived and his cheerful smile brightened the day. I really enjoyed his company. He had a very simple outlook on life and felt that what was not achieved today could wait until tomorrow.

I was beginning to understand that tomorrow never actually came in Ethiopia. The shop fittings were due to be delivered tomorrow, and once they were installed, the new cash desk which I had designed would be delivered, and then all we could need was a cash till.

I was discussing this with Asgers when I noticed that he had assumed his embarrassed look again. He was very sheepish as he explained that he had failed to negotiate the supply of a till. NCR would not give the Imperial Ethiopian Air Force credit for the purchase of one of their tills. They had experienced problems from the Air Force previously, and required cash.

We set off to the airbase in my beaten up old Renault car, to see the Colonel, to at least get a deposit for the till. It took us both a considerable time to persuade the Colonel that NCR really would not give us a till on credit unless we gave them a large deposit and a letter of promise to pay. At last, the Colonel got the message and reluctantly gave us some money, and a letter signed by the Base General, no less.

We arrived in Addis and went to the main NCR agency. I managed to persuade them that I was an honest Brit, and that on my word they would receive full payment for their till, within three months, either from the Air Force or from the NAAFI organisation.

It was agreed that within two weeks, they would supply a top of the range till, and would send a trainer with it to get us and our staff up to speed. It had all gone surprisingly well, and we decided that we deserved a nice lunch after our efforts.

We returned to our shop and carried on with our work. I explained to Asgers the basics of our accounting system, and soon it was time for me to depart for my ride on the Stallion. Asgers thought I was mad, as it was dangerous to ride such a spirited animal.

I bade him farewell as if we would not meet again, at least not in this world. I went back to the hotel, changed into my riding gear and set off for Ruth's house. Ruth greeted me like a long-lost friend and took me around to her stable. She had a groom whom I took an instant dislike to. He obviously thought the Stallion was his and resented my daring to come and ride him.

The Stallion was magnificent and really well kept. The harness was well polished and the groom obviously took great pride in his work. He had evil dark eyes that matched those of the Stallion. Ruth introduced me to the groom and to her beautiful Stallion. I thought she was very brave, trusting such a lovely animal to me.

The horse was soon tacked up by the groom, and I was ready to mount. I asked Ruth where I could ride, and she led me to a grassy field at the back of her residence. It was obviously a training area for her Stallion. I lowered myself gently into the saddle, took up the slack on the reins, and gently squeezed my legs into the sides of the horse. He responded immediately with a snort, and we were off to a gentle trot around the paddock.

He really was a magnificent creature and Ruth was obviously happy that I could manage him. He had an amazing gait and responded immediately to my hand and leg instructions. Ruth was very happy. I was really enjoying the experience too, apart from the groom, who was staring at me with hate in his eyes. Satisfied, Ruth left me alone, and I decided to stay in the paddock to get to know her horse.

We took a considerable time to get to know one another and to see who the master was. The Stallion was determined to show me that he was the boss, but I was equally determined to master him. I worked him really hard, making him go from walk to controlled canter and back again. I made him change rein and generally made him work in a way he had obviously not been used to. As the time went on, a small crowd gathered to watch this crazy Englishman, dressed in riding boots and jodhpurs, exercising this magnificent Stallion.

By now, both of us were covered in sweat, and the Stallion knew he had met his match. He was responding well and concentrating on the work in hand. He seemed to be enjoying himself and really showing off in front of the crowd. I enjoyed it but eventually felt that we had both had enough. I led the Stallion back to his stable, to be met by the evil-looking groom. The Stallion was covered in sweat and dust from the exercise and the once immaculate saddle and harness were now covered in grime.

The groom looked daggers at me. I ignored his evil stare and told him to give the Stallion a wash down and make sure he was well looked after. The evil groom obviously didn't like my instructions, but decided not to argue.

I returned to Ruth's house and thanked her for the fantastic experience of exercising her horse. We set on the veranda and drank tea. I needed a shower, so I thanked her once again, and set off for my hotel, feeling tired, but very happy with my riding.

Following my shower, I had a light supper and turned in for an early night. I felt exhausted and fell asleep quickly.

***

Day broke and I set off in good spirits to the shop. The previous day's exercise had done me good, and I was on top of the world. Asgers arrived soon after me and said that he had been to the Air Force base to collect a signal from NAAFI. The signal said that our first consignment of supplies would be arriving at the Port of Assab in some three weeks' time. The projected date would be 23rd September 1973.

We were quite excited at the thought. Today was the day that the shop fittings would arrive, and things were looking good.

And the word of royalty could be trusted. At nine o'clock, the Mitchell Cotts vehicle arrived. Together with an installation crew, they all worked very hard and by the end of the day, they had installed the complete shop fittings, and both Asgers and I were delighted. The next day, we arranged for the cash desk to be installed, which the Base carpenters had made. It was all beginning to come together.

The shop would be the most modern outside of Addis Ababa, and Asgers was rightly proud. All we needed now was refrigeration, a cash till and staff. Even the Colonel was becoming more pro-active and actually offering help. It seemed that he was now convinced that the project would get off the ground, and he obviously thought he could earn Brownie points by taking credit for its implementation.

Time flew by. I had cussed and cajoled and made myself a general pain in the arse to everyone, but now we had a shell of a supermarket, things were really looking up.

The Colonel had found some staff for us. They were wives of two SNCOs of the Ethiopian Air Force and were really nice ladies. There was little that could be done, as we had no stock, but we started to train them in what would be required, and got one of them interested in the clerical side of the business. I explained the basic accountancy that we would employ. Then the NCR till arrived, together with a trainer. We were really moving forward. But we needed the business to be up and running and to start earning money. We had debtors to pay and even staff salaries owing.

We employed a store man on the insistence of the Colonel, and both Asgers and I took an instant dislike to him. He was a shifty character and always seemed to be listening in to our conversations. Asgers was convinced that he was a spy. Or even part of the secret police – an informer working for the government agencies.

There were obviously dark clouds looming over the whole of Ethiopia. Not only the fact that the rains had failed and more and more people were starving to death, but there was general dissatisfaction with the government. Although the majority of Ethiopians loved and respected their King, his government were considered corrupt, and only interested in lining their own pockets.

The civil war in the North was escalating, and rumours started filtering through that real trouble was brewing. Even Asgers started carrying a pistol, and this did nothing to reassure me.

Asgers was a Tigrayan from the North of the country, and he was obviously very upset at the way things were taking shape. As Asgers grew to know me and trust me, he confided to me that the situation was getting bad. I was too busy to worry too much about it. I had stock to get and to arrange for supplies of local goods. We needed refrigeration urgently and the fridge promised by the NAAFI organisation was on board the ship that was due in Assab the following week.

At last we were informed that our ship had arrived.

'We must go to Assab tomorrow to clear the goods and get them back to the shop,' I said to Asgers.

Once again, Asgers looked very sheepish.

'It would be better if you went, Mr Lupson, and I'll stay here and carry on with our work. You are the expert at clearing goods through customs,' he said.

Asgers was embarrassed at me having to go alone to Assab, but he assured me that it would be better if he stayed behind and took care of the progress in the shop.

I packed sufficient clothing for the anticipated few days I thought I would be away in the port of Assab. I was slightly perturbed at the thought of travelling alone to a place that was at the other end of the world, and close to where the rebels were growing in confidence.

It was during this time that the Suez Canal had been closed and all goods had to travel around the Cape, hence the delay in our goods arriving at Assab. It had actually helped us, as if the ship had arrived any earlier, we would not have been ready for them. It was decided that the goods would be flown back to the Air Force base in the ageing 119, a forerunner to the Hercules Transport Aircraft.

The Imperial Ethiopian Air Force's first trading establishment was well advanced, and with its new fittings, cash desk, and highly polished floor, it looked very smart. Asgers would continue the staff training and would locate local supplies while I was away.

I was a bit worried, to say the least, as the more I thought about it, I felt I was being set up by the Air Force. I suspected that the Colonel had been behind my travelling alone, realising that there would be problems in clearing our goods through Customs and it would be better if his Major was not involved.

Asgers picked me up at the Hotel, and drove me to the Base. He chatted nervously and I realised that he was also upset at my having to go to Assab alone. He kept reassuring me that I would be alright, as an Air Force Lieutenant had been assigned to me and he would take care of me, including my personal protection. The more he babbled on, the more I realised that the next few days would be very interesting.

He drove on through the Base and onto the runway, on which stood a very old 119 freighter plane, bearing the ensign of the Imperial Ethiopian Air Force. The crest was the best part of the aircraft.

I was greeted by the pilot, who was from the same tribe as Asgers, and they were obviously great friends. Asgers told him that I was a good friend of his and to make sure that I was well taken care of. We climbed on board this ancient ex USA Air Force plane, which was well past its sell-by date, and I was given a parachute. This did nothing to reassure me. I was shown how to strap on a parachute and instructed on what to do if we should have to bail out.

The pilot was a short but good-looking chap, with a reassuring smile. At least he had a sense of humour and if we were to die, at least I would be in cheerful company.

I was introduced to the rest of the crew, who were also a nice bunch. They all seemed in good spirits, and were very friendly.

They obviously thought it strange that this reasonably young Englishman had come to Ethiopia and was helping them to have their own welfare organisation. They were all keen to know when we would be open for business, and if we would be cheaper than the supermarkets in Addis.

At last, it was time to depart, and I was shown the Navigator's seat. I sat behind the pilot and had an extremely good view. I waved my goodbyes to Asgers, who, for some strange reason, came smartly to attention and saluted me. This increased my worries. It was as if he was saying goodbye. I grinned at him and returned the salute.

I hoped the pilot realised that my navigation skills were limited and I joked to him that it was no good asking me the way. We all laughed and he turned to the task of getting the aircraft airborne. It took him several minutes to go through the pre-flight checks and at last seemed satisfied enough to attempt to start the first of the four engines. The engine turned, coughed and belched black smoke out of its rear, but did not start.

The pilot tried again and this time, it did manage to start, and continued to run. The same thing happened with each engine in turn. First the belch of black smoke and then spluttering into life. The engines were certainly noisy, but the pilot seemed happy, and gave the "thumbs up" to the ground crew.

We began to taxi to the top end of the runway and took up position for our take-off. The pilot did a final check with his crew and then pushed all levers to full chat and the monster roared into life, charging down the runway. We soon gathered sufficient speed for the giant aircraft to jump into the air. It was a strange runway, as halfway down, it suddenly had a steep slope that gave the appearance of being the end of the runway. I later learned that this had caused a major problem to a visiting Air Force which was invited to land at Debre Zeit. A number of the visiting pilots had actually thought it was the end of the runway and had slapped on their brakes and reversed engines. A number of aircraft had been damaged. Much to the embarrassment of the Imperial Ethiopian Air Force and the visiting force. I think the visiting force was the RAF, but they were too polite to tell me who it was.

I had never heard or seen a runway with a steep slope on it, and obviously the visitors had not been aware of this anomaly. Our pilot pulled back heavily on the stick and the aircraft roared its disapproval and climbed just in time over the trees at the end of the runway. The pilot came through on my headphones, explaining that it was difficult to take off with a full load of fuel on this runway. I smiled and congratulated him on a job well done.

I had a fantastic view from my navigator's seat, and Africa never looked so good. Our aircraft continued to climb and we circled south over the village of Debre Zeit, over the volcano and lake. To the south stood the favourite weekend retreat of his Imperial Majesty King Haile Selassie. The King of Ethiopia. The palace was magnificent. And in direct contrast to the mud huts that surrounded much of Debre Zeit.

The pilot continued the circle and started to head north. We were to fly to a military landing strip, just outside the port of Assab. The old 119 flew very low over the land, and as we flew north, I noticed how parched the land appeared. The rains had failed again and the crops had failed. Villagers had been forced to slaughter their animals and begin a long trek to try to find food. Many thousands were dying and as we flew further north, we saw village after village with no sign of life at all. It was an awful sight and one that would stay with me forever.

We could clearly see the bones of dead animals from above, and occasionally, human skeletons. It was hot and the ground was barren. I later discovered that the northern part of Ethiopia is the hottest place on earth, and was the home of the Danakil, a very fierce tribe of warriors. It was a very harsh but very beautiful country, and I sat there fascinated by it all. I could not believe my eyes. I was deep in thought when a member of the crew appeared, with a grin from ear to ear and offered me some coffee and a large packet of sandwiches. They really were a great bunch, and had taken time out to ensure there were sufficient supplies for me. I thanked them and sipped the coffee. It was strong, hot, and sweet. The sandwiches were made from thick rough Ethiopian brown bread and thick slices of best beef. The coffee and sandwiches went down well, and my spirits rose.

The old freight plane lumbered on and we climbed over another mountain range, and then dipped towards the desert plains which stretched before us. We flew over village after village, abandoned because of the drought. It was an awful eerie sight, not seeing a living soul for many miles.

The first sign of life I saw was a camel train, and it was a sign that we were nearing our destination. Although we were still high up, it was very warm – and getting warmer. The desert seemed to stretch forever, and we seemed to be standing still. I looked down and saw the reflection of our aircraft casting a shadow over the parched landscape.

We were heading for the Red Sea port of Assab, and at last, we saw signs of habitation in the far distance. The pilot was busy talking to the local control tower, giving our call sign, and ensuring that they realised we were a friendly aircraft. We were fast approaching the rebel areas of Northern Ethiopia and the last thing we needed was to be attacked by our own forces.

We circled around Assab, and I caught my first sight of the Red Sea shimmering below us. The port looked quite busy, and one of the freighters had our stock on board. It was good to see a bit of life after all the deserted areas that we had flown over.

The aircraft suddenly banked, and dropped at speed, towards the landing strip. The engines grew increasingly loud as our pilot reversed thrust, and the huge freight plane lurched onto the ground. He had made a perfect landing, and the crew were obviously happy to have reached the safety of the ground in one piece.

They all chatted excitedly and busied themselves in getting the aircraft tidy.

Chapter 7
Assab: Customs and Corruption

With Charlie in Assab

The aircraft ground to a halt and the doors were opened.

I could not believe the heat that gushed in. It was like sucking on a hair-dryer: bloody hot and uncomfortable. The pilot was in good spirits and we chatted while awaiting the arrival of our transport into town.

The aircraft was due to stay in Assab overnight and then return to Debre Zeit the following morning. Hopefully, my stock would be ready by then. How naive I was.

An old Jeep bounced over the runway towards us, and there sat my appointed Lieutenant: very smart and quite young. He got out of the Jeep, came briskly to attention, and saluted me.

I stepped forward, and we introduced ourselves. This young man would be my "right arm" for the period that I would be in Assab, and would ensure that all of my needs were met. He had not dealt with importing goods into Ethiopia before, so at least we had something in common.

He was a nice chap, and as I can't remember his name, I shall call him Charlie.

He helped me to load my bags into his Jeep. I bade farewell to the pilot and crew, and we set off for the port of Assab. We decided to go straight to my hotel so that I could rest after my journey and we would start the business of importation the following morning.

The hotel was of typical Italian influence, but had obviously deteriorated since its Italian owners had departed.

There was a strange dank smell about the place, but my room appeared clean, and had air conditioning, which appeared quite affective, thank God! The Red Sea port of Assab really was a hot place, and one to be avoided if possible. No wonder Asgers didn't want to come. Although I also suspected that he was scared of flying. An Air Force Major scared of flying was not a thing to admit to, but he did have a wife and many children, and the aircraft were old.

I agreed to be picked up by Charlie at 0830hrs the following morning, and gratefully fell asleep on my bed.

I awoke some two hours later feeling thirsty and hungry, and decided to have a shower and go through for something to eat. I tried to have a cold shower, but even the cold water was warm. I had not realised that it was salt water. I washed my hair and it went really weird, and caked with salt. My normal shampoo was useless. In desperation, I went through to the reception. The young lady was obviously trying very hard not to laugh. They were obviously aware of the problem, and had a special local shampoo, which they quickly gave me.

I returned to my room, and tried again. This time the shampoo worked, and I looked quite normal, thank God!

After two showers, I felt much better and I went through to the dining room. It looked reasonably clean, and the waiter was at least in clean clothing.

There were a number of other guests in the hotel, and two of them were young Chinese men. They were having great difficulty in making the waiter understand what they wanted, as their English was very bad, and the Ethiopian waiter was having difficulty with their Chinese accents. I managed to decipher what the Chinese guests wanted, and I translated on their behalf. They were very grateful for my help, and asked me to join them. They became very interested in the reason I was in Ethiopia, to the point where I began to suspect their motives. It was a strange time in the life of Ethiopia, and I felt I should be very cautious of what I divulged to them.

I ordered my meal of soup, steak, vegetables, boiled potatoes, and a large, cool beer. The food tasted good and the beer even better, so I ordered another one.

It transpired that my companions were from Chinese Peace Corps, and had been sent by their government to work in the port of Assab as engineers. They had both graduated from their engineering college, and as a matter of honour, had volunteered for the Peace Corps. They did not like the place, or the work, or the fact that they could not make themselves understood to the locals. Most of the locals spoke broken English, but the Chinese accent was too much for them. I felt sorry for the two young chaps, who had to serve two years in Assab, with very little money and a language problem. They both said they missed their home and family, but it would be a matter of honour, and they would have to stay where their country had sent them.

I suspected that they kept their government aware of everything that was happening on this part of the African continent, including the arrival of a strange, youngish Englishman. We enjoyed each other's company. At least it was someone to talk to.

The evening passed, and I felt tired, so I bade my Chinese friends a good night, and went off to bed. The air conditioner was working well, and apart from the damp, dank smell, my room was reasonably comfortable. Bottled water was placed by my bed, and having drunk half of it, I fell into a fitful sleep.

The images of this vast, barren, dry land, where thousands of people were dying, kept returning to my thoughts, and it was a considerable time before I fell asleep. I awoke to the shrill of my trusty alarm clock, dived into the shower, and again tried to have a cold shower, and failed. The creases at the tops of my legs were sore and red with the heat. Obviously, the hot atmosphere and the sweaty seat in the aircraft hadn't done my parts much good, but a liberal application of talcum powder over the tender areas helped a bit.

I went through to breakfast. I had some watermelon, fresh orange juice, hot coffee, and toast, and felt ready for the day ahead.

Charlie duly arrived on time, and we set off for the Customs Office. We drove through the Assab port area, and I was struck by the number of shanty bars there.

Charlie explained that the makeshift bars played host to all of the visiting ships, and that there were many bar girls, plying their trade, and, bearing in mind that the sailors were a long time at sea, were in great demand.

On the way to the Customs Office, the girls were everywhere, and waved at us as we passed by. They obviously knew Charlie and cheered and as he passed by. In his smart uniform and Ethiopian Air Force Jeep, he cut quite a dashing figure.

I felt a bit strange and decided that it was the heat and the change of food. My crotch area was beginning to feel worse, and even though I was dressed in the lightest possible clothing, and had changed regularly, I was sweating by the time I reached the Customs Office.

I told Charlie of my plan of campaign to get the stock cleared through Customs free of charge, and he looked a bit worried, but didn't say anything. I had been warned that the Customs Officials would only respond if I bribed them to do so, and this was common practice by the civilian clearing agents. But I represented the Imperial Ethiopian Air Force, and as a member of the Services, albeit seconded to them, I was not going to bribe anyone.

I planned to ask to see the Chief Customs Officer, and explain our mission. We were here, after all, on behalf of His Imperial Majesty's Air Force. Charlie looked a bit sheepish, in the manner of Asgers. They were obviously trained in the art of looking sheepish in the Air Force.

Charlie explained that the local Chief Customs Officer was a very powerful man, and could not be upset. He had obviously heard of my run-in with the MD of Mitchell Cotts. I assured Charlie that I would not upset the Chief of Customs, but it was very important that I got his support.

We entered the main Customs clearing office, and were met by a cacophony of sound. Agents and Customs officials were in deep discussions regarding the importation of everything from tractors to toothbrushes. Charlie managed to find a free member of staff, who, after a lot of discussion and strange looks at me, arranged for us to meet the Chief of Customs.

They were obviously wary of me, as I stood out like a sore thumb in amongst the local agents. Charlie and I were ushered upstairs, and into the smart, air-conditioned office of the Chief of Customs. He was a small, fat, greasy-looking man; sweaty, even with the air conditioning. He had gold teeth and a lot of other signs of wealth. He obviously made a lot in his position as "boss man", and not all legally, I suspected.

He rose to greet me, and I took an instant dislike to him. I had promised not to upset him, so I hid my feelings, and we were ushered to a coffee table area. An assistant brought us cups of coffee. It was a good start. The man spoke very good English, and I explained my mission to him, how the grandson of His Imperial Majesty had arranged for NAAFI to supply the Air Force, and how our stock was in his harbour and that I needed it to be cleared through Customs with some urgency, as the shop was waiting to be opened.

I explained that the shop was for the sole use of the Ethiopian Air Force Personnel, and as such, it should be allowed to import the good free of any duty. The Customs Chief smiled politely, showing his gold teeth.

'No,' he said. Just like that. No. The Air Force could not have duty free goods, and that was final.

More coffee arrived, and I tried all avenues to try to change his mind. I failed. He was adamant that the Ethiopian Air Force would have to pay duty if they wanted their goods imported into Ethiopia.

After much more discussion, I conceded defeat and asked how I was to achieve this. He suggested that I appoint a clearing agent. I said that we could not afford this, and I would clear the goods myself. It could not be that difficult.

I should have taken the advice of this sweaty little man.

I asked how I should proceed, and the Chief of Customs said that he was too busy to explain all the procedures, but he would organise a member of his staff to explain the systems to us. We were dismissed from his office and waited for one of his men to come and explain all.

Another small man appeared and he proved to be a very helpful person. Two hours later, we were totally confused, but I was determined to show these chaps that I would not be beaten. I was after all, British.

I should have listened to the advice I was given, but I was younger then, and, I suppose, arrogant. Our helper had spoken of Bills of Laden, Invoices, Tariffs, Duty, Duty Stamps etc. etc. and Charlie and I were confused, to say the least.

I had fortunately brought a set of invoices sent to me by NAAFI HQ. Unfortunately, my British colleagues were also unaware of the Importation requirements of the Ethiopian Customs Office. All the goods were mixed on the invoicing. It transpired that each category of goods had a different Importation Tariff, and had to be individually calculated. I could not believe it. It was an impossible task that I had set myself, and Asgers and the Colonel had really dropped me in it.

The only concession I managed to get out of the Customer was the use of an air-conditioned office in the main block. It did not seem much, but it saved the day, as I was about to spend considerable time there as their guest.

I was worried, as I was feeling the effects of the heat, and my stomach and crotch area were getting worse. I seemed to be spending more and more time in the loo, and this was not a pretty sight.

Charlie did his best to assist me as we started sorting out the paperwork, but it really was an impossible task. It transpired that there were fourteen different procedures to go through to import each category of goods. It was very different indeed, as an example, Heinz Beans in tomato sauce should have had two tariffs, as the bean element had a tariff of 20% but the tomato element had a

83

tariff of 114%. When I asked why, I was told that the Ethiopians grew their own tomatoes, and the tariff ensured that the local market was protected. I had great difficulty in persuading the Customs Officials that there was only a very limited amount of sauce in the beans and that I should only be charged 20%. I eventually won. This was the type of argument that I was to endure, in sickness and in health, for the next two weeks. Thank god that the Air Conditioning worked, otherwise life would have been impossible.

We worked hard on creating a system. I calculated what I thought the duty for each item should be and Charlie wrote out the item and the amount that we should be forced to pay. As already mentioned, the invoices contained a mixture of goods on each page, and this made our task nearly impossible. Thank god, the day passed and I felt awful. We had learned a lot, but there was much more to learn.

Charlie took me back to my hotel, and suggested that we meet for a drink later, to get over the day. Although I felt awful, I agreed that we should meet at 8 o'clock for a quick couple of beers and a look at Assab.

The heat was really getting to me. My nether regions were covered in a rash, and felt like they were on fire. I should have gone to bed and stayed there, but instead, I had an hour's nap, got up, showered, and had a snack, even though I didn't feel like eating. There was no sign of my Chinese friends so I had a coffee and waited for Charlie to appear. He arrived punctually at 8 o'clock, and we decided to walk into town. It was not too far before we reached the start of the bars, and one looked much the same as another, with lots of girls hanging around, and most of the places didn't look so bad in the poorly-lit night.

As we turned a corner, I was accosted by a strange looking chap, who wanted to sell me a bottle of whisky. I wasn't interested until I noticed that the bottle had a NAAFI stamp on it. The man refused to tell us how he had got hold of it. Even though our goods had only just been landed in the secure Customs warehouse, some of our stock had already been stolen and was up for sale in the back streets of Assab. Charlie and I could not believe it and we thought it quite funny. We were having problems trying to import it into Ethiopia, but it had already reached the streets of Assab. We had to laugh.

We found a reasonably clean bar with some nice looking girls and ordered a few beers. The girls were very friendly and kept offering themselves to us, but both Charlie and I were too tired from our day's toil. We had an enjoyable evening talking to the girls, bought them a couple of drinks, but decided that as we were both worn out and faced another hard day, we would go back and have an early night.

Charlie agreed to pick me up at 0830 the following morning. I crashed out on my bed and fell asleep almost immediately.

It seemed like I had only just gone to sleep when the alarm went off. I staggered out of bed, got under the shower and stayed there for a considerable time. My rash was getting worse and was very uncomfortable. I would have to get something done about it. My stomach was also playing up, and I would also have to get something for that.

Charlie arrived on time. I explained my problem, and he took me to the chemist. The chap at the chemist was of Indian descent and he seemed to understand my problem. He suggested some special cream for my crotch, and pills for my stomach.

On arriving at the Customs House, I went to the loo and applied the cream. I took two pills with some black coffee and I felt a little better. Charlie and I set about the task of Importation documentation, and it didn't seem any easier than it had the previous day.

I managed to get to see the Head of Customs, and lodged a complaint about the way our stock had been stolen and was already for sale in the "free market" of the streets of Assab. He greeted me with am insincere smile.

'Still here, Mr Lupson?' he asked.

I confirmed that I was, and intended to stay until I had completed the job. The man's eyes looked quite evil.

'You must understand, Mr Lupson, that this is a very rough area, and there are lots of very nasty people about. People are corrupt and stock gets stolen from time to time, no matter how careful we are.' The Customs Chief maintained his smile. 'Do you understand, Mr Lupson?'

I confirmed that I understood, but was not happy about what had happened, and I left his office.

Charlie and I continued in our task of trying to sort out the categories of tariffs applicable to our stock, having to add the CIF Carriage, Insurance, and Freight, to each item. It was like torture, and trying to concentrate when feeling ill did not help.

There were fourteen different procedures that had to be applied to each section, to compile the necessary documentation, and it was Hell. It took us a further three days to complete the paperwork and I was becoming increasingly ill. On the fourth day, I could not get out of bed. I had hardly eaten for three days, and had spent a considerable time in the loo. My crotch and rear end were raw, and I was very weak. As I lay in a deep sweat on my bed at the hotel, they finally managed to find a doctor, and I was diagnosed with dysentery. I became worse and was now being sick as well as ever-increasing visits to the loo. Charlie visited me regularly and kept Asgers informed.

It should have taken a few days to clear the goods, but we were now into our third week, and I was seriously ill. It was a good way to lose weight, but not one that I would recommend. The next few days were a blur and all I wanted to do was die. I must have lost at least a stone during this time, but I don't remember much about it.

The continuing trips to the loo played havoc with my rear end, and my sores were now bleeding. The doctor made regular visits, and on the third day, I returned from the dead. Thank God the immune system seems to click in after a while, and starts to fight back.

The following day, I managed to get up, and after a long, long shower, to go through to the dining room. I managed to take some soup and bread, and staggered back to bed.

My head ached, my body ached, and I was totally dehydrated. Lesser people had died from dysentery, and if I had not been so fit, I would probably have joined them.

I later saw the state of the hotel kitchens, and I was not surprised at getting dysentery. Birds were allowed to fly around the kitchen, there was little or no sense of hygiene, and it was bloody awful, to say the least. The locals had obviously built up a resistance to the poor state of hygiene in the area, and managed to survive.

On the fifth day, I felt fit enough to return to the task in hand. As we arrived at the main Customs Office, we were met by the Head of Customs.

'Still here, Mr Lupson?' he asked, with a grin. The bastard was gloating at my obvious poor state of health. I assured him that I was still there, and went through to our office. We completed the documentation, and presented them to the Customs Officer. He was very helpful and surprised that we had managed to complete the task.

'We must now inspect the goods,' he said. 'But unfortunately, this will not be possible today.'

They were obviously enjoying mucking me about. I didn't let my feelings show, but underneath, I was seething with anger. Asgers had obviously been aware of what I had been in for, although he denied it when we eventually met again. I should have paid the clearing agents and bribed the Customs Officer, and this would have saved me considerable pain and anguish. But I was British after all, and would not be beaten.

The following day, we arrived early, and were escorted to the secure Customer area. Our stock was there and there were cases and cases of stock, all neatly packed in Tri-Wall cartons. All very well packed, with serial numbers showing the contents of each box. Some had been damaged in transit, hence the sale of our whisky.

The customs officer made us unpack a number of cases to verify their contents. And this is when the arguments started concerning things such as beans in tomato sauce etc. etc.

But at last the Customs Officer had enough, and agreed that the invoicing and documentation agreed with the content of the cases, and we returned to the Customs Office.

At last the documentation was correct and all the stamps and import procedures were completed, and my frustrations were coming to an end. All it needed now was for the Customer Officers to calculate the amount we owed, and that was that. How naïve can you get? Two days later, I was still at the Customs HQ.

I met the Chief of Customs, and confirmed that yes, I was still here, for what felt like the millionth time. I had begun to detest the man, and it was with great satisfaction that I felt that Charlie and I had won. Against all the odds, we had completed the importation documentation.

The next step was to get the money transferred from NAAFI HQ to the head office at Addis, but this could be done once I was back at Debre Zeit. I must confess that I was looking forward to returning to the cooler climates and to getting away from the Chief of Customs.

I decided that Charlie and I deserved a night out on the town after all our efforts, but first, I arranged for my return to Debre

Zeit. The Air Force confirmed that they would not have any transport returning South for at least a week, and they kindly arranged for me to fly back with Ethiopian Airlines, and I would return the following day, thank God!

The Imperial Ethiopian Air Force would arrange to transfer our stock from Customs to one of their own warehouses and then arrange to fly the stock down to Debre Zeit.

I said my reluctant thanks to the Chief of Customs and bade him farewell. He grudgingly said that he had not thought that we wold be able to complete the importation procedures, and there was a slight sign of admiration from him as I said goodbye. I thought it best to try and stay on reasonable terms, as I felt sure I would have to return for the next shipment.

Charlie and I had a superb night out on the town, and even our Chinese friends joined us. I decided that I would host them, as they had very little funds. They were very interested in how I had achieved so much, and insisted on taking a photo of me with them. It probably was quite innocent, but it didn't feel like that in the Cold War climate. They were asking me all sorts of questions that did not seem normal at the time. I was suitably vague at answering their queries.

We toured the low-life of Assab, and met loads of girls. We had a fantastic time, much of which was lost due to the amount of alcohol we consumed. Some of the girls attached themselves to us and we really had a tremendous party.

I awoke to find one of the most attractive girls wrapped around me. I do not remember taking her back to the hotel, but I must have done. I slowly released myself from her and she stirred and smiled. I suppose I must have enjoyed myself, but I did not remember. She had a magnificent body and obviously had some Italian blood mixed in with the Ethiopian. Even pissed, I could apparently still pick them. I realised that she was a bar girl, and gave her some money, thanked her and escorted her out of the hotel. It was only six o'clock in the morning, and there was nobody about. Not that it mattered – they were used to guests bringing girls home.

I returned to my room, had a long, hot shower, and packed, ready to leave. I couldn't remember what time we had arranged for Charlie to pick me up, but I assumed it would be around nine o'clock.

Walking into the dining room for breakfast, I felt distinctly hung over. It had been a night to remember, but unfortunately, I could not. I consumed lots of coffee and toast, and began to feel much better.

My flight was arranged for eleven o'clock that morning, and Charlie had promised to take me to the airstrip that was shared between the civilian and military aircraft.

Reliable Charlie arrived at nine o'clock, and he looked worse than me. I invited him to join me for more coffee, and we sat and chatted. He couldn't remember much about the previous night either, and he had also awoken to find a girl wrapped around him.

He had apparently managed to smuggle her into the Air Force accommodation, and also to smuggle her out again. He also could not remember if he had enjoyed her, so we were both in the same boat.

With all our trials and tribulations with trying to import the goods, we had become good friends, and I was quite sad to say goodbye at the airport.

We had arrived in good time to see the Ethiopian Airline plane arrive in a cloud of dust. Unloading its occupants, refuelling and getting ready to fly again – it was all done within forty five minutes. Not bad. The plane was largish, with four engines and painted in the livery of the Imperial Ethiopian Airlines. It looked smart, but quite old.

I bade farewell to Charlie, who once again came to attention, and smartly saluted, as if saying goodbye forever. I returned his salute. Even though I was not in uniform, it seemed the right thing to do. We grinned at each other, and wished each other well. I said that I would see him again on my next visit, and I assumed that he would be allocated to the task of getting the stock loaded onto the Air Force transport.

I was welcomed on board by the very smart Ethiopian Airlines stewardesses, and I strapped myself in. The plane was three-quarters full, with a mixed crowd of businessmen and others. Our aircraft roared into life, and sped down the runway in a cloud of dust. I was on my way back to civilisation.

Our aircraft headed south, and coffee and a sandwich was served. I fell asleep, still suffering from the night before.

I was rudely awakened by a sudden shudder and roll of the aircraft. The pilot was having great difficulty in controlling the plane. We had hit a tropical storm, and looking out of my window, there were very black clouds and some spectacular lightning. I thought that stewardesses were supposed to keep us all calm, and ensure that we, the passengers, were safe and comfortable. Instead, it was the other way round. The young stewardesses were in a real state of fear, and we, the macho men, did our best to comfort them. The stewardesses were convinced we were about to crash, and it was like something out of the movies.

The aircraft was being tossed about, and I had never experienced anything like it. Items of clothing and luggage were flying around, and we all had to take care to duck the debris. The pilot was having a terrible time, and was too busy trying to fly the plane to let us know what was happening. After what seemed like an age, we reached the far side of the storm and the aircraft seemed to settle down.

It soon became clear that our pilot was hopelessly lost. He continued to head south, and flew very low to try to gain his bearings. He found a road that he seemed to recognise, and proceeded to follow it at a very low level. The stewardesses calmed down and thanked us for our help and understanding.

The road appeared to head towards the capital, Addis Ababa, and our airport. The pilot managed to find the time to address us, and apologised for the very rough flight and the inevitable delay in our arrival.

We in turn, asked the stewardesses to thank him for his courageous flying skills, in taking us through one of the worst storms I had ever seen.

Chapter 8
Geeta

I arrived at Addis International Airport, a thinner, wiser man, and this time I had no problems with immigration, as the flight was an internal one.

I walked out of the main building expecting to find the smiling face of Asgers, but there was no sign of him. I was tired and parched, so I found a coffee stand in the airport, and waited for Asgers to appear. Half an hour went by, and there was still no sign of him. I'd had enough, so I found the best taxi I could, and instructed him to take me to Debre Zeit. It must have seemed like Christmas to the driver, because I was probably the best fare he was likely to get that month.

The car was an old Opel, similar to Asgers' and in a similar poor state of repair. The car smelled of an insect killer which was peculiar to this part of the world. It gave me a headache, and although the driver was a pleasant chap and obviously wanted to talk, I soon fell asleep.

The journey was quite rough, and took over two hours to complete the forty odd miles, but I arrived, safe and sound. I paid the driver the equivalent of his month's salary, and entered the hotel. I was too tired to worry about what had happened to Asgers, and I decided to have a light snack and turn in for the night. Tomorrow was another day, and I needed my sleep to regain some of my strength.

The following morning, I awoke, showered, had breakfast and the world seemed a better place. At least I had escaped the heat of Assab.

I walked out of the hotel and walked to the shop. I was only a hundred yards away from the shop, when Asgers appeared, driving my car. He looked shocked, and as if he was about to burst into tears.

'Mr Lupson, what are you doing here? What is wrong with you? Are you ill?'

He jumped out of my car and bounded towards me. Concern was etched into his face. His questions came thick and fast, and he was not giving me time to explain or to ask him why he had not picked me up at Addis. I managed to calm him down and I suggested he drove me up to our supermarket. We would sit down with a nice cup of coffee, and I would tell him of my adventure, and he would tell me what had happened here.

We were greeted by the new staff and everyone expressed concern over my appearance. I assured them that I was now well. Asgers and I ordered some coffee and went through to our office.

Asgers explained that he had been informed that I would be arriving today and had arranged to meet me at the airport later in the afternoon. He had obviously been given the wrong information, but this was Ethiopia and this sort of thing happened all the time.

I spent the next two hours drinking lots of coffee, and telling Asgers of all the details of what had befallen me at Assab. From the lack of help from the Chief of Customs, to the dysentery, the heat of Assab, the helpfulness of Charlie and the poor state of hygiene at the hotel. I told Asgers how we had managed to clear the Customs documentation without the need of bribery, and he was really impressed.

'We did it, Mr Lupson,' he kept saying excitedly. 'We did it!'

All of a sudden, he had adopted the royal "we".

I toured the shop, and saw with satisfaction that Asgers had managed to put the final touches to the fabric of the building. It looked very smart with the new fittings, some local stock, and the new cash desk and till. All we needed now was the stock from Assab.

I told Asgers that we must go to the Colonel, and enlist his help in ensuring that the Customs would release our goods on a promissory note from us that they would get the Duty that was due on our goods.

I still felt weak from my troubles in Assab, and I allowed Asgers to drive us to the Base. We entered the Imperial Ethiopian Air Force main gate, and the guard came smartly to attention when he recognised Major Asgers. It was obvious that Asgers was help in very high esteem by the junior ranks. They saw him as a sympathetic officer who was doing his best to improve their lot with the opening of their own retail organisation.

Their respect of Asgers was to prove very useful in the coming months, and it probably saved my life on more than one occasion.

We met the Colonel, and even he showed concern that the state of me. I had obviously lost a lot of weight, and still looked drawn from dysentery. I confirmed that I now felt much better and spent the next hour briefing the Colonel about my trip to Assab.

He was obviously disappointed that the Chief of Customs would not allow us to import our goods free of Duty. I suspected that the Colonel was well aware of the fact, but had thought it was worth a try.

He agreed to signal the Chief of Customs, and once agreement was received that they would accept a promissory note that NAAFI would pay the duty, he would arrange for the Air Force to fly our goods to Debre Zeit. He then said that he thought it would be a good idea if I were to return with the aircraft and ensure that the goods were delivered properly. I reluctantly agreed, but on the grounds that we would do the return journey on the same day. There would be no need for me to stay overnight, and I was glad to hear it.

Asgers and I returned to our shop, having thanked the Colonel for his support.

Later that day, the Colonel confirmed that the Chief of Customs had agreed to release our stock, and the Colonel had arranged for a flight to Assab in two days' time. It would be an early start, but I would be back in time for tea.

We finished work for the day, and I felt in need of some company: people on my own wavelength. I had another shower, a quick meal and set off for the sanctuary of the ex-pat club.

I was given a hero's welcome by all of my friends. They had been extremely concerned that I had not returned within the few days as promised and all expressed concern over the state of my health. I did not feel bad, but I obviously looked it. They all plied me with drinks and sat around to hear about my adventures in Assab.

The Indian contingent had arrived at the club shortly after me, and they were all worried about my health. Geeta's eyes looked sad and concerned at my obvious poor state.

'You are very thin, Derek,' she said, and she looked as though she was about to cry. I assured her that I was now well, and thanked her for her concern. As we all talked, and I related my adventure to the gathered members, Geeta's eyes met mine, and there was a strange feeling between us. Once again, her protectors got in our way when there was a danger of us getting too close. It was very frustrating to us both, but they felt it was their duty to protect her from me.

The evening passed all too quickly, and as I was about to leave, Geeta's protectors approached me and said that I obviously needed fattening up after Assab, and asked me to join them the following evening for a meal. Geeta had also been invited. I could not believe my ears, and once I confirmed that I would be delighted to join them, Geeeta's eyes began to gleam. She had a devilish secret smile, and she looked very happy, as was I. We bade each other goodnight, and I returned in good spirits to my hotel. The day had turned out well.

The following day was spent preparing for my return to Assab and writing reports to our HQ in London, and to Norman Lee in Kenya. At last, I was able to confirm that providing all went as planned with regard to receiving the goods from Assab, we would be able to start trading within the next two weeks. We planned an official opening of our first trading establishment, with the Base General cutting the ribbon.

It was all very exciting. Providing of course, that all went as planned and the curse of the promised Ethiopian Tomorrow did not occur. I felt sure that I had covered most aspects of the business, but time would tell.

Asgers was behaving rather strangely and still carried his pistol wherever he went. It was about this time that I started carrying a rather large knife, although I was unsure what I would actually do with it. But it made me feel better. There was obviously something stirring and Asgers attended numerous secret meetings. On his return, he would only say that the situation was getting worse.

On the local front, the rains had certainly failed, and starvation was evident everywhere. The world was beginning to wake up to the potential disaster, but it was already far too late. Thousands were dying, even in this reasonably prosperous part of Ethiopia, with the Air Force Base bringing wealth to the area. It began to be obvious that all was not well with the country.

The day passed very quickly and we achieved an awful lot. We cleared up a lot of the admin, sent my reports, and got the store ready to receive our precious goods.

Asgers agreed to pick me up at 0700 the following morning, to take me to the Base for my 0830 flight to Assab.

I arrived back at my hotel, showered and dressed for my evening with my Indian friends, Raj and Janine, and of course, Geeta.

I drove to their house and all were gathered to greet me. Geeta was smiling, and looking beautiful in her very best sari. My hosts were also in their best clothes, and I felt honoured that they had gone to so much trouble. I was introduced to Petra, their four year old daughter. She was a lovely little girl, but had her head shaved. Her parents explained that it was quite usual for them. The Indian community did this to their young children, as they believed it made their hair stronger and healthier in the long run. It appeared to work, as most of the Indians I had met had beautiful long black hair and it certainly looked healthy.

I had not realised that Janine and Raj had a daughter, but Petra had a local nanny who took care of her every need, and they had not yet taken her with them to the ex-pat club.

We sat and chatted on the veranda, while Janine and her maid put the finishing touches to our meal. It was a good start to the evening, and Geeta and I sat as close together as we were allowed by our hosts. We chatted about our experiences to date. I told them about England, and they told me about India.

It transpired that all three of them originated from the Northern part of India, not far from Nepal. They were all highly trained teachers and had worked at the same school in India. They had seen an advert for teachers at the Ethiopian Air Force Base and had decided to give it a try. Janine and Raj had arrived first of all, and in view of the problems that Geeta was having with her drunken husband, who beat her on more than one occasion, she was persuaded to join them.

Hence the reason why they felt very protective towards Geeta, and why they kept me away from her. They did not want to see her hurt.

We all got on very well and I understood their concerns with regard to the welfare of Geeta. I would be patient and would see what developed. In any case, I had an awful lot of work to keep me occupied over the coming weeks and months.

The meal was fantastic. Janine was a very good cook, and this was the best meal I'd had in months. It was at times like this that I felt quite guilty. Here we were eating as much as we could, drinking as much as we wanted, and yet, less than a mile away, many people were starving to death. It did not seem right.

All too soon, the evening passed, and I explained to my hosts that I had an early start and that I had to fly to Assab the next day, to collect our goods, and that it was important that I was fit for the trip.

Geeta also seemed disappointed that I had to leave so early. As was I. She really was a lovely young lady, and although she was technically still married to "the bastard" in India, her experience of a very rough, but thankfully short married life, had not succeeded in destroying her. She had kept her sense of fun, and was really good company.

My hosts escorted me to their front gate, and I bade them all a very good night. Geeta was not allowed to be alone with me, so we all shook hands, and I thanked them for a superb meal and for a really enjoyable evening in their company. Geeta had a mischievous glint in her eyes, and that lovely sly little grin.

I felt the need of her, but realised that I would have to wait. It was very frustrating for both of us.

I returned to my hotel and had great difficulty in getting to sleep. Geeta kept entering my thoughts.

I awoke to the shrill of my alarm clock, showered and went down to breakfast. Although my hotel was pretty grotty in comparison to UK standards, it was five star, when compared to the hotel in Assab.

I had a large breakfast to prepare me for the day ahead, and Asgers arrived on time. He looked at me quizzically. I felt different – did I look different too?

'How was your evening, Mr Lupson?' he asked, in an all-knowing way.

'A very pleasant experience, thank you,' I replied.

We both laughed. We were getting to be like brothers and I really enjoyed his company. He had a great sense of fun, even though the situation in his much-loved Ethiopia, and his home province of Tigray in particular, was deteriorating fast.

We drove along to the Base, and once again, the guard came smartly to attention as we passed through. The old C-119 freight plane awaited our arrival, and once again, we were greeted like long-lost brothers by the pilot and his crew. They were a great bunch. I climbed on board, was strapped into my parachute, and was ushered to the navigator's seat once more.

I chatted with the members of the crew. Most of them had been trained by the US Air Force, and so obviously spoke very good English. They were looking forward to having their own PX Store, which was the American equivalent of NAAFI. The pilot busied himself, completing the final checks, and I bade farewell to Asgers, who saluted me as we set off down the runway. The salute seemed more like a last farewell, which did not exactly boost my confidence that I would actually return to Debre Zeit this time.

Chapter 9
The Goods Arrive

A C-119 "Flying Boxcar" freight plane in its original USA livery.

The old freight plane roared and belched black smoke as it accelerated down the runway, our pilot eased back on the stick and we climbed into the early morning sunshine.

Once we had done the usual tour around Debre Zeit, we again headed north for the port of Assab. The sun shone brightly and it was a beautiful day, and the crew were in very good spirits. It was going to be a long day, but it had begun well.

As we levelled out, and our course north was set, a member of the crew served hot coffee to us all. As we travelled north, I once again witnessed the lack of movement on the ground. For mile after mile, there was no sign of life. The mud-hutted villages had been abandoned and the fields were parched dry. Apart from the odd buzzard clearing up the dead animals, nothing stirred. It was an awful sight, this harsh, beautiful country that was dying before our very eyes.

We had heard that World Aid had at last started to arrive in the port of Assab, but there was a problem with transporting it to where it was needed.

Our aircraft lumbered on, and it grew hotter and hotter. It felt worse than I remembered, and that was only a few days ago.

At last, the runway of Assab came into view, and once again, our aircraft made a perfect, but very dusty landing. The pilot turned and gave his usual cheerful smile as we ground to a halt near the small terminal building.

Charlie was waiting to greet us, but there was no sign of the transport with our stock. My heart sank. After all this time and effort, and the stock had still not arrived. The doors of our aircraft were flung open and the intense heat flooded in. It was nearly impossible to breathe.

Charlie appeared in the doorway and saw my look of anguish. He immediately reassured me that all was well. The transport was being loaded with our stock, and it would arrive within the hour. There had been a slight hiccup, as the Ethiopian Air Force had just received a consignment of US-made rockets, and these were urgently required back at Debre Zeit. They would have to be transported back with us, and part of our cargo would have to wait, possibly until Tomorrow.

It was disappointing, but there was nothing that I could do. It would take a couple of hours for the aircraft to be prepared and loaded for our return flight.

Charlie would take me into town for lunch and give me a chance to refresh myself. I thanked the pilot and his crew for their help and assured them that I would be back in good time for our return trip.

We drove along the coast road, towards the port of Assab, and passed the General Hospital, which was situated on the outskirts of the town. As we drove along, we noticed a steadily increasing crowd of Bar Girls, all heading towards the hospital. They were laughing and waving to us as we passed. It was a very strange sight; dozens of glamorous prostitutes all heading towards the hospital. I assumed that some sort of plague or disease had broken out, but Charlie explained that it was Friday. Friday, as if I knew what he was talking about! He saw my look of confusion and explained that it was law that each Friday, the girls had to go to hospital to have their parts checked for any signs of venereal disease. Those who were OK were given a permit to practice their profession. The girls who showed symptoms were not allowed to ply their trade, and had to have treatment. It all seemed very civilised, and the girls certainly took it in good humour.

The local police checked the girls' permits from time to time, and if the girl did not have the necessary permit, she was taken to hospital, checked, and then put before a judge, who usually gave them a heavy fine and a few days in jail.

It was in everybody's interest to ensure that the girls were clean and free from disease. It was strange but AIDS was not known at this time. It was, after all, the early seventies, and the world was unaware that the awful HIV would break out, not too many years later.

It seemed a very good idea that all the bar girls and prostitutes had to have a weekly check-up, but I did wonder what would happen if the girl slept with an infected man immediately after her check-up and he didn't use a condom. She would obviously become infected, and could pass on whatever to whoever.

Here we were, going into town on a beautiful, very hot sunlit day, watching this strange procession of long-legged ladies on the way to have their parts checked, all laughing and enjoying their day out together. It was a very strange sight. We laughed and returned their waves, and they blew the odd kiss towards us.

Charlie found a suitable restaurant and we had a local curry lunch. It was a hot, spicy dish, and I wondered as to the wisdom of eating in Assab, following my bout of dysentery. But Charlie assured me that the food was good and I would be alright. He had often eaten here with no problems. We chatted for a good hour or so, and Charlie related the story of the Danakil natives, who lived some ten miles up the Red Sea coast.

They were a very primitive tribe, who scratched a living in the hottest, most desolate place on earth. They still kept their tribal traditions: wearing loincloths and using spears and home-made machetes to hunt, and in some cases, to kill their enemies. They had not changed in hundreds of years, and it sounded fascinating.

Charlie explained that one of the rituals that they still practiced for the young bucks to prove their bravery, and show that they were ready for marriage, was to hunt down an enemy of the tribe, kill him, cut off his parts, and present them to the family of the girl he wished to marry.

I found it hard to believe, but Charlie assured me that it was true. We agreed that on my next visit, when I would have much more free time, he would take me to the nearest Danakil village and we would try to trade for one of their machetes. I was keen to visit, and it all seemed quite an adventure to look forward to. I was a lot younger then.

Time flew, and it was time to return to our aircraft. True to their word, the goods had arrived, and had been loaded, together with the US rockets. It was disappointing that quite a number of our boxes had to be left behind, as the US rockets were needed for the fight in the north, against the rebels. I suddenly realised that we were in the north now, with the rebels not that far away.

The province of Tigray was slowly being taken over by the rebels, who were fighting for home rule. They were being backed by Russia, or at least were being supplied with Russian-made weapons. The situation was getting worse by the day, and the Ethiopian Air Force was making daily bombing raids against the rebel-held areas.

An hour later, we said our farewells to Charlie, and I dutifully strapped on my parachute and sat in the navigator's seat. Our aircraft climbed into the clear blue skies, circled over the Red Sea port of Assab, and headed south. After a while, I needed to use the loo, which was strapped onto the cargo deck of the 119. I gained permission from the pilot, and was escorted to the loo by a member of the crew. The 119 was a massive aircraft, and it was interesting to see our stock strapped in, and next to it, crate after crate of US made rockets.

Here we were, flying very low over potentially rebel-held territory, loaded with high explosives. All it needed was a lucky shot from the rebels and we would be no more. Fortunately, there was no sign of any rebels on this day, and our aircraft lumbered on, over the harsh deserted land, where thousands were dying, and thousands were apparently migrating, in search of food.

Although I had been told that food had arrived in the port of Assab, and that people were on the move, there was no sign of life for mile after mile, as we headed south.

The beautiful harsh land was an awesome, yet eerie sight.

At last our aircraft began to climb, as we reached the hills and the approach to higher ground. Here, the desert gave way to a greener land, and the occasional animal trying to scratch out a living. We saw our first humans, who were also trying to survive. Even from this height, we could clearly see that they looked in a pretty awful state, and they took no notice of our lumbering aircraft.

As we grew ever closer to Debre Zeit, the countryside looked better and more locals appeared, many herding their surviving goats, and the odd cow could be seen.

Debre Zeit came into view, and our pilot and crew began to prepare for the landing. They were in their usual good spirits, as our pilot banked our aircraft and headed for the runway. It was becoming dusk, but I could see my car, just off the runway, with Asgers standing by to greet us.

Our pilot made a perfect landing, with the usual roar, as the engines were put into reverse thrust, and we ground to a halt. Our pilot did his usual turn, and smiled broadly. I think it was always a relief to them all that they had landed safely, but they never admitted it.

The doors were opened and the cool evening air entered the aircraft. It was good to be home and not in the extreme heat of Assab.

Asgers arrived at the aircraft, excited that we had managed the return journey safely, and that the stock had arrived – some of it, at least. It was quite an achievement to have beaten the system of bribery and corruption. We had imported goods into Ethiopia without paying a bribe to the Customs officials, and without the use of a clearing agent. I felt very proud of our efforts.

In view of the pending darkness, it had been decided to lock up the aircraft and arrange to unload it the following morning. Asgers was in good humour, and I allowed him to drive my car to take me to my hotel. Even though it was a bit of a wreck, it was in better condition than his vehicle, and I think he got a kick out of driving the firm's car.

We arrived back at my hotel, and Asgers gave me some post that had arrived during my trip to Assab. I invited Asgers in for a beer, dropped my bag off in my room, and joined him downstairs.

There was a letter from Norman Lee, my supposed boss in Kenya. He was proposing a visit within the next three weeks, to attend the official opening of our shop, and also to pay a visit to the Navy Shop in Massawa. He wanted talks with the Base Commander and other Naval Chiefs, to discuss the non-payment of the NAAFI Account. In addition, he wanted to meet Admiral Scinda Desta, the Grandson of His Imperial Majesty, to have talks on NAAFI's future involvement with the Ethiopian Forces. Would I arrange everything and advise him as soon as possible the proposed dates for the official opening etc.?

Asgers and I thought it was a bloody cheek. Norman Lee had shown little or no interest since my arrival, and here he was, wanting me to arrange a VIP visit for him.

Asgers obviously couldn't stand Norman Lee, and asked if it really was necessary for him to visit.

I assured him that it was, as Norman Lee had the ear of our HQ in London. Asgers was not happy with the idea, but agreed that we had no other option.

We sat chatting, and enjoying our beer, before Asgers bade me goodnight and went home, having agreed to pick me up at 0830 hours the following day. I went through for supper, and opened the rest of my post. There was a letter from my girlfriend in England, and it was really nice to hear from home. I had been busy, and that had kept me from feeling sorry for myself, but it was good to hear that I was being missed. I had managed to write a couple of letters to her, but this was the first letter that I had received from home.

Even the promised "we will be behind you all the way" from NAAFI HQ had not happened. I had nearly died in Assab, and nobody had even enquired how I was getting on with my task, let alone thought to ask if I was still alive! I suspected that HQ relied on Norman Lee to keep them informed, and knowing the way Norman Lee worked, he had probably told HQ that he had everything under control, even though we had not heard from him until now, some six weeks into the project.

I retired to my room, had a quick shower, and fell into bed. It had been a long, tiring day, and I was soon fast asleep.

I awoke to the sound of my alarm, showered, had breakfast, and waited for Asgers. He arrived on time and was in his usual high spirits. He was a hell of a character, and even though he still carried his gun wherever he went, he appeared not to have a care in the world. It was obvious that he trusted me implicitly, and considered me a very good friend, although he thought he should continue to call me Mr Lupson. This had been ingrained in him by Norman Lee, and Asgers obviously feared Norman.

Asgers had been in touch with the Base, and transportation of our stock would commence at 1000 hours that morning. We went to the shop, and made sure the staff had their tasks allocated, and then went down to the Base to watch the unloading of our first consignment to our shop.

We spent the rest of the day unloading the crates into the stores, and I commenced the task of merchandising the shop in a logical Western system that seemed to bewilder Asgers and the rest of the staff. They were not used to a supermarket type of operation. Most of the local shops were very small, and they provided an over-the-counter service. It was therefore strange to see stock placed on open sale for self-service operation, with stock laid out in a logical manner, with shelf space allocated to each item, proportionate to expected sales.

The day zoomed by, and I realised that it was obviously going to be hard work for me to train the staff and ensure that a disciplined lay-out of the shop was made and maintained. I was, after all, trying to take them from the 1930s to the 1970s in one fell swoop.

We had a lot of fun, and frustration in the next few days, as the staff tried to master a merchandising concept that they had not experienced before. Even Asgers got the odd rollicking for not doing as I wished. This was much to his indignation – he obviously felt that I had no right to reprimand an Ethiopian Major, but he managed to bite his tongue.

Chapter 10
A House of my Own!

The fact that Norman Lee was due a visit within the next three weeks must have alerted the Colonel to the fact that he had done little to assist us in recent days.

The Colonel appeared out of the woodwork, and announced that they had at last found a suitable house for me. Would I be ready to move in Tomorrow?

I readily agreed. I'd had enough of living in the hotel, and it would be good to have my own place.

Work was continuing on the shop, and Asgers agreed to take me to the house that been allocated to me. It was situated on the road to the main market, but it looked in a good state of repair. It transpired that this was the Ethiopian Air Force Officers' patch and my house was next door to one of the Base Colonels.

The house had its own high-security fence and I was to have my own local guard and a maid to take care of me. The house was made of wood and brick, with the usual tin roof.

We couldn't enter, as we didn't have the keys. But Asgers appeared satisfied that I had been looked after as befitting the advisor to the Imperial Ethiopian Air Force.

It was agreed that I would move in at ten o'clock the following day. My maid and guard had been employed by the Base, and much progress had been made.

Even though Norman Lee was disliked, he was obviously feared by the Base authorities, and all of a sudden, everyone was interested in ensuring we got full support for our project, pending the visit by Norman.

I awoke as usual, and went to the shop, to ensure that the staff members were progressing with the layout of the shop as I wanted. I had devised a system to aid to replacing stock, which would ensure that everything was restocked in the correct manner, as per my original plan. It sounded complicated, but it was actually a very basic system, and our local staff could easily understand it.

We were progressing very well, and the rest of our goods, including the refrigerator, would be delivered from Assab that week. We had achieved an awful lot in a very short time, but I had been working 14-hour days to achieve it. It had to be all work and no play, but we were winning.

At 0930hrs, Asgers and I set off for my new house. I had packed the night before, and all my worldly goods were in my car.

True to his word, the Colonel had arranged for the Quartermaster to meet us at my new house, and he was a friend of Asgers. The house was in good order, with two bedrooms, a bathroom, loo, kitchen, and a large lounge. My compound was quite large, and there was a shed with a mud floor just outside the back door. It was much more comfortable than the hotel, and all of my needs were taken care of, with blankets, bedding and a fully furnished kitchen and lounge. Asgers' Quartermaster friend had personally ensured that all had been provided to the highest possible standard, and I was really grateful for his help. Asgers was held in very high esteem by all of his colleagues, and this had once again proven beneficial to us.

My maid duly arrived, carrying a large canvas bag, which obviously held all of her possessions. She was a plumpish young lady, with a motherly look about her. She had a lovely smile and assured us that she would be delighted to take care of her new master. I was worried about where she would live, and to my amazement, it transpired that she would live in the mud hut and that she was very happy to have a place of her own.

I insisted that she should at least be provided with a decent bed, and that she should use the bathroom facilities in my new house.

The bed was agreed and supplied by the Quartermaster, but all the Air Force would agree to with regard to her bathing needs, was to supply her with a large steel bowl. She would not wish to, or be allowed to use the loo or my bath. It all seemed very strange to me, but I was assured by Asgers and Alice, the maid, that she was delighted with the arrangements.

I found it difficult to accept that this nice person should be expected to live in a mud hut, some 8ft by 8ft, with no sanitation, but all were insistent that compared with a lot of her fellow maids, she was living in a top class hut, with a tap outside.

One day I might accept that I was living in a different world, but it was very hard.

My maid set to work immediately, ensuring that she had everything she needed to look after me. She was delighted that I had a fridge, a gas cooker, and an electric iron, and lots of new pots and pans.

She was a lovely lass, and had been the maid of an elderly English vicar, living in Addis Ababa. I never found out for sure why she had left his employment, but rumour had it that he had tried to have his evil way with her, and the vicar's wife had found out.

Alice asked me what I liked to eat, and I said 'most things', but that my favourite food was egg and chips. It was all that I could think of at the time, and it was a safe food to eat. It transpired that I would eat egg and chips at least three nights of the week for the rest of my stay in Ethiopia, and sometimes I ate two eggs and chips for a change. Fourteen months of egg and chips has still not put me off the meal – I still enjoy it!

Alice busied herself, making my bed, sorting out my clothes, washing, and making the house a home. She had a nice, cheerful outlook on life, which really helped to keep me sane over the following months.

One problem I found was when I lifted the loo seat. There were frog-type creatures in the bowl. Alice managed to get rid of them, but they returned from time to time.

There was a noise outside, and Asgers and I went to investigate. We were met by a scruffy, poorly dressed individual, with no teeth, carrying a large spear and a machete. This was to be my personal guard. He would guard the compound and ensure my safety.

He didn't look very strong, but Asgers assured me that he would do the job. I didn't take to this individual, and he obviously didn't like me very much. He did not speak English, but Asgers informed him of his duties. He was to lay down his life to ensure my security. He was to stay awake and alert during the hours of darkness. He was to man the gate and ensure it was opened and closed securely, as and when I needed to come or go. During the day, my maid would ensure that the gate was secure, and that my property was protected.

The house was on the main route to the market and there were some very rough and tough people about, who would cut your head off to steal your tie.

'It's very important to maintain your security,' Asgers said.

I must confess, that although I lived in a very dangerous part of the world, I never felt unsafe. But I was younger then, and fit and arrogant. I thought I could protect myself against all comers, and I never felt fear.

All seemed in order, and I thanked the Quartermaster for arranging for me to be so royally taken care of, and Asgers and I returned to work.

Chapter 11
The Great Day Dawns

The next week flew by, with me settling into my new home, and getting used to a maid and a guard.

It was all very strange, but I was fully involved with the pending visit of Norman Lee, and getting the shop sorted out.

In addition to the basics of retailing, we had to arrange for supplies of local requirements. Coffee beans, dried beans, local spices and local fresh fruit and vegetables.

We were fortunate in finding an Italian wholesaler, who was conversant with the needs of the Ethiopian people. The majority of stock provided by NAAFI catered for European tastes, but the majority of our Imperial Air Force customers had never been out of the country, and an awful lot had not even visited Addis Ababa, and had never entered a supermarket.

One of the major problems was the supply of fruit, but Asgers discovered that there was a banana market at Addis every morning. But we had to be there at 0600hrs and compete with the local traders to buy some decent stock. Bananas were in very short supply, but were very popular with those who could afford to buy them.

We decided that we must attend the market, and try to obtain supplies. A few days later, Asgers and I set out from our homes at 0400hrs and drove to Addis Ababa. The roads were deserted, and it was an interesting drive into town. Dawn was breaking by the time we arrived on the outskirts of Addis, and the locals were beginning to stir.

We drove to the northern part of Addis, towards the main market and the banana auction building.

The building was packed with local traders, and the bidding started. It turned into quite a fight, and the strongest traders got the best bananas. Asgers and I stood back initially, until we realised that we would not get any unless we fought our way to the seller and grabbed the amount that we needed. I was taller than Asgers and I managed to force my way past a lot of the traders and got hold of a large stalk of bananas. There must have been about 50lb on this stalk, and I had great difficulty in holding onto it, paying the trader, and getting them back to Asgers. Asgers obviously thought it was unbecoming for an Ethiopian Major to fight and struggle to buy bananas, and he never volunteered to visit the market again.

We had a good laugh at our exploits and managed to get our load back to the car. Even though the bananas had obviously been purchased by us, the local traders still tried to take them off us, and we had to use force to stop them from pestering us. We felt a bit guilty, but our customers were also entitled to some quality fresh fruit. The bananas were green and would last in the cool of our stores for at least a week. It was just as well, as the official opening of the shop was due to happen the following week.

Time was speeding by, and we still had an awful lot to do.

The last of our stock was being delivered by the Air Force later that day, and this included our prized refrigerated cool cabinet.

We made a safe return journey home from the banana market, and I went back to my house for breakfast. Alice made me some strong coffee and toast, and the world began to feel better. She apologised for not getting up when I had left for Addis, and said that in future, I must tell her if I was leaving early, so that she could prepare breakfast before I left. She seemed upset that I had not done so on this particular day, so I promised that I would inform her in future. She was a very caring soul and was determined to look after me.

I returned to the shop, refreshed after our early morning start, and Asgers informed me that our aircraft had landed and they were about to commence unloading it. I was concerned about the refrigerator, and suggested that Asgers and I should visit the Base and ensure that our goods were unloaded safely.

Our friendly pilot was there to greet us, and assured us that all was well. The refrigerator was in one piece.

We watched it all being safely loaded onto the lorry and then arranged for the forklift truck to be driven up to the shop to enable the refrigerator to be placed in the shop. The vehicle arrived, as did the forklift, and we unloaded the rest of our stock and manhandled the fridge to the tailgate of the lorry. The forklift truck driver moved forwards to get under the pallet, and miscalculated the height – and put the blade through the motor compartment.

I stood there, speechless. There was my beautiful refrigerator, having travelled safely for thousands of miles, just outside our shop with a fork through its inner workings.

Asgers saw the grief in my eyes and dashed forwards to ensure that I didn't inflict any damage on the driver.

I really could not believe it. I began to shout my disbelief at how somebody could be so stupid. I was really upset, and let the world know it! Asgers managed to calm me down, and the forklift driver, who had gone very pale, reversed his truck, and managed to get under the refrigerator on the second attempt. He duly lifted my prized, but damaged refrigerator to ground level and we got it into the shop.

Everyone was very upset and sorry to see me so devastated. They all assured me that it would be alright. It would be repaired tomorrow.

The day had started so well, and now I was totally fed up. In retrospect, there were far worse things that were happening, and would happen in the future. So I shouldn't have been so upset. But I suppose the pressure of the last few weeks and months was getting to me.

We managed to trace an Italian refrigeration engineer, who assured us that he would visit the next day, to assess the damage, but he felt confident that he could repair my pride and joy.

I felt a bit better, and decided that as it had been a long day, I would go home to rest. My maid was waiting for me, and she prepared my bath. This entailed boiling buckets of water in the kitchen, and pouring them into the bath. The system worked, and I enjoyed a reasonably hot bath on most days. I stripped and got into the bath, and promptly fell asleep. I awoke to hammering on the door, and my maid shouting. She was concerned that I had been in the bath too long, and was trying to open the door, fearing that I'd drowned! I assured Alice that I was well, and that I would be out soon.

I dressed in fresh clean clothes, went through to the dining area, and really enjoyed my two eggs and chips, washed down with lots of tea.

The world felt good again, and I decided that it was time to visit the ex-pat club for a beer or two. I had been exceptionally busy and had not socialised for a couple of weeks, although I had seen quite a few of the ex-pats in town, and explained that life was too hectic to go out. They all understood, but said I should take time out to relax.

I arrived at the club, and it was great to see them all again. They all welcomed me like a long-lost friend, and it felt good.

We sat and chatted over numerous beers, and life felt good.

It was great to relax with my own kind of people, who spoke the same language and thought the same thoughts. I ended up sitting with Texan John and his Anglo Indian wife, Angie. They were already planning for Christmas. Angie was already getting excited because her mother and sister were planning to visit from India.

I had already heard of her sister, Lavender, who was employed by Air India as a hostess. Angie described her as fantastically beautiful. The plan was for Lavender to accompany her mother from India to Ethiopia. Her mother would stay with Angie and John for a few months, before returning to India. Lavender could only stay for the Christmas holidays, as she had to return to work.

Lavender had visited once before, and all the young Ethiopian Officers, who were also friends of Angie, were queuing up to escort her. Alfred, the ex-Kenyan farmer, confirmed that she really was a beautiful, elegant young lady, who was full of fun. Everyone was looking forward to Christmas, and Lavender's visit. I too became intrigued at the thought of meeting this young lady.

I was told about the Christmas celebrations at the ex-pats' club. Traditionally, they held a carol procession around its members' houses, meeting up at the club first, and then touring the area. Each ex-pat would arrange refreshment at their respective houses, and would entertain the carol singers. It was always very boozy and good fun, and the ideal way to start the festive season. It was definitely something to look forward to.

The evening soon passed and I set off for home. As I drove up to my gate, there was no sign of my guard, and I was pissed enough to be annoyed. I got out of my car, and shone my torch, to where my guard was laid out, fast asleep. Alice had heard me arrive and came out to unlock the gate, by which time, my guard had come to, and was staggering towards the gate.

It was obvious that he, too, had been on the booze, and was quite pissed. I could see the funny side of it. There was the toothless wonder, who was supposed to lay down his life to protect me, hardly able to stand up, let alone fight off any would-be robber.

I gave him a rollicking which I know he did not understand, thanked Alice for letting me in, and staggered off to bed. Alice insisted on making me a cup of coffee, which I gratefully accepted. All too soon, Alice was knocking on my door, saying that breakfast was ready.

I quickly washed, shaved and dressed, and went through for breakfast. After lots of strong hot coffee, I felt fit to face the day ahead. My night out had been good for me, and my usual good humour had returned. There was, after all, more to life than a broken refrigerator.

The Italian engineer arrived as promised, and quickly assured us that he would be able to repair my pride and joy. He would have to return to his workshop to get some spares, but would return within a few hours, and with a bit of luck, would have the fridge up and running by the end of the day.

In addition to the usual items that required refrigeration, like milk, fats, cheese etc. Asgers was very keen to sell fresh meat. I had spoken to John Murray, the Texan running the experimental beef farm, and he said that the farm was more than willing to supply us with the best beef in Ethiopia at a very low price. It all sounded very good. John suggested that I visit the farm for a cup of coffee, and select the beast that I wanted. They would then shoot the animal and rough butcher it into quarters, and they would also deliver it to our shop. I told Asgers of this, and he was very happy with the arrangement. He suggested that I went to the farm that very day.

I duly set out for the farm, which was situated some ten miles outside Debre Zeit.

The farm was in a very good state of repair and it was obvious that America had invested heavily in this experimental farm. The fencing was in a very good state, and they had also arranged for the fields to be irrigated. It was in strict contrast to the surrounding area, and was well protected with armed guards. The experimental herd was worth an absolute fortune to a local, and attempts had been made by local tribes to rustle parts of the herd. Things had become quite vicious, and a number of the would-be rustlers had been shot dead.

It was after all, like living in the Wild West, and life was very cheap. I met the main guard at the gate, and explained that I had been invited by John the Chief Scientist, and he escorted me up to the main farm building. John was every bit the Texan, with his large Stetson, cigar and cowboy accent. He welcomed me and took me though to his office.

They were prepared to supply us with as much beef as we wanted, and it would be used as part of the experiment, to ascertain the quality of their efforts.

One of his lads brought in coffee, and John explained how they were trying to improve the local breed of cattle, and trying to eradicate disease from the local herds. It was a near impossible task, as the local herds were fed on a very poor diet, and a lack of water did not help. The local herds would also have to be inoculated, and although the World Aid programme was helping towards the cost, training local farmers in stock management would take many years.

The task would not be helped by the fact that Ethiopia consisted of some fourteen major tribes, most of which had their own language or at least dialect, and most of the tribes were fighting one another for the best grazing areas and water. It really was like the Wild West.

Most of the local cattle grazed an area until it became barren, and then moved on. There was little or no land or pasture management. Each farmer was only concerned with the survival of his own small herd, just wanting his cows to be as fat as possible, without thinking of the long-term consequences.

John and his team of scientists really did have an impossible task. We finished our coffee, and John was keen to show me around. We visited the breeding pens, and saw the most fantastic looking animals I'd seen since my arrival in Africa. John was justly proud of what they had achieved, as were his team. Their beasts were extremely well cared for, and the results showed just what could be achieved in this rough, unforgiving land.

During the last War, Mussolini had said: 'Give me Ethiopia and I will feed the world'. John had proven that with massive investment, the local situation, where millions were about to die from starvation, could have been averted. Poor management, lack of investment, corruption, and a lack of will from the rest of the world, was killing millions.

John completed our tour of the ranch. It was more of a ranch than a farm, but a fantastic achievement. An oasis, surrounded by parched land, decay, disease, and death.

John showed me a selection of animals which were ready to become our beef, and asked me to make my selection. They all seemed to be looking at me with their big beautiful brown eyes; magnificent animals, and I was being asked to select one to be slaughtered. It was at this moment that I realised how soft I was. I confessed to John that I couldn't condemn one of them to be made into beef. I felt awful at the thought, and told John, who looked at me a bit strangely, but he said he understood. This hard Texan must have thought I was a real softie, but he did not let his feelings show. He said he would select one for me and have it delivered to our shop the day after tomorrow, by which time, our display cabinet would be repaired. I thanked him for his help, and he arranged for the beast to be slaughtered and delivered.

Asgers was well satisfied with my efforts to arrange a supply of fresh beef.

***

We spent the next two days finalising Norman Lee's visit. It was arranged that on the second day, we would hold the official opening of our first Imperial Ethiopian Air Force Supermarket, and the launch of the IEAF Trading Organisation. The Ethiopian Air Force

General had agreed to cut the ribbon, and we were to have a reception at the Officers' Mess.

In addition, we had arranged to visit the Imperial Ethiopian Navy HQ at Addis Ababa, and were even successful in arranging to meet Admiral Scinda Desta, the grandson of the King Haile Selassie.

Norman wanted to visit the Navy shop at Massawa, and the Admiral heard about our visit, and arranged a cocktail party at his HQ. It had all fallen into place quite easily. I think this was due to the fact that Asgers and I had been successful in our efforts, in spite of everything, and the promises of "Tomorrow". The supermarket was finally completed, to a very high standard, and now the Base Colonel and all his "hanger-ons" wanted a piece of the action and to take the credit for our hard work.

The great day dawned, and Norman Lee's aircraft appeared on the horizon, heading for the main runway at the Addis Ababa International Airport. Asgers and I had arrived some half an hour previously, and we enjoyed a relaxing cup of coffee together before the madness started. I was dressed in a suit and Asgers was in his best Major's uniform.

This time, Norman Lee had to join the customs queue like everyone else, and he stood out from the rest of the crowd. He was a short, plump, grey-haired individual, and his arrogance shone through.

I greeted him and welcomed him back to Ethiopia. He expressed his concern that I looked thinner than he had last seen me. I assured him that I was fully recovered from my exploits in Assab and that I really was fit and well.

Asgers was in his usual nervous state and was only willing to salute and greet the leader of NAAFI Africa. We led him out towards our car, having been assured that Norman had been well fed and watered on the plane. He was keen to get to Debre Zeit and get down to work.

Asgers and I loaded Norman's luggage into the car, while Norman inspected it. He noticed the repaired wing, and I told him the story of how it had become damaged.

Norman decided that he should drive us back to Debre Zeit. I was not happy at the idea, but he was supposed to be my boss, so I let him. We set off at a very fast pace towards Addis, and to the west of the city and the road that would lead us to Debre Zeit.

Norman drove like a maniac. I told him to slow down, but he totally ignored me, and sped on. As we approached a particularly busy junction, there was chaos ahead, and we saw a very drunk soldier, trying to get from one side to the other. Asgers shouted at Norman to stop, to enable him to sort the soldier out. We stopped at the side of the road, adjacent to the spot where the soldier was in real danger of being run over.

Asgers opened the window and shouted at the soldier, who immediately noticed Asgers' rank and stood rigidly to attention in the middle of the traffic lanes. Cars screeched to a halt and how they missed the poor drunken soldier, I shall never know. The soldier was rigid with fear, having been shouted at by a Major, and even though he was drunk, could not or would not move. Asgers jumped out of the car, and in front of all the stopped traffic, approached the soldier, who immediately insisted on saluting Asgers. It was very funny.

Asgers returned the salute, grabbed the soldier, and dragged him to the side of the road. He was staggering all over the place, much to the embarrassment of Asgers. Asgers managed to get the soldier to safety, much to the amusement of the drivers who had stopped, and witnessed it all. Needless to say, a massive traffic jam had built up, and the police had arrived. Another fine mess that Asgers had got us into. If he had left the soldier alone, he would have probably made it to the other side of the road, and the chaos we were witnessing would not have happened. Asgers told the police what had happened, and they all seemed to see the funny side of it. Even Norman Lee managed to laugh at it all.

Asgers was embarrassed as the drunken soldier was led away by the police, having been assured that they would deliver him back to barracks safely. Asgers got back into our car and both he and I couldn't stop laughing. This sort of thing seemed to follow us around.

Norman Lee set off again at a very fast pace, driving like a fiend. I again asked him to slow down, and he again ignored me. It was at this point that I lost my temper, and Norman got the message. I had been in serious accident some ten years earlier, when a friend of mine had died because of a speeding driver, and I was not amused at Norman Lee's performance. He got the message and slowed to a safe pace, much to the relief of Asgers and I. Norman was beginning to learn that he had met his match, and that I was not impressed with his stupid, arrogant attitude.

I could not face the thought of sharing my new house with Norman, so I had arranged for him to stay at the local hotel. He was obviously not happy at the thought, but I really did not want his company for twenty four hours a day.

I agreed to join him for supper, and, having dropped him off at his hotel, I returned home. Asgers had made his excuses for not joining Norman and I for supper, and I dropped him off at his house.

I was greeted by Alice, who had prepared a bath for me. It was good to be taken care of. I had a good soak and a snooze.

I returned to Norman's hotel, and we went through to the bar and had a couple of beers. I spent the next couple of hours bringing Norman up to date on the progress we had made, and we went through the programme for his visit. He seemed well pleased with the plans, and we enjoyed a few more beers and a very nice meal. Norman began to relax, and was quite good company. I think he realised that I considered him my equal, and that I would not put up with any crap that he thought he might dish out. I had managed a very difficult task, with little or no help from him, or our HQ in London, so I was not going to let him off lightly.

The following day, I picked up Norman Lee from his hotel, and took him to our first Imperial Ethiopian Air Force Establishment. Asgers and I had worked very hard, and the whole place was immaculate. I had even managed to start a vegetable garden at the back of the shop, to provide tomatoes and lettuce for us to sell fresh in our shop.

Norman Lee was obviously very impressed with everything, from the accounting system to the merchandising of the shop, the new till, and new staff with our own uniforms. It really did look impressive, and Asgers and I were justly proud of our achievements.

We were ready for the General to officially open our shop.

Tomorrow would be a great day.

Norman Lee was very satisfied with all that Asgers and I had achieved, and was like a dog with two tails. He asked if I would take him to the ex-pat club that night, so that he could meet my new friends and family again.

We arrived at the Club, and most of the ex-pats were there, apart from the Indian family, Raj and Janine, and of course, Geeta. I had not seen Geeta for weeks. I had been so busy that I had found no time to socialise. The rest of the gang were in good spirits, and made Norman very welcome.

Norman was obviously in a very good mood, and he bought everyone a drink. A party mood soon ensued, and it was a superb evening. Texan John and his wife Angie arrived. Angie was in her usual full of fun mood and insisted that I danced with her. She really was a sexy bird, and insisted on forcing her womanhood into my groin. Only a thin layer of clothing, her Sari, and my cotton slacks, separated us. It suddenly became very hot, and Angie was really enjoying arousing me.

She was laughing and grinding her body into me. I was really hot, and extremely bothered. I was reasonably well-endowed, and my erection would have stood out if I had managed to escape from Angie. She knew exactly what she was doing to me, and ground her body even harder into me. She was a temptress, and surely I was tempted. We had moved to a darker part of the floor, away from the prying eyes of the crowd, which included her husband. She started nibbling at my ear, and grinding her crutch even harder into mine. The music got louder, and we were all but making love. It all became too much. When the rest of the gang appeared not to be looking, I managed to push Angie away, on the excuse that I had to go to the loo. She reluctantly released me and I made a dash for the sanctity of the Gents' loo.

It took me several minutes to cool down and for my erection to subside. I had a quick wash, tidied myself, and returned to the fold.

Angie sat next to John, the total picture of innocence, as if nothing had happened.

'Feeling better now, Derek?' she asked, with a sly smile on her face.

I assured her that I felt much better. Angie had obviously decided to add me to her list of conquests, and had made it very painfully obvious that she was willing and ready to relieve my frustrations. She was very sexy, and very attractive, but I could not bring myself to the thought of having John's wife. I was still quite young and naïve then, and did not make a habit of seducing unfaithful wives. Even if they were handed to me on a plate.

Norman appeared and enquired about my health. Angie had told everyone that I was feeling unwell and had to dash off to the loo. I explained that I felt much better now, and that the heat must have got to me.

I made a mental note to try to avoid being alone with Angie in future, and to try not to dance with her. She was 110% woman, and if her sister was anything like her, we were all in for a treat at Christmas.

All too soon, the evening passed, and it was time for Norman and I to leave. We had a busy day ahead of us the following day, so we reluctantly said our farewells and set off for the hotel and my house. The gang from the ex-pats club were all eagerly awaiting the opening of our shop, as they wanted the European goods they'd been missing. They all promised to visit, as soon as we were officially open. We had quite a captive supply of potential customers.

I dropped Norman off at his hotel, and watched him stagger off to his room. He was quite pissed, but happy.

Chapter 12
Grand Opening – and a Lucky Escape

The General opens the supermarket – with my money!

I got up early the following morning and went straight to the shop.

I had arranged for Asgers and the rest of the staff to meet me there at 0730hrs to put the final touches to our project. I must confess that it all looked very good.

I had the store man supplied with two large pieces of felt, and he was skating up and down the shop floor, polishing it for all he was worth. He was not liked by anyone, and had grown fatter and lazier as he began to earn money, which had gone right to his head. According to Asgers, he had been seen out at the locals' bars, late at night. He would have to be watched.

I went back to the hotel and fetched Norman Lee. He was a bit hung-over, but in good spirits.

All was now complete, and we awaited the arrival of the Commander of the Imperial Ethiopian Air Force. A Jeep swung into the entrance of the shop compound, and two guards got out and took up security positions by the front door. Another Jeep appeared, followed close behind by a black limousine, bearing the standard of the General. It seemed a bit over the top to have so much security, but it was a sign of the times. It appeared that the General was not a well-liked man, and needed bodyguards wherever he went.

The General approached our shop, and Norman Lee and I moved forward to greet him, closely watched by his bodyguard. Asgers was in his very best uniform, as was the project's Colonel.

They all came smartly to attention, and the General wished us a very good morning. Everyone seemed in very good spirits, and we invited the General to cut the ribbon. A number of Junior Rank Airmen and their wives had been invited to attend the official opening, and they were all excited at the prospect of having their own trading organisation. The General made a long speech, in which he thanked the marvellous NAAFI organisation, Mr Norman Lee, the Manager of NAAFI Africa, and of course, their own Mr Lupson, for making this wonderful supermarket possible. He thanked Asgers, whose chest visibly swelled, and of course the project's Colonel. It went amazingly well, and we were all very pleased with our efforts.

Against all odds, we were up and running.

We invited the General to be our first customer, and a member of staff accompanied him around the shop, carrying his shopping. He selected a number of items, which included two bottles of whisky, and when he got to the till, he suddenly remembered that he had no money with him. I dashed forward and avoided embarrassing him by insisting that as he was my first customer, I would pay.

We then invited the Junior Ranks and their wives to shop. They all seemed reluctant and unsure of what to do. Asgers explained that most of them had not experienced a supermarket before, and did not know what to do. Our local staff came to their aid, and explained how the system worked, and in no time, they were all happily shopping away.

The young officers discovered our meat, which was sliced into strips, and packed in plastic trays. As they stood in the queue at the cash desk, one of them could not wait to taste this wonderful fresh meat, and opened the packet and began to chew the raw beef as it if was the best thing he had ever tasted. It looked bizarre to me, but nobody else seemed to notice as he chewed away on the raw meat, with blood dripping down the side of his mouth. I looked at Norman and neither of us could believe what we were witnessing, but the airman did pay for the meat, and that was the important thing.

The whole official opening ceremony went very well, with Asgers proudly showing off all that he had achieved. He stood tall, with his chest puffed out and his head held high, as he explained to the General all that had been done to achieve the opening of the first Imperial Ethiopian Air Force trading establishment.

It was a very good day, and it was good to hear the nervous laughter of the wives of the Junior Ranks, as they enjoyed their very first experience of shopping in a Western style supermarket. Against all the odds, Asgers and I had achieved a minor miracle.

Having admired all of our efforts, the Colonel invited the General and Norman Lee and I to join him in the Officers' Mess for lunch and drinks.

The Officers' Mess was a fantastic building, built for the Ethiopian Air Force Officers by His Imperial Majesty, who was very proud of his Air Force. The building was constructed in the best marble and was equal to most palaces that I had seen in the movies.

The lunch was a hot spicy curry, followed by many glasses of local beer. The General and all concerned were enjoying the day.

Norman Lee was also enjoying himself, taking the plaudits for supporting the project and explaining to the General how well he knew Admiral Scinda Desta. In fact, he knew the Admiral so well, we were going to fly to Massawa the following day to meet the Admiral at a cocktail reception he had arranged for us at his Naval HQ.

The General was obviously very impressed with Norman.

It was arranged that following our visit up North, we would hold a series of meetings with the General and his staff, to continue the expansion of the Imperial Ethiopian Air Force Trading Organisation. More work and headaches for Lupson and Asgers.

Having consumed lots of beer, thankfully Norman decided that we should have an early night as we would have a very busy day tomorrow.

We thanked the Colonel for an excellent lunch, said our farewells to the General, and departed to Norman's hotel, with Asgers doing the driving. He had stayed the most sober of all of us, thank goodness. We arrived at Norman's hotel and ordered coffees all round. We sat with Asgers and discussed the arrangement for the following day. Asgers would collect Norman from the hotel, and me from my house at 0900hrs the following day, and we would then be taken to the Air Force Base and flown to the Red Sea port of Massawa. Transport would meet us at Massawa and take us to our hotel. We would then be taken to visit the Imperial Navy shop, and we would return to our hotel, in time to prepare ourselves for the cocktail reception, arranged for us by the Admiral Scinda Desta, the Grandson of the Emperor Haile Selassie.

The plans were discussed in fine detail, as the Admiral was not one to cross, and even Asgers was afraid of him.

After more coffee, Asgers drove me home. He was a very happy and proud man.

'We did it, Mr Lupson, we did it!' he kept repeating, as I began to fall asleep.

My faithful maid was waiting to greet us, as was my guard. She had prepared my egg and chips, which I had to decline. She had also prepared my bath, which I gratefully accepted.

I said goodnight to Asgers, went through to the bathroom, and promptly fell asleep. As usual, I was awoken by Alice hammering on the bathroom door. I awoke, still in the bath, which was now very cold. I thanked Alice, asked her to wake me at 0700hrs, and fell into my bed.

Tomorrow was another day, but this day had been very good!

***

The morning arrived all too soon, and Alice was knocking at my door with a strong cup of coffee. I had a breakfast of boiled eggs and toast, and felt ready to face the world.

Asgers arrived with Norman, who was still recovering from the previous day's celebrations. Asgers was his normal cheerful self, and I suspected that part of the reason was that he was going to be rid of Norman Lee for a while.

Asgers drove us to the Imperial Ethiopian Air Force Base, where we were met by a very smart NCO, who saluted Asgers and wished us a pleasant day. We carried on towards the airstrip, and there stood our transport. It was a 1950s Dakota, straight out of the old movies. The only difference was that it bore the crest of the Ethiopian Air Force, and was quite smartly painted.

Asgers helped us to load our cases onto the aircraft and introduced us to our pilot. Once again, he was a very good friend of Asgers, and he would take good care of us. The aircraft was amazingly small, with metal seats that ran the length of the aircraft.

It held some twenty people, who sat facing one another. It felt strange and very claustrophobic.

We bade our farewells to dear old Asgers, who assured us that he would be very busy with the shop, and wished us a pleasant trip to Massawa. Once again, he came to a very smart attention, and saluted us as if we were never going to meet again. It made me wonder if he really did have confidence in his own aircraft and colleagues, and why he always managed not to accompany me on flights. Perhaps he really was scared of flying.

We strapped ourselves into this strange old aircraft, and the pilot started his pre-flight checks. One by one, the engines reluctantly coughed and spluttered into life, with great clouds of black smoke belching from the rear. It did nothing to reassure us that the aircraft was safe.

Asgers had disappeared, and our pilot put the engines at full chat, and sped down the strange runway with its small hill halfway down it. The aircraft was very noisy and Norman sat there, obviously still suffering from the day before. It was a beautiful hot and sunny day, and we had a clear view of Debre Zeit as we climbed into the blue skies. We circled the village and headed North West.

The countryside fell away beneath us, and once again, we could clearly see every detail below us. There was little sign of life, even in the part of Ethiopia which was greener than most parts. We continued North, and a member of the crew produced some hot, strong coffee, which both Norman and I really appreciated. We flew even further North West, and the terrain turned more mountainous. There was no sign of life, even though we saw numerous villages. They had been abandoned as their population went in search of food and water.

It was a truly beautiful country. Very harsh, but very beautiful. The mountains seemed to get even higher as we travelled north and then all of a sudden, they stopped and the ground fell away to the desert below. Norman was half asleep, but did manage the odd grunt of appreciation at the view.

We saw a few camel trains, making their way South, with their cargo recently collected from the Red Sea port of Massawa. There was even the odd truck, trying to make its way South over very poor terrain. It was like looking back into history. Camels, 1930s trucks, and us, sitting in this old Dakota. All very exciting.

It seemed to be getting very hot, and the metal seat was very uncomfortable. We were still heading North West, and had flown over some amazing countryside. We had witnessed the extremes of Ethiopia: the greener pastures around Debre Zeit, the jagged mountains, the burnt grassy plains that led into desert, and now the rocky deserts as we approached Massawa. We witnessed that the drought had affected this part of Ethiopia too, and many villages were deserted. There were dead animals scattered around the outskirts of the villages. Many locals had perished from starvation, and lack of water, and nobody seemed able to help. It was very sad to see such a beautiful country in such a terrible state. The world was beginning to respond, but it was far too little, far too late.

The Dakota began its descent towards the airstrip that was jointly used by the Ethiopian Air Force and the civilian airlines. It was strange – we had heard of very serious fighting between the Eritrean Rebels and the Ethiopian Forces, but there was little sign of it. We had seen the odd burned-out vehicle, but not much more. We found out later that the majority of the fighting had been further along the coast, some fifty miles away. Ethiopian Air Force Bombers had strafed the rebels and caused many casualties. Our old Dakota bounced along the runway and its engines roared as it was put into reverse thrust and we came to a grinding halt. We taxied towards the airport terminal, which was virtually a large hut, and our pilot switched off the engines. The engines coughed in gratitude and once again, large clouds of black smoke belched out from their exhausts.

The door was opened by the crew, and a small set of steps were placed to help us to get out. The aircraft was suddenly very hot, and Norman looked very uncomfortable. We were, after all, in one of the hottest part of the world. And it really was hot, and very humid.

Keeping us to our itinerary, a military car was on hand to take us to our hotel, and onto the Navy shop, once we had freshened up.

We retrieved our luggage, thanked our pilot, and set off for our hotel. The immediate area around the airport was quite smart, and the roads were good. The buildings had an Italian influence, and most seemed in a good state of repair.

We travelled on, and saw the inevitable poor parts of the area, with starving people and animals, and no water or sanitation. We saw the Italian influence in the population, and there were some very beautiful women, tall and elegant with European features, but very poorly dressed. It was sad, but I was beginning to get used to these sights.

Our car journey continued and we started the descent towards the Red Sea. The road was amazing incredibly steep with treacherous hairpin bends. It felt like we were being tossed from side to side, as our driver struggled to control the car, with brakes screaming and tyres trying hard to keep a grip on the hot surface. Thank God the military driver was obviously used to the road, and we made it safely to the main port area and our hotel.

We were both in a hot, tired, sweaty state and we were in dire need of a rest, shower, and refreshment. Our driver agreed to collect us two hours later, and we checked into our hotel. We were met by a very beautiful lady, who was obviously half Italian, and she spoke very good English. Even Norman was impressed.

We disappeared to our respective rooms and agreed to meet an hour later. I have seldom enjoyed a shower as much as I did that afternoon. I lay down on my bed and set my alarm.

Thirty minutes later, I awoke to the sound of my alarm, had a quick cold shower, and dressed. Norman was already waiting for me in the restaurant, and we had a quick snack, lots of coffee and prepared for our trip to Norman's Naval Shop.

Our driver arrived, and we were whisked off to the Imperial Ethiopian Navy HQ. The Navy had an ageing frigate and a couple of Torpedo patrol boats, and that was all. It certainly did not warrant an Admiral of the Fleet, but Admiral Scinda Desta was, after all, a grandson of the King, and needed the rank for his status. He had, after all, passed through Davenport Royal Naval College. He had not passed any major exams, but the fact that he had attended college warranted his high rank.

The Admiral was not liked by any of his fellow Officer or men, and tended to use the base as his private Yacht Club, and the Officers' Mess as his private residence. The Base was immaculate and was obviously designed on the principles of the British Royal Navy. Our car swept through the main gate, and we were obviously expected, as the guards came smartly to attention as we passed by. Our car headed towards the administration area, and Norman's Shop. The manager was waiting outside, and greeted Norman and I as though we were VIPs. Norman had certainly installed fear into his naval operation.

The manager invited us in, and we spent the next hour inspecting his stock range and ordering systems etc. Although the Ethiopian Navy had not paid NAAFI at all for the stock or the service it provided, many hundreds of pounds of stock were on order from our HQ and were about to arrive. I broached the subject with Norman, who was rather embarrassed that he had allowed this to happen without any action being taken. We had arranged to visit the Imperial Ethiopian Navy HQ at Addis Ababa, and this was not the time to discuss financial matters. Norman was obviously a little upset that I had dared to raise the matter in front of his manager.

The day was flying by, and it was soon time to return to our hotel to prepare ourselves for an audience with Admiral Scinda Desta, grandson of the King of Ethiopia.

We thanked Norman's Manager, and said that we would return the following day, for a trip around the Naval Base.

We returned to the hotel, washed, showered, and dressed in readiness for our cocktail party. We both looked very smart in our best suits. Even Norman had made a special effort.

Our transport arrived on time, and we were whisked off once more to the Naval Base, the Private Yacht Club of the Admiral. The Guards once again sprung to attention as we sped through the main gates. We drove to a very smart building, surrounded by lush lawns and flower beds, immaculately kept. It was becoming dusk and laid out on the patio in front of the building was a sumptuous buffet, attended by numerous waiters, all dressed in their very smart white naval uniforms.

Numerous guests were already there, including many incredibly elegant ladies, dripping with jewels and the very best cocktail dresses. It was an amazing sight. A royal reception, with no expense spared. Even if NAAFI were paying for part of it.

We were very warmly welcomed as VIP guests, and our host explained that he was the Mess President, but the Admiral could join us soon. In the meantime, he was instructed to attend to our every need.

A small band played suitable music and it was an incredibly civilised sight. Beautiful women were attending to us, to ensure we were well looked after with food and drinks.

It was a very impressive occasion, with the warm evening and glow of the patio lights glinting off the jewels of the lovely tall half-Italian ladies; a magical event that I will never forget.

We were busy talking to the hosts when the music stopped and everyone turned their attention to the arrival of the Admiral. I was still gazing into the eyes of a particularly beautiful girl, and had not noticed the arrival of His Highness. I suddenly realised that it had gone quiet, and my dreams were suddenly broken by a voice with a perfect Oxford accent:

'My dear fellow, how lovely to see you again.'

I turned and there stood Admiral Scinda Desta, immaculate in his Saville Row suit. It all seemed very strange. Here we were in the poorest country on earth, sipping cocktails, surrounded by beautiful women, all the food that you could wish for, and now, being greeted by Royalty.

Norman moved forwards and shook the extended hand of the Admiral, and bowed his head. I was very impressed. I did not think that Norman could bring himself to bow to anyone.

The Admiral was certainly a very smart, good looking man, and was obviously a player. I was summoned to meet the Admiral and I did the same as Norman. I shook his hand and bowed my head. The Admiral was delighted to meet me. He had heard of my exploits with the Air Force and assured me that his Grandfather was very appreciative of our efforts to establish an Ethiopian Military Trading Organisation. The Welfare of his servicemen was of prime concern to His Majesty and to the Admiral. No mention was made of financing, but there were plans to extend our activities further in the very near future.

Admiral Scinda Desta was an extremely smooth operator, and he obviously ruled by fear. He was surrounded by beautiful girls, and his aides were waiting for any signal of whatever he should wish. Although I did not take to him, as I had a moral conscience, thinking of the many thousands of starving, dying people, all within a few hundred yards and miles of where we stood, I could imagining him mixing in the highest circles wherever he went.

Black clouds were, however, on the horizon, and although no one could have predicted the future events on such a beautiful regal occasion, the Admiral would be dead within the year.

The charm oozed from the Admiral and Norman was like a puppy dog, listening to each and every word that the Admiral uttered. The Admiral thanked Norman for his outstanding work. His grandfather would hear of it, and Norman beamed with pride. The Admiral wished for the naval shop to be extended and perhaps Derek could arrange to order extra stock and supplies through the Air Force shop. Everything the Admiral suggested was readily agreed to by Norman.

I turned my mind to more important things and returned to the lovely lady. I didn't manage to escape for too long, though, and was soon ushered back to the Admiral. He was making arrangements for us to tour the Base the following day. Unfortunately he would be busy, but would arrange for one of his aides to escort us. I was not really that bothered about getting the VIP treatment, but Norman readily agreed, and so it would be.

We sat chatting to the Admiral, enjoying the drinks and food, and the cocktail party went on and on. It was a truly magical night.

But as the evening progressed, I grew to dislike the Admiral even more. He was obviously very conscious of the power he had, and under the warm exterior, he was a particularly nasty person, who obviously only cared for his own personal wellbeing and wealth.

He was part of the Royal Family, and he could have eased the load of his oppressed people by using the Navy to transport food and aid to the dying, but it had obviously not occurred to him that he could have made a difference. People were dying through lack of clean water and food, and all he cared about was creating the right image for his foreign guests. It made me feel sick to the stomach.

At last, the evening drew to an end, and somehow I had managed not to insult the Admiral by bringing the plight of his country to his attention. He must have known what was happening, but chose to ignore it.

The Admiral stood and said that he must retire, as he had a very busy day tomorrow. He thanked us most profusely for coming to his reception, and wished us a pleasant trip around his private yacht club on the following day. The admiral departed, escorted by two very beautiful, long-legged girls, with his aides in attendance.

Norman was well satisfied with all that the Admiral had said, and he felt buoyed by the fact that the Admiral would tell the King about all the help that Norman and NAAFI were giving to the Imperial Ethiopian Forces. Norman was a little gullible, and could not see through the exterior charm of Admiral Scinda Desta.

Our driver was summoned, and drove us back to our hotel. I joined Norman for a coffee, and listened while he told me how good he was. He really thought a lot of himself, and insisted on telling the story of how he had set up the Navy Shop, and how popular he was with the Ethiopian Authorities. I thought that his gullible and naïve outlook seemed rather strange in this much older man – who had been around a bit, and should have known better.

The following day, we packed our bags, ready for our afternoon flight back to Debre Zeit, and having had a superb breakfast, we awaited the arrival of our driver, who was to take us on a tour of the Ethiopian Naval Base.

The Car arrived, and was driven by a very smart Navy chap, who sprung from the car and saluted. Norman and I placed our bags in the boot. We set off for the Naval Base, and were met by a Junior Officer, who was to be our escort for the morning.

The Admiral had given instructions that we were to be given every courtesy as his VIP guests. The young Officer was obviously very nervous and determined that we should be well looked after. The Admiral was not one to be crossed, and was held in fear by all concerned.

It was a very pleasant morning, and we were shown the Naval Torpedo boats, and taken to the pride of the Navy; the Admiral's frigate. It was a very smart vessel that had once been owned by the British Navy. It was at least thirty years old, but had been refurbished prior to being sold to Ethiopia. We were welcomed on board by the Captain, who was a very smart chap, who had been trained at Davenport, and had actually passed all the exams, and was qualified to the standards of the British Naval College, unlike the Admiral, who had just passed through the college!

The frigate was in first class condition, and the Captain was obviously very proud of his ship. We complimented him on his very high standards, and he glistened with pride, and invited us to join him in his ward room for refreshment.

It transpired that the Captain had spent many years in England and had completed his education at Oxford, prior to joining the Imperial Ethiopian Navy and training at Davenport. He was a really interesting chap, and unlike his boss, was a genuine and caring person. We discussed the plight of his country. He was aware of the millions starving, but didn't know how it should be put right. The problem was too great. He appreciated that the world was beginning to respond, and that World Aid was shipping thousands of tons of food into the ports, but he was aware that it was not reaching the millions who needed it. He was really concerned.

Our conversation continued on the theme of aid being brought to his country, and he asked if we had met the ladies from the Red Sea Mission. We were intrigued, and he explained that there was a religious group, living in the worst slums of Massawa, caring for the sick and dying. He said that they were English girls, and he really admired the work they were doing. He secretly supported their efforts as much as he could.

As we had a few hours to spare before our flight to Debre Zeit, he suggested that we visit the girls and see for ourselves the good job they were doing. I thought it was an excellent idea, although Norman was not quite so keen.

Our driver was summoned, and the Captain joined us. He had changed into civilian clothes, as the area was a little unsafe, and he did not want to become a target.

Our car entered the outskirts of Massawa, and headed for the west of the city, where the city changed. The stench of decay was awful. Open sewers were the norm, and rubbish and filth were piled up all around us. We stopped at one of the smarter-looking stone buildings, that had windows and a door, and the Captain got out. We joined him.

We knocked on the door. It was opened by a young lady. She recognised the Captain, and he introduced us, explaining who we were. She invited us in, and to our amazement, another five young ladies appeared. They were wonderful people, obviously very religious, living with the very bare essentials to survive. It was very, very hot, and the smell from outside could not be hidden, but the girls were clean, and although thin, they all seemed fit and well. We were invited in to take tea, and we sat on the rough wooden furniture, as the leading girl explained their mission. They were all well-educated and from good family backgrounds in the UK, but had decided to dedicate their lives to God's work. They had joined the Red Sea Mission, and had been sent here to Hell on Earth.

I found it amazing and asked how they could live in such a squalid area, surrounded by filth, with no sanitation. They had no obvious signs of security, and they were surrounded by desperate people. How could they sleep at night? Weren't they afraid? To a woman, they all agreed that they were doing God's work, and He would protect them. Their faith was amazing, and it had obviously worked so far. They had experienced some awful sights. With people dying all around them, they had done their best to provide a little comfort with very limited means, and God had protected them.

I gazed in disbelief at the oldest girl, who couldn't have been more than thirty, and the youngest, perhaps twenty, but they all had the same sparkle in their eyes, true believers that God was on their side. I believe that he was and is. If there was ever a case for believing, this was it. To give up one's life for the good of others. These young ladies were doing exactly that. I felt very guilty and very humble to be in their presence. Even Norman was speechless.

We gave them as much money as we had on us, and told them how much we admired them, and thought they were very brave.

The young English girls thanked us for our gifts, and our well-wishes, and they again assured us that all was well and that God would take care of them. They had an inspirational glow about them as they spoke of their faith in God, and I wished I had the faith that they obviously had. God had called them, and they had answered that call. They were amazing people. I left them, but I will never forget them. They were real Christians.

I hope God has kept his promise and that they were all kept safe and well. Whether in Heaven or on Earth, they deserve all the peace and joy possible.

The Captain, Norman, and I were strangely quiet as our car navigated the slums of Massawa. There were signs of how Hell was really on Earth: ragged starving children and adults, trying to survive amongst the heat, filth, and stench of this little Hell. While all the time, the Admiral lived the life of luxury. Our Captain realised what we were thinking.

'One day, this will change. It has to change.'

The Captain offered to escort us to the Air Force plane that was waiting to take us back to Debre Zeit. Chatting to the Captain, I was very impressed by him. I thought that one day, he might be able to make a difference to his country, and I hope he has. The situation was going to get far worse in the not too distant future, and Ethiopia needed educated, caring people to help guide it through the difficult times ahead.

Our car began the climb from the Red Sea port to the Airport. It was an amazing landscape. The road was virtually sheer, with bends every few yards. We were being thrown from side to side as our car laboured in its task to try to reach the top. On each bend, the tyres screeched as they tried to maintain grip. It was quite a frightening experience. I was later told that the road was in the Guinness Book of Records for being the steepest in the world, with the most bends in the shortest distance. I could well believe it.

At last, we reached the top, and felt relieved. We headed towards the airport and our awaiting Dakota. The driver dropped us off with our luggage, and we bade farewell to the Naval Captain, and thanked him for his kindness throughout the day. He saluted and assured us that he had enjoyed the day, and wished us a safe journey home. The car departed in a cloud of dust, and Norman and I turned our attention to our plane. The Dakota looked even smaller than I remembered, and looked like something out of a 1930s movie.

The pilot and his crew welcomed us on board, and ensured that we were comfortable. Norman and I sat on the metal seating that ran each side of the length of the old plane. We had settled in and were awaiting take-off, when some other passengers arrived. An Ethiopia General was joining the flight, and he was accompanied by his wife. He was a tall, well-built middle aged man, and he smiled and said good afternoon. We exchanged pleasantries and settled down, awaiting the pilot to complete his checks before take-off. It seemed to take longer than normal, and the inside of the plane was very hot. We were all covered in sweat as we waited and waited.

At last, all seemed well and our pilot started the engines. They turned, coughed, and spluttered into life. One of the engines seemed to take longer than the other. The pilot tested them at maximum revs, and seemed satisfied, and we began to taxi to the other end of the runway. We stopped, awaiting instructions to take off. The pilot pushed the controls to full chat, released the brakes and we sped down the runway in a cloud of dust. The aircraft was very noisy, and it climbed towards the blue sky. We were some twenty feet off the ground, when there was a very loud bang.

The aircraft filled with smoke.

Everything that happened next took a matter of seconds, but it seemed to be taking place in slow motion. The aircraft buckled and twisted as the pilot wrestled with the controls. The General, sitting opposite us, began to panic, and his face drained of blood, his eyes popping out of his head.

'Smoke! Smoke!' he shouted. He was stating the obvious, but there was nothing that any of us could do other than pray that the pilot was a good one. The Dakota fell from the sky, and we were still travelling at quite a speed. It hit the ground and bounced into the air again. The pilot was having the fight of his life to stop the aircraft and bring it into a safe landing.

The General had regained control of himself, and Norman and I sat there with the "stiff upper lip", pretending to be brave, as the aircraft again tried to land.

It was like the world had gone into slow motion. People say that this happens when you think you're are about to die, and it's true. The aircraft hit the ground again and bounced a few more times, before deciding to stay on dry land. The brakes screeched and the pilot put the one remaining engine into reverse, and we slowly, very slowly, ground to a halt.

The pilot had managed to stop the Dakota, only two yards away from the boundary fence, and we were well off the tarmac surface.

I really believe that if it had not been for the design of the Dakota, with its glider type design, we would have been in a much worse condition.

We looked over to the General, who was comforting his wife sheepishly. It had been a lucky escape for all of us.

The smoke had cleared a little, but the acrid smell lingered. We were delighted to have landed in one piece, and the crew opened the doors and we all scrambled out. We were all nervously chatting, trying not to show how scared we'd been. Outside, a number of military rescue vehicles had arrived, but thank God, we didn't need them.

The pilot came out of the plane, looking equally scared, and drenched in sweat, but smiling broadly. He was also very pleased to be alive. We crowded around him, and congratulated him on his sterling efforts in bringing the old lady under control and landing her in one piece.

One of the would-be rescuers produced some coffee, which we all readily accepted. We were very lucky that the engine had blown when it had. Another few minutes of flight would have seen us crashing into the shanty village adjacent to the airfield.

The old Dakota stood, very close to the boundary fence, and it looked as if nothing untoward had happened to it.

After much discussion, it was decided that the aircraft would be recovered and taken back to the service depot. The pilot apologised for the inconvenience, but it was obvious that we would not be able to travel back that day. Maybe Tomorrow.

It was arranged that we would be returned to our hotel for the night, and we would be informed the following morning what arrangements had been made for our return to Debre Zeit.

Our luggage was unloaded and our transport arrived. Once again, we had to experience the winding road down to the port and our hotel. The Air Force had contacted the hotel, and arrangements had been made for our rooms. Norman and I were both recovering from our ordeal as we set off for the unexpected return to our hotel. The road was as steep as ever, and seemed even more terrifying, as dusk was falling, and the bends appeared sharper than ever.

The lovely young receptionist was waiting for us, and her smile and concern for us, raised our spirits. Norman had chatted non-stop during our journey, and was obviously as shaken-up as I was. We settled into our respective rooms, and I went down to the bar for a large brandy or two.

Our nerves began to settle and we went through for our evening meal. This was followed by another couple of brandies and we both staggered off to our rooms at the end of the night, feeling at peace with the world. It had been a long, tiring, and stressful day. The last image I saw before I fell asleep was of the young English girls taking care of the poor and dying on the outskirts of the city. Compare our lot with theirs, and we had no problems at all. They really were an amazing bunch. We should feel very humble and very proud that some people can give up their lives for the benefit of others, especially in circumstances where it seems to be an impossible task.

Chapter 13
"Mr Lupson! What happened to you?"

I woke to a knocking at my door, and a young lady, a hotel employee, appeared with a large mug of coffee.

The hotel had heard of our escape, and saw us getting rather pissed, and decided that we would appreciate an early morning coffee!

Our Navy Captain had contacted them, and said that our transport would arrive at 1100hrs, and our return flight had been scheduled for 1400hrs. The plane had been repaired overnight, and all was well. He had wished us a safe return to Debre Zeit. He really was a gentleman.

I'm sure that all concerned shared my thoughts on the wisdom of flying in an aircraft that had the previous day dropped out of sky with a blown engine, but we were British, and decided not to mention it.

I arrived at the Breakfast table, to find Norman, tucking into a hearty breakfast, fully recovered from the previous day's ordeal. He was in a good mood, and we chatted about our experience with the Red Sea Mission ladies and how we both admired them.

Our transport duly arrived, and we thanked the hotel staff for looking after us so well, and set off once again, to climb the winding road to the airport. Our car did its usual screaming of tyres as it did its best to navigate the awful road. We made it safely to the top, and arrived at our departure hut.

Our poor old Dakota stood, looking even smaller than ever, and slightly ashamed of itself for breaking down.

It was once again, a very hot day, and both Norman and I were beginning to feel the effect of the previous night's drinking.

The Air Force staff offered us some sweet black coffee, and this made us feel a little better. It was time to load ourselves and our luggage onto our little friendly Dakota, and we climbed on board and strapped ourselves in.

The General and his wife arrived, and greeted us like long-lost friends. We had all survived a rather frightening experience, and this had formed a bond between us. They smiled nervously at us as they strapped themselves in, and the General still looked a bit embarrassed, obviously conscious of his behaviour the previous day.

Our pilot went through his usual pre-flight checks, and he seemed totally unconcerned about the fact that we had crash-landed less than twenty four hours previously. He seemed satisfied that all was in order, and started up the engines. This time, both of them sprang into life at once, but there was the inevitable black belch of smoke.

He taxied the Dakota to the end of the runway and awaited clearance for take-off. He pushed the controls to full chat, and our aircraft roared its approval and lurched forwards at full speed down the runway. This time, the Dakota soared into the clear blue skies. Although we were all awaiting another bang, nothing happened, and a crew member appeared and assured us that all was well. He even produced more coffee, and we were all happy and content. Our Dakota was purring along and in good order. It was a relief to us all, bearing in mind that we had a considerable distance to travel, over hostile deserts, mountains, and over some rebel territory. We all seemed to be listening to the engines to ensure that they really had been repaired. Thankfully, the ground crew had done a first class job.

It was very hot inside the aircraft, and it was not long before I fell asleep. It seemed like I had just nodded off, when we were told that we were about to land at Debre Zeit. I had been asleep for at least three hours.

We circled the village and turned towards the runway. I soon recognised my car at the side of the runway, with Asgers waiting beside it. Our aircraft made a perfect landing, turned and taxied back to the reception area and came to a halt. We waited for our pilot to turn off the engines. Before we left the aircraft, we went to thank the pilot and the crew for taking such good care of us.

Asgers appeared and once again, saluted me nervously. We shook hands, and he even gave me a bit of a hug. He was obviously glad to see us returned in one piece. He had heard of our narrow escape, and also thanked his brother pilot for his skill in landing the aircraft so skilfully in such a difficult situation.

One thing I found difficult to get used to was the fact that true male friends in Ethiopia held hands when walking along. It was a way of demonstrating friendship and nothing else, but it took a bit of getting used to. Asgers and the pilot walked back to our car, holding hands, and it seemed a bit strange to this Western person.

Asgers was still very nervous, and had given me his usual greeting, saying.

'Mr Lupson, what happened to you?'

It was beginning to be a habit, but I did seem to be experiencing a lot of adventures in quite a short time. The greeting was always followed by a long spell of laughter from us both. Asgers was a great guy, and I felt a bond between us. I wouldn't hold his hand though!

I dropped Asgers and Norman off at their respective accommodation, and gratefully arrived home.

Alice was waiting for me with my inevitable double egg and chips, and a hot bath. Asgers had visited her during the day. Asgers had told her about our lucky escape, and she was obviously very concerned that I was alright. It was nice to be cared for, and I assured her that I was perfectly well, and thanked her for her concern. My guard showed little concern at my delayed return, and obviously didn't give a damn.

I enjoyed my meal and my bath and turned in for the night. All too soon, Alice was knocking at my door with some hot coffee. I shaved and prepared myself for the day. We had a number of meetings arranged, and it would be a long day. I collected Norman on the way to the shop, and we were greeted by the ever-smiling Asgers.

He was wearing one of his better uniforms, and still carried his small arms. We spent the next half hour discussing progress to date, and we were delighted that the shop was going so well.

The major problem was the lack of suitable local food items to which the Ethiopian Air Force Personnel were used to. We obviously had to increase our product range to cater for all of our customers' needs. The ex-pats were very happy with the range, but we were here for the Ethiopian Air Force, and not really for them. We decided to prioritise obtaining a regular supply of local foodstuffs.

We departed for the Air Force Base to meet the Project Colonel. He was also very pleased that all was going so well, and he was obviously getting a lot of Brownie Points for its success, even though he had done little towards the project. There followed a number of meetings to discuss the future, and how the Imperial Ethiopian Air Force Trading Organisation should expand.

During our various meetings, I was interested to note how the locals responded to Norman. He seemed skilled at getting up everyone's nose, and it was obvious that his arrogant attitude was not liked by the people we met. He obviously thought he was superior to them, and it showed in the way he treated them. He played the white man to the hilt, and dictated future policy. I squirmed and felt sorry and embarrassed for all concerned.

The sooner this little man returned to Kenya, the better. We had managed quite well without him, and he was doing more harm than good with his attitude. There was a young lieutenant whom he seemed to take a particular dislike to, probably because he was more "switched on" and educated than Norman. They certainly clashed whenever they were in the same room. But unfortunately for Norman, the lieutenant had the ear of the General, and this did not help matters.

The day flew by, and we returned to our accommodation, quite tired by the day's work. We dropped Asgers home and decided that we would pay a visit to the ex-pats club. I had my usual bath and egg and chips, and returned to the hotel to pick up Norman. We discussed the day's events on the way to the club, and Norman seemed very pleased with the situation. He had not picked up the vibes that he was not liked. I suspect that he would not have cared, even if he had done so.

The club was full of the ex-pat community. Everyone was there and enjoying themselves. We were greeted like long-lost heroes, and the beer soon flowed. The ex-pats were really appreciating our efforts and were surprised that such a high standard had been achieved in such a short period of time. We chatted and related our experiences in Massawa: of the Admiral's reception, the Red Sea Mission Girls, the plane crash, and they all sat and listened.

The music started, and Angie, wife of Texan John, tried to persuade me to dance with her. I managed to delay the inevitable, but she was not taking no for an answer. On the second attempt, she grabbed me, and led me into the darkened dance area. She had an evil glint in her eye, and was obviously intent on mischief. The music slowed and she pulled herself close to me – very close. The music grew louder, and she started to grind her body into mine. She knew what she was doing, and the evil smile reached her pouting lips as she felt my arousal.

It had been a long time since I had been with a woman, and she really was sexy, an expert in the ways of arousing a man. In spite of my efforts, I could not control my old man, and it stood, very rigid, to attention, as she ground her body into mine. She laughed, noticing it, and started to nibble my ear. I did my best to get away from her, but it was a hopeless task. Thankfully, other people had joined the dance area, and they shielded us from the rest of the clientele. I felt like I was going to burst, and Angie was really enjoying herself. She knew I really wanted her, but I could not take her. John was a really nice bloke, and I would not be able to face him if I was screwing his wife. I needed a woman, but I would resist Angie. At last, the music changed tempo, and I managed to disentangle myself from Angie.

I made the excuse that I had to go to the loo and made a dash for it. I looked into the mirror in the Gents, and realised that Angie had made me break out into a sweat. My shirt and trousers were soaked. It took several minutes before I felt that I looked reasonable to return to the fold. Fortunately, I had not been missed, and nobody seemed to notice my appearance.

When I returned, Angie was sitting next to her husband, with a sly, satisfied smile on her face.

They were talking about the impending visit of Angie's mother and her sister.

'Derek, you must meet my sister,' Angie said. 'She's very beautiful, and will need to be escorted.'

Angie was enjoying her moment and realised what she'd done to me. She was determined to nail my scalp to her belt.

While Angie and I had been busy on the dance floor, some of the ladies had gone home and made snacks. It was going to be a long night, and the atmosphere was great. Even Norman seemed to be enjoying himself, and was busy chatting to the Russian. It was obviously a meeting of minds, and they seemed deep in conversation. Probably about how they would rule the world if they ever got a chance.

Angie was still after me, and was trying to arrange to come and view my new house and possibly improve the décor a bit.

'All houses need a female touch,' she said. Even her husband, John, was trying to persuade me to let her help. He was obviously more naïve than I thought. The only thing that Angie was interested in was making love.

I needed a woman, and here she was, handing herself to me on a plate. I told her I would consider her offer.

The night soon passed, and it was time for us to depart. It was the early hours of the morning, and we all started to say our goodnights. Angie was still hot, and, as we said goodnight, she kissed me fully on the lips, and her hand "accidentally" grabbed my parts. She laughed as we both went our separate ways. John was staggering a little and Angie supported him. She really was a hell of a sexy woman.

The next day was full with meetings about the project to date. It was when the issues about the Importation of Goods were raised that I decided to get a grip on Norman. I told him that I would not try to import any more goods into Ethiopia unless our HQ reorganised the invoicing system and grouped similar items together. This would enable me to sort out the various tariffs and make life much easier, especially in the hot, humid climate of Assab, where it was difficult enough to breathe, yet alone calculate the Import Duties.

Norman reacted as though I was asking for the moon. It would not be possible for NAAFI HQ to do this. Our voices were becoming raised as I told him what I thought about his stupid attitude. It was far easier for some clerk in HQ to sort out the groupings and invoice us accordingly. Neither of us was going to give in. We were really giving each other "what for", and I noticed that Asgers was standing, bemused at the other end of the office. I told Norman that unless he supported me on this, and insisted that NAAFI got its act together, he could stick his job right up his arse! It was a simple request, and I'd had enough. Norman finally got the message, and agreed to my requests. He needed taking down a bit, and I had won.

I looked over at Asgers. He was pretending not to listen, but he had a satisfied smile on his face. He really could not stand Norman Lee, and was delighted to witness someone giving him a hard time. I was not amused at the way that Norman had treated Asgers and the rest of the Ethiopians, and I really enjoyed getting my own back.

The next two days flew by, with planning meetings, and our trip to the Naval HQ in Addis Ababa, where Norman was assured that payment for the goods supplied to his naval shop would be sent to NAAFI HQ. Possibly Tomorrow. How gullible can you get? Norman appeared to accept the promises of the Naval Finance Officer. I suppose he had little choice, as there was nothing else he could do.

In our last meeting with the Imperial Ethiopian Air Force authorities, it was decided that we should expand our range as soon as possible, and that we, i.e. me, should become involved with the running of the Airfield restaurant, and the HQ tea bar. Norman readily agreed that we should take over the restaurant as the next phase, and that we should make contact with local wholesalers to try to increase our range to cater for the needs of the local airmen and their families.

At last it was time for Norman to return to Kenya, and I must confess that I was not sorry at the thought. At least Norman had got the message that I would not take any crap from him, and that HQ London had better keep to their promise and support my efforts. Asgers and I escorted Norman to the airport at Addis Ababa, and we bade our farewells.

Norman was in one of his better moods, and actually complimented Asgers and I on our efforts to date. We shook hands, not exactly good friends, but there was understanding between us.

Little did I realise that it would be six months later before Norman would be allowed to return to Ethiopia. During the coming months, the country would be in turmoil, and millions would die from starvation and disease. There were very dark clouds on the horizon, and Asgers was becoming even more uneasy as each week went by. He often hinted that something was about to happen, but did not go into detail, even if he knew.

Now that Norman had left, I turned my attention to myself. Letters from my girlfriend in England were becoming less frequent, and this was probably because I had been too busy to write to her. It also took a long time for mail to travel from the UK to the remote Air Force Base. She said that she was missing me, but I got the feeling that her feelings were changing. I couldn't blame her. It had been over four months since we had parted and she was obviously feeling lonely.

I missed not having a woman, and carnal thoughts were beginning to enter my head with regard to the local girls. Asgers was always trying to get me sorted out.

'It is not good for you not to have a woman. You must taste Ethiopian girls,' he kept urging me on. I began to agree with him. I needed a woman.

The shop was now running very smoothly and we had been successful in obtaining local goods, sacks of coffee beans, local spices and produce, and even our own little vegetable patch was going very well. We were averaging one cow every two weeks, and the good quality fresh meat was appreciated by all concerned.

Especially by the young airmen who insisted on eating the meat in its raw state.

Our store man was now well fed, and had money, and had become even more idle. Asgers was convinced that he was spying on us, and reporting to the Project Colonel. We found him asleep when he should have been working, and decided that it was our chance to get rid of him. He felt that he was protected by the Colonel, but Asgers took great delights in sacking the idle, sly sod.

Asgers soon found a suitable replacement and he was a much nicer, hard-working lad, who really appreciated the chance to earn a crust. It was by some strange chance that the lad was from the same tribe as Asgers. I couldn't pronounce his local name, so I called him Jim. He immediately made a difference to the whole area, and never stopped working. Even our vegetable patch seemed to thrive, with ample supplies of fresh lettuce, carrots, and tomatoes, all growing incredibly quickly.

It just showed what could be done with ample fertiliser and irrigation. As we were going to establish a café, we would need fresh produce, and Jim worked wonders. He was also liked by all, and Asgers assured us that he could be trusted.

Chapter 14
Madam Mocambo

Having got the main aspect of the project up and running and settled into a routine, I decided that it was time to sort out a routine for myself.

All work and no play was making Derek a very dull boy.

My social life improved considerably. I managed to be available for a number of supper parties, and even managed to find time to ride Ruth's stallion a few times. He was superb and it was a hell of a challenge to control him and keep him calm. He needed a lot of exercise, and really enjoyed our outings. Looking back, it was quite dangerous to explore the outback on my own on a fiery beast, but I wouldn't have missed it for the world.

Socially, things were warming up. The men-folk tended to gather at the club on a Thursday evening and then go into town on a pub crawl. It became a regular event and was really good fun. Dave (the teacher with the lovely young wife) and I soon became good friends. And although I fancied his wife, I never tried it on, and respected them both.

Robert, the teacher who was into young boys, also fancied the odd young girl's company, and joined the Thursday gang, to my disapproval.

Our regular dive was the one owned by Madam Mocambo. It really was a very basic mud and wooden hut, with mud floors, and the loos were just a hole in the ground. I don't know why we liked the place, but we always seemed to end up there.

Madam Mocambo was a really interesting character, who took a shine to me. She was a real momma figure, larger than life and full of fun.

Even though she spoke very limited English, we all got on very well. Her establishment was really a brothel. She took in girls of all ages, and took care of them until they were fit and well. She never insisted on any of the girls plying their trade, but they used to join us for drinks etc. It was a very strange, poor place, which frequently ran out of beer. She often had to send one of the girls along the road to another club to buy cool beer for us.

Robert spoke the language perfectly, and translated Madam Mocambo's words for us. As a young girl, she had been very beautiful, but her family was very poor, and she had been forced into prostitution to support them all. She'd had a very rough life, and because of this, she wanted to take care of other unfortunates. She had become pregnant at a very young age, but following a beating, and knee in the stomach from a very drunken would-be client, she had lost the baby and as a result, was unable to have children, although she really wanted them. She really was a mother hen, and a very caring person.

During her work as a prostitute, she had managed to hide some of her hard-earned money and managed to escape the clutches of her grabbing family, and she left home in search of freedom and a new life.

She eventually arrived at Debre Zeit and had been taken in by the then owner of the club in which we now sat. The previous owner was also a friendly person who also took pity on those waifs and strays who had fallen on hard times and had taken to prostitution to survive.

The owner of the club took in all that arrived at her door, fed and watered them and provided them with a home for as long as they needed it. They were not forced to continue the life of prostitution, but could do so if they wished. Those who earned the money were expected to contribute towards the running of the club, and the others were expected to work in running the club. It was a place of safety for those who needed it, and the owner, who had lots of local contacts, protected them. It was a family affair, with those girls earning supporting the rest of the family.

The owner of the club had died and left the club to Madam Mocambo, who continued the tradition of looking after the less fortunate. It was all very strange, but it worked, and everyone seemed very happy with the situation. The girls were there to please the clients, and could sell sex if they wished, but only if they wished.

We chatted to Madam Mocambo, and poor old Robert was working hard to translate our questions and the answers that Madam gave. She really was an interesting character, and a lady to boot. If things had been different, she would have been a real lady. She had educated herself in the University of Life, and in spite of all the knocks, she had risen above all the Hell and stayed sane.

We ran out of beer, and Madam Mocambo sent one of the girls to buy some more cool beer.

Madam was telling us that her latest arrival was a very young girl, barely thirteen years of age. She had been heavily pregnant on her arrival. She had recently given birth to a healthy bouncing baby boy. Madam Mocambo and her girls acted as midwives.

Madam Mocambo summoned the young girl. She was obviously very young, and very pretty. She carried her baby on her hip and was obviously a very proud little mum. The girl was very shy, and sat down beside Madam Mocambo. One of the other girls was asked to look after the baby. The girl chatted to Madam Mocambo and Robert. It soon became clear that Robert had taken a fancy to the girl, and in his drunken state, was beginning to become a menace. The young girl was declining his offers. But Robert was becoming more and more persistent in his endeavours to have this poor little lass.

I decided to intervene, but Robert wasn't taking no for an answer. I told him that it was time to leave, but he became even more abusive. I nodded to Peter, and we both grabbed him and dragged him outside. We apologised to everyone for our friend's bad behaviour.

Madam Mocambo appreciated our intervention, thanked us, and bade us goodnight, telling us to return soon.

I gave Robert a sharp jab in the ribs to ensure he got the message, and we frog-marched him home. He really was pissed, but we managed to dump him at home, and he was last seen being taken care of by his house boy.

There followed many visits to Madam Mocambo, and we were made very welcome by all of the girls.

Chapter 15
A Change from Egg and Chips!

It was soon time to start the next phase of the Imperial Ethiopian Air Force Trading organisation project, and I turned my attention to the café at the Airfield, and the HQ tea bar.

The tea bar would not be a problem at all – it just needed a change of staff, a coat of paint, and the purchase of new equipment, suitable for the HQ staff.

The big problem would be the airfield café. It was basically a filthy run-down hole that needed to be completely refurbished and re-equipped. The present owner would not go easily, and the café was his only means of income. But he had to go. He had rotten teeth, and rotten standards of hygiene to match. I inspected the operation and made notes on what was required. I gave my detailed report to the Base General, who assured me that all would be taken care of Tomorrow.

I had begun to learn that Tomorrow never came in Ethiopia, but I had to give the General a few days to see if he would respond. Needless to say, nothing happened, and I began to get annoyed with everyone concerned. Even Asgers got the sharp end of my tongue, and disappeared whenever he saw my temper rising. It was frustrating.

I had very little time to do a lot of work, and I was getting no support from the Base authorities. They wanted an upmarket supermarket and facilities for their Air Force, but could not get off their backsides to support me. I was really annoyed and demanded to see the General. The inevitable meeting was called, and the General sat at the far end of the table from me. He had been informed that I was in no mood to be fobbed off with Tomorrow, and he made sure there were officers placed between me and himself.

I opened the meeting by demanding to be informed about the progress that had been made with regard to my report. There was a deathly hush, and all eyes turned to the General. To my surprise, he reacted very well to this demanding young upstart.

He had learned the art of "sloping shoulders", and asked the Project Colonel what progress had been made. The Colonel looked sheepish, and turned on poor old Asgers and demanded to know what progress had been made.

Asgers swallowed hard and said that he had been awaiting instructions on how to proceed from the Colonel. It all got a bit embarrassing as they all began to argue amongst themselves. It was at this point that an orderly arrived with coffee and biscuits. This broke the strained atmosphere and the meeting calmed down.

The coffee and biscuits seemed to cheer everyone up, and they continued to discuss my report in their own language. While the meeting relaxed, another orderly appeared with our mail. All of our mail came through the HQ, and I noticed that amongst the official mail from NAAFI HQ, there was a private letter to me from my girlfriend in England.

As the General and his staff were still discussing progress in their own language, and seemed to have forgotten that I was there, I decided to read my girlfriend's letter. It had been a long time since I had heard from home, and it was not good news.

The letter began: 'My Dear Derek. I'm sorry to have to tell you that I have met someone else, and I fear that we must end our friendship.'

Here I was, in the middle of a crisis meeting, and I had started reading a "dear John". I could not believe my eyes. I knew that I had not written very often, but I had been very busy, and here I was, being dumped, in the middle of a conference. It was a bit of a shock, and Asgers was the first to notice that I was not looking quite so happy with life.

'Mr Lupson, what happened to you?' he asked – his usual question.

I told him that all was okay, and that I would tell him later.

The members of the meeting realised that I was still there, and reverted to speaking English. I was thanked by the General for my comprehensive report, and he assured me that I would receive their full support starting tomorrow. I thanked them all, knowing full well that Tomorrow would never come. Tomorrow came and went without any response.

So I demanded to see the Project Colonel again. Asgers and I went to the Base, and I confronted the Colonel. I left Asgers outside the Colonel's office, as I did not wish to embarrass them both. I closed the office door, and told the Colonel about my frustrations, and how I would leave the project if I did not get the immediate support I needed. Five minutes later, I left the Colonel's Office. The Colonel had made a few hasty phone calls and things started to move. The present incumbent had agreed to vacate the café within two days, and it would be handed over to me the following Monday.

Asgers looked a little surprised at my success, and also a little pleased. He didn't like the Colonel either and a moral victory was a good thing.

We spent the next few days working at the shop, and getting ready to take over the café. The first thing was to get it thoroughly cleansed, so we assembled all our cleaning materials, ready for first light on Monday.

The café had been closed and it would not open until we had transformed it. The Air Force Personnel accepted this, but they needed a refreshment place as soon as possible. Monday morning dawned and Asgers, I and our store man set off, fully laden with gallons of bleach, scrubbing brushes and mops.

The café was even worse than I remembered, and the toilets were awful. We set about the task of cleaning and I was not surprised that Asgers soon found an excuse to depart. It was after all below the dignity of an Ethiopian Major to get his hands dirty. I had to laugh, and pulled his leg, but let him go.

Asgers was right. It was unbecoming for a senior Ethiopian Air Force Officer to be seen scrubbing walls and floors. So it was down to me and Jim, the store man, to get the first layer of filth off the walls and other surfaces. It was an awful job, but I was determined to get the project up and running no matter what.

I told Asgers that we needed a lot of new equipment, and as he was not doing any of the basic work, it was his job to find the equipment and supplies.

We needed nearly everything, from a new stove to a coffee making machine, and new furniture. It became evident that the whole building required decoration, and I went back to the Colonel. Once again, I was promised that Tomorrow painters would be sent over to me. I knew I was being fobbed off, so on the way home, I got Asgers to stop at a local hardware shop, and I bought paint and brushes from my own pocket.

Asgers protested, but I ignored him. Tomorrow arrived, but as predicted, the painters did not. I started to work on the walls, preparing them for paint. I continued to ignore Asgers.

My efforts drew considerable attention from the passing airmen. They could not believe that this white man was doing such menial tasks, and was now actually about to start painting their restaurant. Little did I realise that this crazy episode would help to save my life.

Asgedom was beside himself with embarrassment.

'Mr Lupson, you should not do this. This is labourers' work.'

I laughed at his concern, and continued. It was only by embarrassing the Air Force that I might get the café decorated.

Asgers disappeared. I later found out that he had gone straight to the General and pleaded with him to supply painters.

'There is this crazy Englishman, who is painting the Imperial Ethiopian Air Force restaurant,' he pleaded. 'We cannot allow a foreigner to do such menial tasks.'

The General responded immediately by ordering painters to be despatched that very minute. The General hated me from that moment on. I had, after all, embarrassed him, and once again won a moral victory. I didn't care if the General was upset. The important thing was to get the restaurant up and running.

The painters got stuck into the job, and I must admit that they did a better job than I.

I was now freed to assist Asgers in finding suitable equipment. We were fortunate in finding a local café that had closed, and all of the furniture was up for sale. It wasn't new, but was in very good condition, and with a good clean, would do the job nicely.

I then contacted our beer and mineral suppliers and persuaded them to supply new refrigeration equipment. Coca Cola came up with a very smart bottle cooler, and I felt like things were beginning to move. The next thing was to negotiate the supply of a decent commercial gas cooker, and an Espresso coffee making machine. Asgers had located an Italian supplier in Addis Ababa, and of course, it was up to me to try to obtain the goods on credit.

We had managed to persuade the Colonel to get the Base carpenters to build a new counter for the restaurant, and our suppliers even gave us some tables, chairs, and umbrellas for our patio area. We were really making progress.

The following day, I set off with Asgers to the Italian equipment supplier. I had a letter from the Colonel, promising to pay for any equipment we might need, providing he could pay for it in instalments.

The supplier had a very good range of equipment, and we soon struck a deal for a new stove, a new coffee machine, and a selection of pots and pans.

Once again, the fact that I was British seemed to work, and the owner agreed to a twelve month credit agreement, but with me and NAAFI. Once again, they were loath to trust the Imperial Ethiopian Air Force with credit.

We returned to Base very happy at our efforts. Our restaurant was progressing very well, and we received many visitors from the Base. The Air Force personnel were all keen to know how we were getting on. They couldn't believe the progress we were making, and the high standards that were becoming evident. It was great fun, and everyone concerned was very happy.

Even the Colonel was getting excited. Even though he had done virtually nothing to help us, he was basking in the glory of how the shop and the restaurant were progressing. He even managed to persuade the Officers' Mess to provide the restaurant with a Hi Fi system to play music.

We were fortunate in finding a suitable manager and cook, who by some strange coincidence happened to be of the same tribe as Asgers. I ensured that the new staff knew what was to be expected, and that hygiene and a high standard of quality food and service were to be the norm. Nothing else would be tolerated.

We arranged for fresh supplies of meat from our shop, and fresh salad items were provided from our own garden. Jim was a very good gardener and he soon had regular supplies of lettuce and tomatoes available for the restaurant.

An official opening of the restaurant was arranged, and once again, the General and the Colonel performed to the official opening ceremony. It was a very good facility and there was nothing better in the whole area. Asgers and I were very proud of our achievements. It had only been three weeks since we had taken over the filthy old building, and we now had something that the Air Force could be proud of.

The Air Force personnel couldn't believe the transformation, and it was an instant success. One of their favourite dishes was a spicy beef dish served in a roll. The meat was cut into strips and was highly flavoured with local spices. The beef was the best that the American farm could supply and it was garnished with fresh lettuce and tomatoes from our own garden. It was a winner from the start, and a change from egg and chips!

***

Christmas was approaching fast, and now that I had got the major projects up and running, I turned my attention to my own needs. Once again, all work and no play was making Derek a very dull boy. Even my new friends from the ex-pat club kept asking me when I was going to slow down and enjoy life a little.

The situation in Ethiopia was deteriorating fast, and even the King was not mentioned in such hallowed terms as he had been. There was a change in the air, and some nasty types began to appear out of the woodwork, including a very young lieutenant. He had strong Marxist views and was feared by all. Asgers warned me to avoid him if possible. It was strange that a young officer was feared, but it transpired that a lot of the young NCOs shared his views, as we were to find out in due course. Ethiopia was on the verge of a major breakdown but we were more concerned about Christmas.

Angie was at the ex-pat club on the first night in weeks that I had ventured there. I'd been too tired from my efforts at work. She ran forward to greet me.

'My sister will be here next week, Derek. She will arrive with my mother, and stay for Christmas. You must meet her,' Angie insisted.

She reminded me that her sister was an Air Hostess with Air India, and that she was also very beautiful, and currently single. I already knew that, as I had done my homework, and found out as much as possible about the coming visit of the lovely Lavender.

The only problem was that I had a lot of competition from the young Ethiopian Air Force Officers, who were also awaiting the arrival of Lavender. She had visited Debre Zeit before, and had caused quite a stir. Although she had accompanied her sister and her Ethiopian Air Force boyfriend, Lavender had not become involved with them, much to the disappointment of the young bucks. The more I discovered, the more intrigued I became.

Although I did not disclose my feelings, I was also getting very excited at the prospect of Lavender's visit – and Christmas. Even Asgers commented on how beautiful Lavender was, and that I should try to escort her. I'd heard it all before – but beauty was after all in the eye of the beholder. I was to eat my words, as when I did eventually meet her, I fell instantly under her spell.

We still had a week before her planned arrival, and Asgers and I were still very busy at work, ensuring that our trading organisation was progressing well. I even made a few trips to Addis to fight for fresh bananas in the market, and to obtain local supplies.

My poor old Renault Four always returned fully loaded with supplies, and even sacks of coffee beans on the roof rack. The car seemed to put up with the abuse and never let me down.

Strangely, Asgers found good reasons for not getting up so early and attending the banana market. I noticed that he seemed preoccupied, and always seemed to be attending special meetings. He would not discuss the problem, but always said that the political situation was getting worse. There was open dissent, and the Marxist elements were gaining credence.

I had worked very hard, seven days a week, and I needed to get some fresh air and exercise. I decided to take an afternoon off, and take the Stallion out. Ruth, his owner was away with her husband for a few days, chasing tsetse fly.

I had heard of a lake some way away that was full of flamingos, and I decided that it would be an ideal place to visit. I arrived at Ruth's house and hammered on the gate. Their guard appeared, saw me and immediately, hate filled his eyes. His Mistress had told him that I would be coming and to ensure that the horse was prepared for me. He pretended not to understand that I wanted to exercise the Stallion. It was after all, his Stallion. I stood my ground and he eventually got the message. He reluctantly brought the tack and tacked up the horse.

The Stallion seemed to recognise me and became quite excited. He also needed a change of scene, and a chance to stretch his legs and show off a bit. He really was a magnificent beast, and I fully understood how the guard felt at having to hand him over to this arrogant white fella.

The Stallion was groomed until its coat shone, and as I approached him, his nostrils flared, and began to dance on the spot. He was impatient to be off and so was I. The Guard reluctantly helped me to mount him, and I barely got into the saddle before the Stallion was fighting me. I made him walk slowly down the track until it was safe to let him go. As soon as I gave the signal, I felt a thump on my backside, as he let rip into an immediate full gallop.

It was a fantastic day, cool but beautiful, with blue skies and clear sunshine. We were travelling at full gallop over the plains of Ethiopia, and it was blissful. We were out of control and the Stallion was really enjoying the freedom.

I was shouting with the freedom of it all, and the local natives scattered and waved as we sped by them. They watched in amazement as this crazy white man dressed in riding boots and jodhpurs sped by, shouting, and laughing. The Stallion was really showing off, and I urged him on. He responded, expecting any minute for me to rein him back. But I was determined to match his enjoyment; the thrill of the gallop. He was a proud Arab Stallion, and he enjoyed showing off. It was fantastic, the sheer power of this magnificent, fit beast. He didn't tire, and sweat was pouring from us both, as we climbed hills and descended into the valleys. The whoops of the locals we sped by was music to the Stallion's ears. He was King of the World.

I eased on the reins and at first, he didn't respond, and we still sped on, past a mud hut where a peasant farmer tried to make a living, living in the same hut as his goats, chickens, and family. They all came out and waved as we sped on. I was beginning to tire, and decided it was time to slow down. The Stallion got the message and reluctantly slowed down to a walk. My shirt was stuck to my back, and the Stallion was covered in sweat.

We began to climb a hill, not far from our goal of Flamingo Lake. We passed vast areas where the farmers had tried to grow their teff grass, a form of local corn. It had been planted in good time for the rainy season, but the rains had not come, and now the ground was parched and the crops were dying. As were the local population who relied on the crops. It was a very sad sight. People had died of starvation for hundreds of years, but this was the worst it had been in the past forty years. Far worse than in living memory, and the world was beginning to hear of it, thanks to the BBC reporters. Food was beginning to be shipped into the ports of Ethiopia. But it was too little, too late.

The day was too good to ponder about the tragedy that was unfolding, and as we came to the top of the hill, we saw before us the pink haze of Flamingo Lake. My Stallion smelled the water and became frisky, as he needed a drink, and he began to pull. I eased him back, and as we approached the lake, I appreciated the fantastic view of hundreds of flamingos. A magnificent sight, an oasis in this parched land. The flamingos were on the far side of the lake, and as I approached them, I noticed that they were not quite as pink as they had first appeared. The drought had also affected the lake and there was not so much food around as they needed. But it was still a beautiful sight.

I pulled the Stallion to a halt and dismounted. The water was murky but seemed safe, and once my horse had cooled, I allowed him to drink his fill. He was no longer as frisky as he had been and seemed content to rest and nibble at the odd blades of grass that surrounded his paradise in the middle of disaster and despair. It was a peaceful scene, and I sat and rested, and refreshed myself from my water bottle. I was alone in the middle of Ethiopia, surrounded by a rugged beauty. The sky was blue and I felt at peace with the world.

After half an hour or so, I decided it was time to head back to civilisation. My Stallion allowed me to re-mount without too much fuss, and we reluctantly turned back towards Debre Zeit. The Stallion was still full of life and awaited my command to break into a gallop. He was really well behaved, and we seemed to have a mutual respect for one another.

I gave him his head for a few miles, and he really enjoyed himself again. I decided that he should calm down for the last few miles home, and I didn't want the guard reporting that I had returned Ruth's pride and joy in a poor state.

The guard was awaiting our return, and eyed me with suspicion. The sweat had dried, but the streaks remained on the magnificent animal. He was obviously tired after our journey, but he was very well behaved and I knew that he had enjoyed himself. The guard had prepared his feed and he ate eagerly, oblivious to us as the guard began to groom him. The guard and I had a mutual dislike for one another, but we both admired the Stallion. I knew that he would be well taken care of, and I thanked the guard and departed.

I returned home to my maid, a hot bath and the usual egg and chips. I was physically knackered, but felt on top of the world. It had been a superb day, and one I shall remember for many a year. I soon fell asleep.

Chapter 16
Haile Selassie

Haile Selassie, resplendent in his naval uniform.

The day after my ride to Flamingo Lake, I awoke to the usual cup of coffee and breakfast. I was really well looked after.

It was a beautiful sunny Sunday, and I decided to drive up to the Base to check on the restaurant.

My faithful Renault Four car was waiting for me, and I set off towards the Air Force Base. As I rounded a bend, a soldier appeared in the middle of the road, pointing a gun right at me. I screeched to a half, wondering what the hell was going on. The soldier directed me to get off the road with a wave of his gun.

I moved the car to the side, onto the mud bank, and as I did so, more soldiers appeared, all heavily armed and filling the whole road. They were followed by many officers, all armed and ready for action. I sat in the car, wondering what to do. There were a number of locals beside my car and they all began to kneel and put their heads on the ground.

The officers were followed by aides in smart dark suits, and there, in the middle of the road stood the tiny figure of Haile Selassie, His Imperial Majesty, King of Kings etc.

I didn't know what to do, but I decided to get out of the car and stand beside it. The King was an amazing sight. No taller than five feet, straight-backed and dressed in a Saville Row suit. At eighty two years old, he was the oldest living ruler in the world, and looked every bit like the pictures I had seen of him.

And here he was, taking his Sunday stroll through his favourite weekend village of Debre Zeit. I obviously stood out like a sore thumb, with all his subjects grovelling in the dust around me.

As the King drew opposite me, he turned and acknowledged me with a lowering of his majestic head. I bowed low in response, and got some very strange looks from his bodyguards.

The procession continued up the road and I stood there in amazement. I had just been acknowledged by a King whom millions thought of as a god. He had stood just a yard away from me, and I was awe-struck. I thought back to what I had learned about this elegant man over the months that I had been in Ethiopia.

This beautiful harsh land of extremes, where the Southern areas around the capital Addis Ababa were reasonably well off for water and managed to grow some food. Compared with the Northern provinces, which were regularly afflicted by severe drought, and the rough mountainous terrain made the movement of supplies difficult, to say the least.

The long-standing conflict between the so-called Eritrean Rebels and the Government meant that scarce resources were diverted to the war front. The country's limited funds should have been used to build the country and take care of its people, but they were being used up to combat the Rebels. Many were dying in the fighting, adding to the tragedy of this beautiful land, where millions were dying through lack of water and food.

For the first time since the Second World War, the world was beginning to hear about the massive famine problems in Ethiopia. The BBC had shown the world some of the problems, but had given the impression that it was a recent phenomenon, when in fact; poverty and starvation had been the norm in Ethiopia long, before Jesus had walked the world.

I sat in my car and thought of the history of this fascinating Kingdom, where the King was God, and his advisors lived the high life, while his people died. The King was kept unaware of the plight of his people. At eighty two, he had become only a figure-head, and needed daily medication to ensure he survived. Without the medication, he would soon die.

At last, the world was beginning to rally around, to give aid to the millions of starving Ethiopians.

Tons and tons of grain had arrived in the Red Sea port of Assab, but little of it had reached those who needed it most. America had worked wonders by providing grain under its Hands Across the World Programme, but some of Ethiopia's corrupt ministers had already found export markets in the Middle East and were exporting the grain and pocketing the money. It would not be long before the world tired of the pictures of dying natives and of being asked to give. Their attention would soon turn to other matters as they became bored of Ethiopia, but the locals would continue to die.

It is a sick world where millions have too much and millions have nothing, not even fresh water. History will repeat itself over and over again, and the hope of Tomorrow will never come to this wonderful land.

Ethiopia, with its cruel past and doubtful future has existed for over two hundred years. Formerly known as Abyssinia, this country has resisted many attempts at being conquered. In recent times, the Italians have been most successful, and their influence is plain to see, not only in the buildings, but also in the inter-breeding within the population. The Ethiopians are naturally a beautiful nation, and when mixed with the Italian looks, the results are quite stunning.

Italy conquered and ruled the Northern Province of Ethiopia from 1890, until it took over the whole of Ethiopia during 1936, at the beginning of the build-up to the Second World War. Some six years later, the allied forced, led by Britain, forced the Italians to relinquish control of both the Northern Province, and rest of Ethiopia, resulting in the triumphant return of King Haile Selassie (the Lion of Judah), Emperor of the United Kingdom of Ethiopia. Thus, re-establishing the line of monarchs that went back through history by direct descent, to King Solomon (932 BC). This incredible man had just passed me, and lowered his head in recognition of my standing there. The King of some 42 million people living in a harsh country of some 470,000 square miles had just passed by, through his favourite weekend retreat.

By a twist of fate, all the countries south of the Red Sea lacked natural resources, including "black gold", oil. As a result, Ethiopia, and its neighbours Sudan in the west, Kenya in the south, and the Somalia in the east, were extremely poor neighbours of the nations to the northern side of the Red Sea, and as a result, they were of little use to the Western World.

Most of Ethiopia is very rugged land, but it does have pastures that could have been cultivated, and with proper irrigation and management could have helped support itself, but it has been left to die.

It would not be an easy task to right the ills of Ethiopia, with its vast areas of land rising to 13,000 feet, and its desert plains of the Danakil, which record the hottest temperatures on Earth, contrasting with the grassy plains of the South. This land of extremes, where some fourteen different tribes try to unite as Ethiopians. Even that is an impossible dream, as they all have their own dialect or language.

Even the country is divided by extremes of nature, where the highlands are divided by the Rift Valley that runs the length of Ethiopia with a series of lakes, along part of which flows the Blue Nile. A land of mysteries and legends with the Christian faith as its prominent religion.

The King of Ethiopia, a massive Land with a military force in excess of 300,000, where life expectancy for men is just 39 years, and for women, 43 years. Where the average annual income is less than £90. Where, in many parts, History has stood still, where the Danakil tribe in the North still perform the ritual of slaying an enemy and cutting off his private parts to present to his prospective bride. Where villagers still hunt with spears and the majority have no access to fresh, clean water; where there is little or no food.

A near impossible task to try and reign over a country so backward and poor. Now black clouds hung over Haile Selassie's reign, as Marxist rebels were plotting his overthrow. This little, immaculate man, who had just passed by, soon to be part of history, and added to the legends. All these thoughts passed through my head as I continued my journey to the Base.

I was delighted to see that the restaurant was up and running, and the manager had it all under control. Even on a Sunday, the standards were excellent and the few customers who were there greeted me, and said how pleased they were with their new facility.

The manager joined me for coffee, and I related my story of seeing the King. He told me that he had seen the King on a number of occasions in Debre Zeit, as the King liked to escape the noise and the heat of Addis at the weekends for the calm and fresh air of Debre Zeit. His favourite palace overlooked the volcanic lake and he always felt safe and well near his pride and joy, his Imperial Ethiopian Air Force.

The manager spoke with pride about his King, how in 1916, the King, then named Ras Tafari, was appointed Regent of the Realm and Heir Apparent, and had succeeded to the throne on the death of the Empress Zewditu.

King Haile Selassie was responsible for the first written constitution of Ethiopia, which called for a bicameral Parliament, a cabinet and an independent judiciary, which set the framework for a complete separation of powers. Totally unheard of in the history of Ethiopia. I was surprised on how well-read the restaurant manager was about the history of Ethiopia, and I complimented him on his knowledge. He explained that he had been educated at one of the English schools in Addis, and found the history of his country very interesting.

I really enjoyed the day, and was determined to find out more about the King and his land.

Well satisfied with our efforts in establishing a clean and well-run facility at the restaurant and the HQ tea bar, I returned home for an early night and my egg and chips.

Monday soon arrived and Alice was there to ensure my every need was taken care of before my departure for work.

I arrived at our shop, and was met by the ever-smiling Asgers. I related my weekend experience of seeing his King, and how our restaurant manager had impressed me with his knowledge of the history of Ethiopia. Asgers was a little surprised that I had made a visit to the restaurant on a Sunday, but was clearly relieved that I had reported that all was well.

We sat and enjoyed a cup of coffee as the staff busied themselves with their routines of setting up the shop. The staff had responded well to our training, and it was a well-run operation and good to see. Asgers was determined not to be outdone by a junior member of his staff and proceeded to demonstrate his knowledge of his country's history.

Asgers explained that after the death of Empress Zewditu in 1930, Ras Tafari ascended to the throne as Emperor Haile Selassie the First. His first act was to promulgate Ethiopia's written constitution. He made a moving speech before the League of Nations in 1935, when he pleaded for help and protection from the growing menace of Fascism. He pleaded not only for help in his own country, but for all small poorly-armed nations. His speech proved prophetic and has become a classic indictment of world injustice. His establishment of an independent parliament and judiciary was to be based on the British system, which he so admired. He had, after all, received most of his education in England, and always had respect for the British.

Asgers was really impressing me with his detailed knowledge, and he glowed with pride as I told him so. He continued by saying that the King was an amazing man, well ahead of his time during that period of Ethiopian History. His Majesty had initiated reforms unheard of in the whole of the African continent, which affected every aspect of life in Ethiopia. He worked tirelessly to try and bring Ethiopia out of the Sixteenth century into at least the Nineteenth, bearing in mind that the rest of the world was well into the Twentieth Century.

He was to suffer a major setback when, as he had warned the world, his country was invaded by the Germans and Italians at the commencement of the Second World War. The King fled his beloved Country and became exiled in his second love, England. He got his revenge when the Germans and Italians were forced to retreat by the British and Allied Forces, and the King returned triumphant to his capital Addis Ababa.

Although the King had a near impossible task, he succeeded in bringing the educated elements of his People into the Twentieth

Century. It was through his personal efforts that Addis Ababa was chosen as the HQ of the Organisation of African Unity, an organisation that was supposed to promote the African continent in a similar mode to the United Nations in New York. The OAU has done a lot of good work, but it has also had its corrupt ministers and has failed in many of its endeavours.

This articulate King of Kings, who has demonstrated tremendous inward strength and enthusiasm, was now a shadow of his former self. At eighty two years, his hard life had sadly taken its toll, and his grip on the realities of this moment in history was passing him by. His medicines kept him alive, but he was unable to understand the realities of the country's situation. His ministers kept him poorly informed and out of the way. He was a figurehead, but that was all. He did not understand that the majority of his beloved people were dying through lack of rainfall and failed crops.

Asgers was becoming quite upset as he related the current situation, and I made the excuse that we should do some work to stop the pain. I had been fascinated by it all, but there was little or nothing that we could do but support them all as much as possible in the coming months. A sad situation.

Chapter 17
Lavender

Our job was progressing well, and all concerned were eager to take credit for the high standards of service that had been achieved through the efforts of Asgedom and myself.

More stock was purchased and all seemed well.

Christmas was approaching fast and the dear old NAAFI had actually managed to send us a few extra Christmas items to generate the Christmas feeling.

Some of the senior officers were also getting excited at the thought of Angie's sister Lavender arriving. She had visited before, and all had endeavoured to escort her. As an Air Hostess with Air India, she was allowed free flights for her immediate family members, and as her sister was in Ethiopia, she had taken advantage to arrange the trip for her mother. Her mother would stay with Angie for three months.

Lavender had been built up by my friends at the ex-pat club as a beautiful girl. I was very intrigued by it all, and the level of their excitement. Surely no one could be that beautiful? And in any case, the Indian community were very close-knit, and did not take kindly to anyone getting off with their own. I had found this with the Geeta, the beautiful teacher, who worked at the Base, who was well protected by Raj and Janine, her fellow Indian teachers. We had exchanged greetings and the odd secret smile, but whenever there was a chance of getting closer, one of her colleagues appeared out of the woodwork.

Getting close to Lavender would be a challenge for Lupson to try.

At last, Christmas Eve arrived, and I had heard that Lavender and her mother had arrived safely, and they would be attending the ex-pat community's parties over the Christmas period. The ex-pats had arranged for us all to meet at the club, and to set off to visit each member's house, to sing carols and enjoy various refreshments. The wives of all of the married Club members had prepared food and drinks, and would entertain the crowd for a while. Then we would move onto the next house.

In view of the fact that I would meet the infamous Lavender that night, I paid particular attention to ensure I that was smartly turned out. I had arrived home early, taken a long bath, dressed in my best clothes and I was ready to face the world.

I was excited at the thought of what the days ahead would bring. Lavender was only in town for a few days, so I had to work fast if I was to succeed in attracting her away from the competition.

I drove to the ex-pat club and there were already quite a few members who had arrived ahead of me. I could hear the excited chatter as I got out of my car. I walked towards the club house and as I rounded the corner, I felt as though I had been hit by a bolt of lightning. There before me, surrounded by her excited family, stood the most elegant, beautiful girl I had ever seen up close.

Asgedom was right. She was the most beautiful creature who had ever walked on Earth.

Just looking at her from a distance took my breath away. It had been a long time since I had been with a woman, certainly one as lovely as Lavender.

The group had not noticed my arrival, and I waited in the darkness to recover my composure. There had to be a way to attract his lovely lady. She was surrounded by friends and family, all excited at her arrival.

In years gone by, my father had told me that in this situation, sum up the opposition and react differently from the herd. It was a way to arouse the female curiosity and vanity. This was going to be very difficult, but it may be the only chance that I had, bearing in mind the attention that Lavender was generating from the male species in our club.

I stood for a moment, admiring her from a distance. She was some five feet six inches tall, very slim, very elegant, with very long, beautifully kept black hair that hung down to her waist. Even at a distance, I could see her large dark eyes and the occasional flash of a smile as she chatted to the group. She was draped in a beautiful sari that added to her overall elegance. I was completely smitten by her, and I had only seen her for a few minutes.

It was time to move, so I strolled out of the darkness, into the light of the patio, and shouted a "hello" to all.

Lavender looked up with mild curiosity, and our eyes met for a split second. I kept walking toward the bar.

'Welcome to Ethiopia!' I greeted her.

'Thank you,' she said.

I brushed past the group, greeting them all as I passed, and I went to the bar. I had decided to try to ignore her, apart from the polite welcome, and I continued on my way. It was a dangerous ploy that could backfire, but I hoped to hell it would not.

I felt sure that her sister would have told Lavender about me as I knew Angie had also fancied adding my scalp to her belt. I had resisted her advances until now, as I respected and liked her husband. It wasn't his fault that he was much older than her and couldn't keep up with her sexual demands.

The teachers, Dave and Nicky were at the bar and were as excited as everyone else at the prospect of our Christmas celebrations. I joined in the excitement, although I wished that Lavender would appear. I knew that whatever I did, I had to try to avoid her. She was obviously used to men falling at her feet, and she could take her pick from anyone within a hundred miles of her at any time. I got a drink from the bar and chatted to Peter and June, making sure that nobody saw my glances towards where Lavender was chatting to some of the Officer friends of her sister. I felt sure that the Ethiopian Officers would not be joining in our Christmas celebrations, so I would get my chance later, providing that my plan worked.

Lavender and Angie's mother joined the group, and it was obvious where Lavender had got her looks. Her mother was in her early fifties, but still good looking. She was also very elegant and looked superb in her sari. She had a sparkle in her eye, and she had obviously passed it onto her two beautiful daughters. I was hoping to make a good impression with her so that she would put a good word into her daughter's ear for me.

We chatted like old friends, and I took an immediate liking to her. She had a ready smile and a glint in her eyes that hinted at her sense of fun. She certainly enjoyed life and was very proud of her family.

The rest of the gang arrived, including Kenyan Alfred and his faithful old dog. Alfred caught sight of Lavender and went to her immediately to welcome her back. They had obviously met before and Alfred, ever the gentleman, kissed her hand. They both laughed and enjoyed the reunion. I felt a little jealous, but I kept out of the way.

I continued chatting to Lavender's mum and kept an eye on Lavender. I made sure that no one noticed me looking at her. Lavender was looking around the room, obviously looking for her mother. She excused herself from the group, and began walking towards us. I made an excuse to Lavender's mother and moved away from her. I had to arouse Lavender's curiosity.

Alfred's dog came to me and I bent down and made a fuss of him. He was a lovely old dog, and worshipped Alfred. I glanced up and noticed that Lavender had joined her mother and was looking in my direction. I pretended not to notice and played with the dog.

Someone announced that it was getting close to the time to be moving off on our round of carols. I was happy to note that the young Ethiopians had left the party. That meant there were less eligible young men competing for Lavender's attention.

There were around twenty of us, all happy and chatting away. The atmosphere was great. We wound our way out of the compound and down the track, leading to our first point of call. As we did, the evil eyes of the jackals reflected in our torches as they scampered off into the safety of the darkness. It was a cool, pleasant night, with the stars shining brightly and the African moon as large and as beautiful as ever.

I joined Dave and Nicky on the track, trying to avoid Lavender. Every time we got close, I moved away, trying not to be too obvious that I was ignoring her. We arrived at the first house, gathered on the porch and sang our first carol. The doors were flung open and Ruth and her husband John welcomed us all with a large glass of hot punch. Lovely Ruth, the owner of my favourite Stallion, had obviously worked very hard and had produced a marvellous display of food. She had succeeded in decorating her house in a traditional Christmas style. It looked lovely and the atmosphere was fantastic. We ate and drank, ate and drank, sang a few more carols and everyone was enjoying the party. I managed to avoid getting too close to Lavender, but we did manage the odd smile and word.

The drink was beginning to take effect when someone shouted that it was time to move on. We thanked our hosts and all departed for the next venue. Ruth and John joined us, leaving the maid in charge of cleaning up all the debris that we had caused. We all joined arms and sang and danced down the track. We were all happily intoxicated by the drink and by the night. It really was great fun. It would be even better if Lavender was close to me.

She was in front of me with her sister, mother and Kenyan Alfred, and they were all very happy, laughing and joking as we went onto the next house. We were all singing and it was then that I noticed how well Lavender sang. She had a lovely voice. It really was a magical night. We had arrived outside Dave and Nicky's house, and they disappeared inside to make the final preparations to greet us all.

'Silent Night, Holy Night, all is calm, all is bright.' We sang our carol to the house. I don't know why but it was at this moment that I felt that Lavender was looking at me. Our eyes met for a brief second, and there was that beautiful face with sparkling eyes, smiling at me. I returned the smile and kept my eyes down, pretending to read the carol, even though I knew it off by heart. I allowed myself another secret look, and there she was, with a smile and a curious look on her face. I broadened my smile and felt as though my heart would burst. My ploy was beginning to work. Lavender's curiosity had been aroused. She saw me looking at her and looked a little embarrassed, but her smile broadened too. She knew I was smitten, as only women do.

I managed to look away from Lavender, but my heart felt as though it would burst. I had never felt so happy. I scanned the rest of the crowd. We had all linked arms, and joining together as one, and the atmosphere was electric.

The doors burst open and Dave and Nicky welcomed us all into their house. Their servant served us with drinks and snacks and it was great fun.

Once again, I stayed a little distance away from Lavender. I didn't want to mess up my plans by being too keen. Lavender's mother came over to me. She had the most sparkling eyes and a knowing smile. She knew that I fancied her darling daughter. Lavender's mother was a lovely lady and had become widowed some years ago. Life had been hard in Bombay, but she had struggled through. She began telling me about herself and her family. She had three daughters – the lovely Lavender, Angie, who was married to John and lived here in Ethiopia, and her third daughter, who was married to a wealthy American in New York City. She was obviously very proud of all of her daughters.

Lavender had joined Air India as a trainee Air Stewardess some two years ago, and had quickly progressed. She was now a fully-fledged Air Hostess. She travelled all over the world and had visited her sister in New York on a number of occasions. I pretended not to be interested in Lavender, but I was dying to know more. I discovered that Lavender had her own small flat in Bombay, but spent a lot of time away on flights. She had the facility to travel for free and to take her family on an occasional trip, so she had brought her mother to Ethiopia for Christmas. It was a shame that Lavender could only stay for a few days. Her return journey would be in just five days' time, just before New Year's Eve. Lavender's mother told me this with a glint in her eye, which told me: 'if you want to get to know Lavender, you won't have much time'.

'It's a great pity,' her mother continued. 'I know that Lavender would love to stay longer, as she enjoys visiting her sister.' Mother had a lovely Indian-accented voice that seemed to sing as she spoke. Her long, greying hair and elegant features showed that she was once a very beautiful young lady. She had an amazing, elegant posture, and seemed to glide along as she walked. Both her daughters had inherited this from her mother. I looked up and saw Lavender walking across the room, her sari flowing behind her. A beautiful sight to behold.

Her mother was watching me with a smile on her face.

'It is very sad that Lavender has to go back so soon,' she continued. I agreed a thousand percent. My eyes met those of Lavender's mother and there was a knowing glint in her eyes. She knew I was smitten by her daughter and she was enjoying it.

The party was going with a swing and somebody reminded us that it was time to move onto the next house. It was time to move to Lavender's sister's house.

Texan John had stayed at home with his servants, to ensure that all was prepared for our arrival. Everything was big with regard to John. He had the biggest house, the most staff: he was from Texas after all. We all set off in very high spirits. We arrived outside, sang our carol, and the lights came on. It really was an impressive house, with well-manicured lawns and gardens. No money had been spared to make the house their home.

John and Angie had a very young family and questions were asked about how middle-aged John had managed to sire three good-looking kids. But they all looked like him, so he must have had the energy somehow.

As a special Christmas treat, they had all been allowed to stay up for our arrival and for us to sing them a carol. The two girls and one boy all spotted their favourite aunt at the same time, and all made an excited dash to greet her. All of them clamoured for her attention and she beamed with joy at their antics.

We all sang another carol and once again, the atmosphere was electric. A beautiful night, full of goodwill. Even the hyenas seemed to be enjoying it, as they could be heard laughing in the distant hills. A night full of magic with a bright moon, and stars that seemed brighter than ever on this very special night.

The doors to John and Angie's house were opened and our hosts welcomed us all. The house had been beautifully decorated for Christmas. Someone had obviously gone to a lot of trouble. The food spread was unbelievable: turkey, gammon, pork, and beef were all in abundance and enough to feed five thousand.

John and Angie had extra house guests for the evening, and we all introduced ourselves and chatted. Their guests were heavily involved with John's experimental beef-raising project and were really interesting people.

The party was really going with a swing, and we ate and drank, and drank some more. I must confess that I felt guilty at the thought that not too far away, people were starving to death. There must have been in excess of thirty of us, all eating, drinking, and enjoying ourselves. John's house was so large that it accommodated us all, with plenty of room to spare.

Lavender was acting as host, along with her sister, mother, and brother-in-law, and she made sure that all of the guests were well-watered and fed.

We decided that as John and Angie, and their staff had put so much effort into the night, we would abandon any thought of moving on and stay there for the rest of the festivities. John and Andie were delighted that we were all going to stay. They had a really comfortable set-up.

Somebody produced a guitar, and we all sang a few more carols.

Lavender was being urged by her sister and brother-in-law to sing for us, and as we all joined in, insisting that she sang, she eventually gave in. I sat with Dave and his lovely wife, away from the main party, but I ensured that I had a good view of the lovely Lavender.

The crowd fell silent and Lavender sat on the arm of a chair that was occupied by her mother, whose arm instinctively curled around Lavender, and she looked up, obviously a very proud mum. Lavender began to sing, accompanied by the guitar. Her voice was soft and lovely. I still cannot remember what she sang, but the whole crowd were enthralled by it.

Within a matter of hours, I was deeply in love with Lavender. Love at first sight was possible, and I had proven it to myself. My body and soul ached for her, and there was moisture in most people's eyes, as they listened to Lavender sing on this magical night.

She came to the end of her song and everyone asked for more. But she would not give in.

As the night progressed, our paths crossed on a number of occasions, and our eyes met. I complimented her on her singing, and she looked genuinely pleased. I still tried to avoid her, and this brought a puzzled expression into those beautiful eyes. She was obviously not used to being treated in such a matter by a man, and I hoped that this would intrigue her. I had, after all, a hell of a lot of competition, all waiting to obey her every wish.

I felt guilty at the way I was treating her, and I did manage the odd admiring glance to ensure she was aware of me.

Some dance music was turned on, and before I had a chance to move, Angie pounced on me and insisted that I dance with her. Even though I say it to myself, I was a fair dancer, and so was Angie. She melted into my arms. I could feel her whole body pressing hard against mine, and she pushed her womanhood deep into my groin. Her eyes were fixed on mine and her lips parted in a sensual manner. I had not realised, but the rest of the party had made space for us on the dance area and they were all enjoying the cabaret. We both turned on the style and the crown joined in the fun, clapping to the beat of the music. Angie smiled a wicked smile, knowing that her antics had aroused me. She was a devilish woman.

Angie knew that she had taken the limelight away from Lavender for a while, and she was making the most of it. Angie responded to the attention of the crowd. She was really enjoying the moment. This must have been the forerunner to "Dirty Dancing". It was certainly very sexy, as though we were making love in front of the whole crowd. We were all half-drunk by this time and the children had long gone to bed, so everyone was past caring.

As we danced, Angie whispered into my ear.

'What do you think of my sister, Derek?' It was the chance I had been waiting for.

'She is the most beautiful girl I have ever met,' I gasped. 'But please don't tell her so.'

'Do you fancy her, Derek?' Angie teased. She was looking at me with an evil glint in her eyes. I told Angie that I was absolutely smitten by Lavender, but that I felt that she wasn't for me. And besides, she would have to go back to India in a few days' time. Angie nodded, but still had a very mischievous glint in her eyes. She was planning something.

The music ended and I made an excuse to go to the loo. I had to cool down, as my old man had responded to Angie's gyrations.

I managed to compose myself, and returned to Dave and his lovely lady Nicky. I asked Dave if I may dance with her, and he readily agreed. As we danced, we chatted like old friends, and once again, Lavender came into our conversation.

'She really is a lovely girl,' Nicky was saying, and I agreed. We had become good friends over the past months and she gave me a knowing smile.

Lavender was dancing with her brother-in-law, and I felt strangely jealous.

The music stopped and I thanked Dave's wife for the dance.

'Go and ask Lavender to dance,' she said. I decided to take her advice.

I approached this lovely lady, and my throat went dry.

'Lavender, may I have this dance, please?' I managed to croak. She turned those big brown eyes on me.

'Yes, Derek. I would love to dance,' she said.

The dance was a slow one, and she tentatively sank into my arms. Like her sister, she was a very good dancer, and we began to enjoy the moment. Her body pressed closer to mine, and her long black hair draped over my arm. There was nobody else in the room, or in the rest of the world.

It was a beautiful moment and we did not speak. We did not need to speak. I moved my head, and my arm tightened around her waist. She looked up at me with her deep brown eyes and pouting lips. Her eyes gazed enquiringly into mine. We looked deeply into each other's souls and liked what we saw. She lowered her head and she nestled ever so slightly closer to me…

The music stopped and I thanked her, and reluctantly returned her to where her mother was sitting. Her mother had a knowing smile on her face.

It was very late and I needed to escape from there, to return home to sanity. I had to get away from this impossible dream…

A lot of the partygoers had already left, and I circled the room, wishing the remainder a very good night. Dave and Nicky were leaving at the same time, and we went over to thank our hosts. It had been one of the best nights of my life, and our hosts had been superb. Lavender was with the rest of our hosts and I did manage to take her small hand to wish her a very good night. My eyes met her beautiful, smouldering eyes.

'Goodnight, Derek,' she said. It was probably the drink, but the way she looked and spoke made me feel on top of the world.

'Goodnight Lavender,' I replied, and I staggered out into the dark night.

Everyone was smiling. Like me, they had really enjoyed the night.

We had drunk a lot more than we thought, and we all staggered down the dusty track with Nicky escorted on either side, by myself and Dave. We sang as we headed for home.

At the last crossroads, I parted from Dave and Nicky and we assured each other that we would find our way home safely. We wished each other a merry Christmas and agreed to meet the following day at the club.

Dawn was beginning to break as I stumbled happily on my way. I was happy, very happy, and I had to keep reminding myself that Lavender was returning to India in four days and in any case there was lots of competition, all fighting to escort her. The younger officers were quite wealthy and all had very smart cars. What the hell, I would win somehow. By fair means or foul, I had to win her heart. I had to.

I was still singing to myself as I arrived at my house. I had encountered a number of hyenas on my way, but they had scampered off into the darkness. The way I felt, I could have destroyed them easily. I was invincible. The drink had really taken effect.

My guard was fast asleep at the gate. He didn't even stir as I pushed past him. I left him in peace. It was Christmas, after all.

My faithful maid was there to greet me and made me a hot drink. I thanked her, wished her a merry Christmas, and staggered off to bed.

I eventually awoke, feeling a bit on the rough side to say the least. I was excited at the prospect of seeing Lavender again. My maid was up and brought some fresh coffee and made breakfast for me. She also prepared my bath.

I gave my maid her Christmas present and she was very excited. I'd bought her some expensive toiletries and gave her a bonus that equated to a month's salary. She was delighted. She had her family to support and the bonus would be very welcome. I enjoyed my coffee and breakfast and felt fully recovered.

I sank into a hot bath and planned the next strategy to try to win Lavender.

The ploy to ignore her had aroused her curiosity, and I felt sure that her mother and sister would put a good word in for me. But time was passing. I would have to try and play it by ear. I finished bathing, shaved and put on my best clothes. It was Christmas!

I walked to the club. I needed the exercise, and life was good.

I arrived to find the ladies all at work preparing lunch for all. Everyone was in a festive mood and we wished each a merry Christmas. I didn't see Lavender at first, but she suddenly appeared from the club kitchen, carrying a tray of food. Our eyes met and she smiled broadly, put the food down, and came towards me. I was in heaven.

She came close to me, raised her head and our eyes met. We seemed to linger there. Time stood still. Our eyes locked and her lips were waiting to be given a Christmas kiss. I bent forwards and our lips touched and brushed lightly together. I dared not linger there, not in full view of the rest of the crowd. We both smiled and wished each other a Merry Christmas.

Lavender's mother called to her and she was gone, busy helping to prepare the Christmas buffet for all the ex-pats.

I went through to the bar to where the men folk were sitting and I ordered a very large orange juice. We wished each other a merry Christmas, and talked about the previous evening's exploits. All agreed that it had been one of the best events that had been organised and everyone had really enjoyed it.

Now and again, I managed to catch glimpses of Lavender as she helped her mother and the rest of the ladies. We exchanged smiles whenever our eyes met, and I felt on top of the world.

The ladies completed their preparations for lunch, and the men were summoned to the buffet. It was a superb spread, and everyone got stuck into it with much gusto.

Most of the men seemed to be drawn to where Lavender was sitting. And I found myself close to her too. It seemed natural that we should be together. I don't know why, but the rest of the gang seemed to have made up their mind that Lavender and I were made for each other.

All the kids were there, showing each other the presents that they had received. One of Jan Ruschin's kids came over to me and proudly showed me what she had got for Christmas. I made a fuss of her. She was a lovely little lass – it was sad that she had such an awful father.

The kids were all very excited and insisted that Lavender and I joined in with their games. It was really good fun and an excuse for me to stay close to Lavender. We all laughed and played silly games, giving piggy backs and fighting and rolling on the ground. The noise was tremendous, with the kids shrieking their delight as Lavender tickled and played with them. Lavender and I felt very close, and that was fantastic.

At around six o'clock, it was decided that it was time for the kids to calm down and go home. They all protested but their parents insisted. It was decided that the adults would return later for an informal barbecue and continue the celebrations. I was also reluctant to leave, as it meant parting again from Lavender.

I returned home, had another bath, and relaxed for a while. I tried to snooze, but my efforts were interrupted by thoughts of Lavender.

When I eventually got back to the Club, Kenyan Alfred and his trusty dog were there. I helped him to clear up from the day's activities and we sorted out the music for the night ahead.

One by one, the rest of the gang arrived. At last, Lavender came in. I was sitting at the bar, and she came straight over to me.

'Hello, Derek,' she said. I turned and greeted her, looking deep into those lovely dark eyes. My god, she was beautiful. She was dressed in another beautiful sari in a greenish blue design and her hair had been brushed back and shone. She had obviously made up her mind that I was going to be her host for the evening and I was over the moon.

Her mother and sister joined us and I made sure they all had drinks. We went over to join the main party. Lavender was close to my side and I felt on top of the world.

The whole group were in fine spirits, and enjoying the day. The music started, and all of a sudden, Lavender was on her feet, dragging me up to dance. I didn't need much persuading. Unfortunately the music was upbeat, and we danced apart. She loved to dance and seemed to know the words of the songs off by heart. We really enjoyed every moment and our eyes never parted. I was captivated by her cheeky smile and pouting lips. The music stopped and we returned to the crowd to catch our breaths.

Lavender's mother was there, with that twinkle in her eyes and that knowing smile. She was justly proud of her lovely daughters, and she was happy that Lavender was accompanying me.

Lavender was in demand and as we talked, she kept being asked to dance by the menfolk. After a while, she apologised to me and asked if I minded.

Of course I minded, but I was also pleased that she felt the need to seek my consent. We were beginning to become a couple, and it was great. I managed to dance with most of the ladies present, and it was a great evening.

At last the pace slowed, and Lavender was in my arms. We were close again at last.

At first, her body was taut, scared to come close to mine, scared of what she might arouse, but as the music continued, she relaxed and snuggled closer to me. We talked as we danced. It felt as if there was no one else in the room, and no one else in the world. We whispered sweet nothings into each other's ears. At last, we found ourselves in a dark area of the room, and Lavender raised her head with those beautiful pouting lips, just waiting to be kissed.

Our lips joined together in a long, passionate kiss. I hugged her closer to me and she responded in full, enjoying the moment.

At last, we managed to break free and catch our breath. Both of us were laughing. We were as one. Lavender wiped the lipstick from my lips, and we tried to compose ourselves. We danced in the shadows until the music stopped.

Lavender went off to the ladies to repair her lipstick, and I went outside to get some fresh air. The night was full of African magic, with the sounds of the wild animals on the prowl. Although there was no moon to be seen, the stars were brighter than ever. The smell of the barbecue and cooking from the local village added to the magic of the night.

Some of the gang wandered outside to enjoy the coolness of the night and its magic. I sensed the arrival of Lavender as she came gracefully up behind me. Her hand rested on my shoulder and lingered there. I reached up in the darkness and clasped it. I gently pulled her closer to me. I wanted to hold her, but the rest of the gang were close by, so I dared not. I could feel the warmth of her body and the smell of her perfume. I longed for more, and she knew it.

***

Soon, the barbecue was ready. It was excellent, and we all sat and chatted. It was now taken for granted that Lavender and I were a couple by all concerned, and it felt great.

Her mother and sister joined us, and we plotted the next day's activities. It was decided that we would have lunch at the Club again, followed by a trip to the thermal swimming baths at Ambo, just outside Addis Ababa. We would take a picnic to the baths and return late in the evening.

Lavender said that she wanted to explore Debre Zeit with her sister's children in the morning, and I readily agreed to escort her.

As my house was on the way into town, we would meet there, and then go into Debre Zeit.

We all began discussing Lavender's short visit. She had only another three days before she had to return to India. I hated the thought of her leaving already, and so did the whole ex-pats club. We were all enjoying the feeling of fun that she generated, especially me.

'There must be some way you can stay longer,' I said, and I felt her hand squeeze mine. There was a glint in her eyes. She was happy. She didn't want to return to India and her job either, but she was determined to enjoy every moment that we had left.

'The only way for Lavender to stay is if she's sick,' her mother said. 'And we don't want that to happen, do we?'

'No,' I replied.

We all chatted for a while longer, and then a nice slow romantic record was put on. I found myself being gently pulled out of my seat by Lavender, and onto the dance floor.

The lights had been turned down, and everyone was in a romantic mood. Lavender pressed her body into mine, and I pulled her tightly to me. Whenever we got a chance, she would raise her body into mine and I pulled her tightly to me. She would raise her lips to be kissed. My body ached for her and I could no longer hide my feelings. We were hot for one another, but it was impossible for us to share the moment.

All too soon, it was time to go home. It had been a long, tiring, fabulous day, and now it was coming to an end. Angie and her mother were waiting to take Lavender home. Most of the older members had already departed, including Texan John. He had been very tired, and was no doubt already fast asleep at home.

I agreed to escort Lavender, her mother and her sister home. As we set off, Lavender's hand found mine, and we strolled home. We arrived at John and Angie's house, and their servants were still up, awaiting their return. I was invited in for coffee, as I had hoped.

We all sat and planned ways of extending Lavender's stay, half-joking, half not. There had to be a way. Her mother kissed Lavender goodnight, and said goodnight to me. Angie would stay to act as chaperone to us. As soon as her mother was safely out of the way, Angie smiled knowingly and wished us a very good night. Angie came over to me, and gave me a kiss, with that wicked look in her eyes.

'Don't you guys stay up too long,' she said, winked and disappeared.

At last, Lavender and I were left alone. She came over to me, turned down the lights and the next moment, we were in each other's arms. Our lips pressed hard together, our tongues exploring each other, our bodies were locked together. Only our clothes hampered our being as one. Our passion was raised to the full. Lavender knew what I wanted, and she wanted it too, but it would not be possible. We were in her family home and her mother was just upstairs. Our bodies writhed in ecstasy and our hands explored each other's bodies.

Lavender whimpered as I caressed her beautiful breasts and I ran my hands down her parted legs. I felt the heat and the wetness of her, wanting me as much as I wanted her.

The fever grew to a pitch, and if she didn't stop, we would not be able to stop. I felt that I would burst if I could not have her. We whispered sweet nothings to each other, and promised that we would fulfil our bodies' wishes as soon as it was possible. She was so beautiful.

She was aroused and this increased her beauty. Her parted lips were eager to return my kisses.

At last, we managed to break loose from one another.

'I must go,' I said. 'Otherwise, I will not be able to stop myself.'

We had a long, passionate goodnight kiss, and I backed out towards the door as quietly as possible. It was at least an hour since her sister had left us, but it felt like minutes of ecstasy.

'Until tomorrow,' Lavender said, and there was a promise in her voice.

I floated home, the happiest man in the whole of Africa. Lavender was mine.

The hyenas laughed and so did I. We were happy. The world was a great place. Africa was a great place.

Chapter 18
A Night of Passion

Dawn came too soon.

It was Boxing Day and I was still recovering from the previous night. Lavender would be coming soon with her sister's children, and we were going on a tour of Debre Zeit.

My maid was up already, busily preparing my bath. I shaved and prepared myself for Lavender's visit. The breakfast and hot coffee revived my aching body and I ate for two.

My maid had noticed how happy I was looking, and she had a knowing twinkle in her eye. It must have been catching.

Lavender arrived and I introduced her to my maid, and showed her around my house. It was pretty basic, but clean and tidy. Lavender was most interested in the sleeping accommodation. My maid Alice gave me a meaningful smile. She now knew why I was looking so happy. It was obvious that Lavender and I were in love.

The kids were impatient to explore the village and after they were served with orange juice and fresh fruit, we set off for the market. We were all acting like children, and we played silly games as we walked through town. Lavender and I exchanged the odd hug and a kiss whenever the kids weren't looking. We cuddled as much as protocol would allow, without the kids being able to report back to their mother.

Debre Zeit was a fascinating place, with hundreds of locals all trying to buy or sell something. Anything from jam jars to live iguanas, fresh fruit to dried spices, worn clothing, and lots more, all piled up in the market place.

The market was full of rich smells – some pleasant, some not. It was hot and quite uncomfortable, but fascinating. The locals looked at us with mild curiosity. It must have seemed very strange to them, seeing a beautiful Indian girl, accompanied by a white man dressed like something out of the past, with bush jacket and stick, with three young children in tow.

The local men carried their long sticks that they used as a weapon. The richer men carried rifles and long knives. It was strange. It could be a very dangerous place, where they would cut your throat for your tie, but I never felt unsafe. I never knew why. Perhaps it was because I was an arrogant young Englishman. I was accompanied by a beautiful woman, and that made me feel completely invincible. I could defeat them all.

It was time to return to the ex-pat club for lunch. The kids were still full of energy, and played tag on the way. Lavender joined in and they all laughed and joked.

The kids really enjoyed the attention of their favourite aunt.

***

The Clubhouse gang had already gathered, and we quickly refreshed ourselves, ready for lunch. Lavender stayed by my side, and the rest of the gang treated us as a couple. It was a lovely feeling, not being alone any more. Her mother smiled her approval as Lavender and I entered the dining area holding hands.

As we arrived, we were introduced to some of Texan John's friends from Addis, who had joined us all for lunch. They were American researchers, working on ways of improving the African cattle and they were very interesting people.

Lunch was served, and time passed quickly. John decided that he would not join us on our trip to the Ambo baths, but insisted that Angie took his station wagon, as that would seat us all, including the kids.

Angie had arranged for her Ethiopian Captain friend to join us. He had very kindly volunteered, according to Angie, but she had that evil glint in her eyes.

It was agreed that Angie would go home to get everything organised, and that she would collect me on the way to Ambo for our swim. I arrived home and got myself ready. I was not a good swimmer, but I had brought my trunks from the UK, so I was as prepared as I could be.

The car arrived, and Angie drove. Her mother and one of her children were in the front, and Lavender was in the back of the car with the rest of the kids. She opened her door and pulled me in beside her, giving me a quick kiss, not realising that her mother was watching me in the rear mirror. I looked up and caught her eye. She had a knowing twinkle of approval in her eyes and she smiled ever so slightly.

We stopped at the Officers' Mess at Debre Zeit, and picked up the Captain. He sat in the front, and Angie's daughter joined us in the back. We all chatted and the kids were enjoying having their aunt at their side. They were also excited by the thought of a swim.

We passed though the outskirts of Debre Zeit, and on through the narrow, twisting road, through the poverty-stricken villages towards Addis Ababa.

We passed the outskirts of Addis Ababa and picked up the road heading north. Angie's Captain gave us a running commentary on the points of interest as we sped through the countryside. Angie was a very fast driver, but she seemed in control. As we travelled north, the country became greener and more hilly. With small pockets of woodland, it all looked quite civilised, compared to the lower, drought-ridden plains we had passed through a short time before.

A little further on, we turned off the main road and passed through some heavy wrought-iron gates that were guarded by security forces. The Captain showed his documents and explained that we were going to the springs to bathe, and the guards saluted and waved us through.

It was like entering a different world. There were well-attended lawns, gardens, and many trees. His Imperial Majesty and the rest of the Royal Family regularly visited the area, which was why it was kept to such a high standard.

The road led towards the natural lake and hot springs. A swimming pool had been created, using the natural warm water from the spring. It was a magical setting and a totally different world from the awful sights we had witnessed as we'd passed through the local villages.

Steam arose from the pools, and it soon became evident that considerable effort had been made to cultivate the area, as the swimming pool was carved out of solid rock.

The whole area was beautiful.

We all stripped off and changed into our swimming costumes. The kids were the first to enter the water. They each swam like fishes, and shrieked with delight as they splashed through the water. As I mentioned before, I was not much of a swimmer, but I managed to enter the shallow end and look as though I could swim. The water was fantastic and refreshed our souls. It was warm and soothing. We were all laughing and enjoying ourselves, and I looked over at Lavender. She was dressed in a full-bodied swimsuit and I surveyed the outlines of her magnificent body, usually covered by a beautiful sari.

Lavender's nephew and nieces joined her, and dragged her into the water, all laughing, and enjoying the moment. It was a perfect day, warm and friendly, and we all enjoyed the coolness of the water. Lavender's mother had prepared a picnic for us all, and she busied herself, laying out the food, and obviously enjoying being with her grandchildren.

The picnic was excellent and Lavender sat close to me as we enjoyed the food and drinks. The Captain had not joined us, making some lame excuse that it was too cold, but his eyes never left Angie, also dressed in a full-bodied costume that left little to the imagination.

As ever, in Africa, dusk began to fall early, and the lights came on, surrounding the pool. It was nearing time for us to depart, but Lavender insisted that we should have one last swim. I dived underwater, and managed to emerge close to Lavender. She squealed with delight as our bodies wrapped around each other. We were locked in a passionate embrace out of the sight of the others. My hands shamelessly groped her body and she moaned with delight, a deep guttural sound that was lost in the sound of the surrounding jungle.

We enjoyed the thrill of each other's bodies for a short, fleeting moment, but all too soon, her sister was calling us to get ready to leave. We laughed and swam to the side. I had to spend a couple of minutes while my body adjusted itself to that I could emerge in a half-decent state. Warm towels were ready for us, and a Thermos of hot coffee. Life felt great as we helped to dry each other, got dressed, and set off for home.

Lavender and I snuggled close in the back of John's station wagon, and the kids soon fell asleep and didn't notice us cuddling. It had been a tiring day for them, and they been very lively the whole time, until now.

We arrived at Angie and John's house. John was waiting to greet us. He was delighted that we'd all had such a great day, and actually thanked the Captain for taking care of us. I thought he was being a bit naïve, but, what the hell. It was nothing to do with me.

Drinks were supplied by the house staff, and we all sat around, talking about everything. John explained that his guests had all returned home to Addis Ababa earlier, but that one of them had been involved in a pretty serious car accident and was under observation in the Addis hospital. The car was badly damaged, but fortunately, no one was seriously injured. They had received slight concussion, bruises, and minor cuts. They had been very lucky.

As they talked, a plot was beginning to hatch in my mind – a plot that could extend Lavender's visit. I would have to discuss it with them later, but it could work…

Angie looked on edge and excited, like a cat on heat. She kept making sly looks at her Captain, and it was obvious that she was also plotting something.

John was wilting fast, and made suggestions that it was time to go to bed. Angie went to him and whispered something in his ear, smiled her evil smile, and gave him a grateful kiss. She announced that her mother and John were feeling tired, and would turn in, and the rest of us, i.e. Lavender, and I, and the Captain and Angie, would go out for a late night drink. The two sisters took the glasses and dishes into the kitchen, while the rest of us said goodnight to John and Lavender's mother.

The sisters were away for a considerable time, and were obviously working out some kind of plan.

John and Lavender's mother departed. Lavender came very close to me, took my hand and we went out to the Captain's car. As soon as we were in darkness, she gave me a long, lingering kiss.

As we drove out of John's compound, Lavender sat very close to me, and we kissed again. Her sister was wrapped around the Captain. Angie turned to us and asked if I minded if they didn't go for a drink. She thought it would be nice if Lavender and I could spend some time together and suggested that they drop us at my place for a couple of hours. Who was I to argue? I readily agreed! Angie obviously wanted to be alone with her Captain, and this suited me fine.

It was agreed that they would collect us on their way back in a couple of hours. The plot had obviously been worked out between them while they were in the kitchen. I thought the idea was an excellent one. Of course I wanted to be alone with Lavender.

The Captain drove into my compound, and my guard came dashing to open the gate. At least he was awake this time. The noise of our arrival had also woken up my maid Alice, and she dashed out of her hut, bowing to meet me and my guests. I explained that two of my guests would be leaving for a while, but would return later to pick up Lavender. Alice opened my house and asked if we would require any refreshments. I thanked her and told her that we would be alright, and she returned to her hut, bowing to Lavender as she left us alone.

I poured Lavender and I a cool drink, and joined her on the couch. At once, we were embracing and exploring each other's bodies. The drinks were soon forgotten. I stood up and took her by the hand, leading her to my bedroom. I stripped down to my underpants and lay on the bed. I watched, fascinated, as Lavender elegantly unwound her sari. She had never looked so beautiful and she took enjoyment in watching me as she tantalisingly removed each layer of pure silk. The sari slipped to the floor and there she stood, in a brief pair of panties, and a kind of bra worn to support the sari. She removed this to reveal her magnificent breasts. Her dark nipples stood firm. She was a magnificent woman.

I thought I would burst, my heart was thumping so hard, and she smiled, wetting those luscious lips with her wicked tongue. We did not speak. There was nothing to say.

I reached up and gently lowered her onto my bed. Her body enveloped mine and we began to writhe in the ecstasy of the moment. She moaned as I kissed her breasts and explored her body with my tongue. There were only two bits of clothing keeping us apart, and we removed them. Our passion and need for one another was raised to screaming point. There was the dark, deep recess of her womanhood. My mouth enveloped her breasts, and she guided my eager tool inside her. She was whimpering and moving like a wild animal. We were both wild animals, making guttural sounds as our passions met new heights. Tears were rolling down our faces as our passion for each other became more ferocious. We were soaked in sweat and the moment. Our bodies were locked into each other, and there was no world. Nothing apart from us, as we rode the wild wind and the ecstasy of the moment. Lavender was in a world of her own and was muttering words of Hindi, a deep, animal sound, almost pleading.

At last, she fell off the edge of the world in a magnificent climax, screaming with delight. I was also falling off the edge of the world and could not stop myself screaming a deep animal sound into the dark African night, as six months of loneliness flowed through my body and into Lavender. She was still writhing beneath me as our climax reached its peak. Tears flowed from our eyes, and it was beautiful.

The turmoil began to ease and we slowly returned to earth. We were wet from the toil of our efforts and we lay, locked together in each other's arms. Lavender opened her eyes, and wiped away the tears of joy. Tears that stung them. She looked deep into my eyes. Her eyes were dark, brooding, and sexy. She smiled and hugged me close. We hugged each other as though there was no tomorrow. Tomorrow would never come. Tomorrow must never come. With our bodies locked together, it would never come.

We lay together, kissing and enjoying each other's bodies for a considerable time, and then we gently eased apart and rose. We went next door to the bathroom and allowed the cool water to ever so gently revive our bodies. We soaped each other from top to bottom and gently washed away the evidence of our love making.

We laughed as we dried and fondled each other. It was a sensual, wonderful feeling, and I felt myself aroused again as Lavender giggled at the sight of my erection.

But we had to stop. Otherwise we wouldn't be able to stop, and Lavender's sister would return soon. The time had gone far too quickly, but there would be other times. There had to be other times. We dressed and went through to the lounge. And as we did so, my ever dutiful maid appeared with a pot of fresh coffee. She had obviously heard our loud lovemaking. The whole of Africa must have heard. But we didn't care. Our passion was too great.

My maid smiled a knowing smile, and Lavender looked a little embarrassed, and we all began to laugh. What the hell – we were young and very much in love, and we could not hide the fact that we were passionate about each other. We laughed and laughed.

The coffee revived us, and with perfect timing, the captain's car arrived. They came into my house, obviously having satisfied each other, and Angie looked a little sheepish, but soon realised that we knew what she had been up to and she could tell that Lavender and I had changed in the past couple of hours. We were now as one; an item.

I decided it was time to put my idea to the test. We all wanted Lavender to stay as long as possible, especially me – and my plot could extend her stay in Ethiopia. The American friend of John's had been involved in a nasty accident on their return to Addis, and my plot was to pretend that Lavender had been in the car. She had not been seriously hurt, but sustained bruising and slight concussion. She could not possibly return by air until she was passed fit to do so by the local doctors. Lavender squealed with excitement at the idea. Angie thought about it and after careful consideration, thought it a very good idea. She even knew a doctor who could be persuaded to compose a suitable sick note. Even the Captain thought it would be a good idea, as he quickly realised that Angie would have an excuse to go out on the town more. After all, she had to chaperone her little sister.

Angie quickly worked out the basics of our plot, and agreed with Lavender to approach her mother and John in the morning. She thought that her mother would agree to the plan. Lavender was on

Cloud Nine, and melted into my arms. She kissed me a passionate "goodnight".

It had been one of the best nights of my short life.

'Until tomorrow,' Lavender whispered, and once again, there was a hint of a promise in her voice.

It was four o' clock as I went through to my bedroom. Tomorrow was already here.

My bedroom smelled of Lavender's perfume, and I lay on my bed and soon fell fast asleep. It had been a day to remember. I slept the sleep of the gods. For once in a long time, I didn't feel lonely, and my body was well satisfied.

Chapter 19
Lupson in Love

Lavender

I awoke to a knocking on my bedroom door.

My maid was there to say that I had visitors, and I asked her to prepare some refreshment for them and ask them to wait in the lounge.

I quickly took a cold shower, shaved, and dressed quickly. The shower revived me and I felt much better. The thoughts of the previous night soon returned and I was happy.

I went through to the lounge and there sat Lavender, her sister Angie and the three kids.

Lavender's face beamed as soon as she saw me, and came forwards to give me a "good morning" kiss. It was restrained, as the kids were watching her every move.

Everyone started talking at once, and the kids were very excited. Did I know that their favourite Aunt was going to stay a bit longer? I pretended not to know, but said that I was delighted, and I winked at Lavender. The kids were really excited about it, and wouldn't leave Lavender's side.

My maid brought some fresh coffee and toast, and we all sat down to a light breakfast. We all talked and laughed and it was great. Life was great. Lavender's mother had been convinced that the car accident scheme would work, but John had been difficult to convince. Angie had used her persuasive talents and he had given in. Lavender would stay.

I had planned to exercise the Stallion that afternoon, and it was soon agreed that Lavender would join me.

Angie suggested that I join them for lunch, and she, Lavender, and the kids would go ahead and organise themselves for lunch and the afternoon's adventure.

I kissed Lavender goodbye when the kids weren't looking, and said I would see them all in a couple of hours.

My guard and maid had washed my beaten-up Renault car, and it looked quite smart.

I set off for John and Angie's house, and as I left my compound, I saw the remains of another donkey that had died under its load on the way to market. The poor beast was an awful sight, having been half-eaten by the village dogs and the odd hyena. Its body had swollen grotesquely in the heat, and the smell was awful. Fortunately, nature would soon get rid of it. The local dogs had the first bite, followed by the hyenas, followed by the buzzards, followed by the rats. It would soon be gone.

I arrived at John and Angie's house. Lavender came out to greet me. She glowed and had a sparkle in her eyes. Her pouting lips were waiting to be kissed, and as she was alone, I obliged. We had a long, lingering kiss, and chatted about the previous night.

'We must do it again soon,' Lavender said, and I readily agreed. She wiped the lipstick from my face, took my hand, and guided me into the house.

The family were sitting at the dining table. Angie gave me a secret wink. I greeted them all, one by one, and Angie's mother shook my hand and let me kiss her on the cheek.

Everyone was excited at the thought of Lavender staying longer. I was ushered to the top end of the table, opposite my host John. Lavender's mother sat on my left, with Lavender on my right. The kids chattered excitedly at the thought of going for a horse ride, and I was surprised to learn that the whole family apart from Mother, was going to join us. Lavender could ride, but not very well, but a suitable docile horse had been sorted out for her. All of the family had riding gear, and Angie had loaned Lavender some jodhpurs.

Lavender and I sat very close, as close as we dared, in front of her mother's gaze. Lunch arrived, and drinks also. I had asked for a beer, and I was really enjoying it. I looked away, and when I reached for my beer, it had disappeared. I looked at Mother, and she sat there, the picture of innocence. Lavender had a secret smile on her face.

'What have you done with my beer?' I asked.

The only person who could have pinched my beer was Lavender's mum, but she sat there smiling innocently. Everyone was beginning to enjoy the joke. I leaned forward and gazed directly at Lavender's mum. She couldn't contain herself any longer and burst into laughter as she produced my beer from under the table.

This elegant, dignified lady had a good sense of humour and devilment.

We all enjoyed her joke, and soon became firm friends. Especially as she realised that her daughter and I were very fond of each other.

After lunch, we all had a siesta. John had arranged for his staff to prepare the horses for Lavender, her sister and the children.

I drove on to Ruth's house, and once again, I met a hostile reception from her guard and groom. But luckily Ruth appeared and asked how I had enjoyed the Christmas festivities. I had to admit that they were beyond my wildest dreams. She gave me a knowing smile, as news had soon spread that Lavender and I were an item. It felt good. Very good.

The Stallion was brought around for me. The groom had polished his coat, and it shone with health. The Stallion looked magnificent. The groom gave me his usual evil stare as I took hold of his prize stallion. The Stallion had not been ridden for a while and was full of himself, prancing on the spot and dying to be off. I thanked Ruth, and said that I would take great care of her horse, and set off for John's house. The Stallion fought me all the way, trying to break free. He really was a handful.

When I arrived at John's house, everyone else was already mounted and waiting for me. The horses had Western saddles and looked strange compared to mine. Ruth was a traditionalist and insisted on an English saddle.

My stallion grew even more excited, as we joined the other horses, and he began showing off in front of the female horses. Prancing around and snorting, eager to get the chance to get amongst the ladies. We all laughed at his antics, and it was quite a struggle to control him. John led the way out of his compound with my Stallion close behind. I warned the rest to stay away from the Stallion's rear end, as he was likely to kick out.

Lavender's mother waved us goodbye and begged us all to be very careful.

My Stallion was not happy at the slow pace of the group, and wanted to be off. After all, he was a Stallion. As we left the village of Debre Zeit, we went out to the countryside and started climbing the hills. My horse was proving to be a pain and I rode up to John and explained that the Stallion needed a good gallop to clear his head. I knew the area, and explained to John that there was a track ahead of us that ran for a couple of miles, and that, as long as he didn't mind, I would go ahead of the group and allow my horse to have his head and get his frustrations out of his system. John agreed, and I rode back to Lavender and told her my plan. I managed a quick kiss. I then rode slowly to the front of the group so as not to upset the rest of the horses. As soon as I was a suitable distance in front, I gave the Stallion his head. He shot off, like a rocket screeching his delight at being free.

The Stallion was magnificent and galloped, full chat, up the path. I urged him on, and we both really enjoyed the thrill of the pace. My thoughts returned to the previous night, and whooped with delight as we sped faster and faster. I knew how the Stallion felt. We were both kindred spirits. Two young stallions enjoying the freedom and the thought of young fillies. It was hot, and the wind brought tears to my eyes as we sped up the track.

The Stallion showed no sign of wanting to slow, and I didn't want him to. It was great to feel the power of this magnificent animal at full speed beneath me.

After another two miles or so, I decided that it was enough and I eased on the reins. My Stallion took no notice. I pulled a little harder and he snorted his disapproval. I pulled harder and gripped with my knees. At last, he began to slow. Slowly, he came back under my control. He reluctantly gave into my command and we were both covered in sweat. I slowed and stopped and allowed him to graze whatever was close at hand. I dismounted and looked back down the track, but there was no sign of my friends. It took some time for them to appear, and this gave us time to cool down.

My magnificent Stallion had enjoyed himself, and was much calmer now that he had got some decent exercise. He really was a magnificent beast, and he knew it. Although he didn't look quite as smart as when we had set out – the sweat and salt on his coat was quite a mess.

My friends were slowly coming closer in a controlled canter, and I was pleased to see that Lavender was a competent rider, and looked as though she was enjoying herself.

The countryside around us was dry but beautiful, and we had a panoramic view of the whole area. We could look down on the grassy plains beneath us, and could see a number of small, mud-hutted villages, with their wood fires, preparing their food. It was a lovely sight, and very peaceful. It even looked romantic, until you realised that these people were on the verge of starving to death.

My friends arrived and were excited at the joy of riding through the mountains. We all greeted one another, and John suggested that we all dismounted and walked the rest of the way up the hill to allow our horses to rest. The horses enjoyed being free from having humans on their backs and tried to graze on whatever was close to hand. My Stallion had proven his prowess, and was now very well behaved.

John and Angie were in a very good mood, and held hands as they walked in front of us. Lavender and I found ourselves at the back of the ride, and as soon as the rest disappeared around a corner, we were in each other's arms, and enjoyed a long, lingering kiss. Her magnificent body pressed itself deep into mine and aroused my soul.

'I want you tonight,' I found myself saying, and she readily agreed.

How we would manage to be alone was another matter, but I felt sure that Angie would organise it somehow.

My Stallion became impatient and pulled us apart with a snort of disapproval.

John said it was time to return home, and we all mounted, turned around, and headed back to Debre Zeit. The kids were really excited, having enjoyed the ride, and the company of their favourite Aunt.

We must have covered some twenty miles in all, and had seen part of the Rift Valley that ran through the heart of Ethiopia, up to Egypt. In the far distance, we had seen the reflections of some of the lakes that lie in the Rift Valley. We had seen buzzards and the lairs of the scavenging hyenas and jackals. The day had been fantastic, and one that I shall never forget. But it was not over yet. I still wanted to be with my Lavender.

We returned, to be greeted by Lavender's relieved mother. She had prepared tea and listened patiently as her grandchildren told her of our adventure.

I was invited to stay for tea, and I agreed, but I explained that I would be a little while, as I had to return my Stallion. Lavender volunteered to come with me, and we set off for Ruth's house, leading the horse.

We arrived at Ruth's house, having had a cuddle on the way, and were met by Ruth's hostile groom/guard. He had hate in his eyes as he saw me with his beautiful Stallion and my beautiful Lavender. Fortunately, Ruth appeared and he became all sweetness and light, bowing to Ruth and taking my mount. As instructed by Ruth, he would ensure that the Stallion was well fed and groomed.

Ruth was pleased to greet Lavender again, and insisted that we joined her for a cup of tea. We agreed, but explained that we could not stay long, as we were expected for afternoon tea at John and Angie's house.

Ruth was keen to learn how her Stallion had behaved, and I told her that once he'd had a good gallop, he had behaved very well. I thanked her for allowing me to ride her magnificent Arabian Stallion, and she said that she was very pleased to find someone who could manage him. Ruth had found him a bit of a handful and had realised that he needed a lot of exercise. I said that I would ride him as often as time would allow. We chatted for a while longer, and Lavender said that she thought we ought to return home as the others would be waiting for us. Ruth understood, and we departed.

Lavender and I hugged each other all the way home. Life was good, very good. It had been a lovely way to spend the day, and there was the evening to look forward to.

Lavender's mother and the rest of the family greeted us on our return. We all enjoyed a late afternoon tea. Lavender and I were puzzling out how we could escape for the evening when the problem was resolved for us. Angie's Captain appeared at the door and invited Angie, her sister and I out for the evening to a very nice club he knew in Addis Ababa. There was a special dinner dance in town and one that we should not miss.

I was a little worried as the next day was Monday, and it was time that I met up with Asgedom to do some work. However, it was too good a chance to miss, so it was agreed by all. Once Angie had persuaded John, that is.

Monday was also the day for us to put our plan regarding Lavender's pretend accident into operation. We had to contact a local ex-pat doctor to get him to sign a sick note, and then contact Air India. Angie assured us that there would not be a problem, and as it turned out, there wasn't.

It was agreed that we would all meet at my place at around 8 o'clock, and go into Addis. John was happy that his wife was enjoying her sister's stay, and as there were four of us going out, he didn't suspect that she could be misbehaving herself.

I returned home for a snooze, and explained to my maid that I needed a bath and a rest, and would be going out at around 8 o'clock, and would she also tell my guard that my guests would be arriving? Three hours later, I was shaved, shampooed, bathed and rested, and ready to fight the world. I was a lot younger then, and could stand the pace. Life was good.

The Captain arrived in his smart new car, and I was greeted by my Lavender, and Angie.

Lavender and I snuggled up close, in the back of the Captain's car, and enjoyed the trip into Addis Ababa.

The Captain was obviously out to impress us all, and we drove straight into the heart of Addis Ababa, to the Wabi-Shebele Hotel, one of the top hotels in Ethiopia. We were greeted like royalty as we entered the hotel, and a lift took us to the fifth floor of the hotel, and into a very smart cocktail lounge with panoramic views over the city of Addis Ababa.

Lavender and her sister had really gone to town, and looked a million dollars. As we entered the lounge, all eyes turned to view the arrival of these most beautiful women.

Waiters rushed to take care of us, and obey the every wish of our arrogant host, Angie's Captain.

Our Captain clicked his fingers and immediately a waiter appeared at our table. We were given the best table, enjoying the best views of Addis, and we all felt like royalty. The Captain was really enjoying the attention he had received on our grand entrance.

It was a very expensive club with fantastic standards, in strict contrast to the degradation we had seen on our way here.

I agreed that we should split the cost of the night. I didn't want the Captain to be too much of a hero.

We sat and drank our cocktails, admiring the views over Addis Ababa with its extremes, extreme wealth, and extreme poverty. People were dying less than a hundred yards from where we sat.

They were dying from starvation and a lack of clean water, and there was nothing that we could do about it. The problem was too vast, and it would take many years to right itself, if it ever would. I felt happy and Lavender caught my mood, held my hand tighter and we snuggled up close.

In the distance, we could see the Kings Palace, with its magnificent gardens, illuminated over the dark skies of his Kingdom. Little did we realise, but the situation would change very soon, and the Kingdom would be no more. That was in the future and we were here to enjoy ourselves.

After cocktails, we went down to the restaurant, and enjoyed a local traditional meal. It was highly spiced, and full of flavour.

It was a magical night, and we were all enjoying each other's company. Lavender was her magnificent self, and I was extremely proud to be the one she had chosen to escort her. Life was good, very good, and I had earned a bit of happiness, after all the hard work I had put into the Air Force Project.

After the meal, we went through to the nightclub, and relaxed as we watched the cabaret. A troupe of Ethiopian dancers accompanied by their own traditional band, and they performed a series of folk dances and songs. It was truly magical. The dancers were dressed in their pure white national costumes, and the performance they gave was fantastic.

We could have been a million miles away from the abject poverty that was just outside the hotel's door.

The cabaret came to an end and a western style dance band took over. They were also first class. No sooner had they started than Lavender was dragging me onto the dance floor. It was a slow dance and Lavender pushed up very close to me. It was reasonably dark, and we took advantage to have a kiss and a cuddle. She looked up at me with those dark, brooding eyes and pouting lips, and I felt that the night must not end. Tomorrow must not come.

We were swaying to the sound of the music and the atmosphere was intoxicating. The music ended and we returned to our table.

Angie suggested that Lavender should sing with the band, but she didn't seem keen on the idea. But the Captain joined in with trying to persuade her. Lavender turned to me and asked if I wanted her to sing for me. I felt like a king. I said I would really enjoy it as long as she didn't mind. The Captain was up on his feet and went over to the band. Lavender had sung a little with a band in India, which I hadn't realised. Lavender again asked if I really wanted her to sing.

I did, although I didn't particularly want to share her with the rest of the crowd.

Lavender was called onto the stage, and introduced to the crowd. She looked magnificent and all eyes were on her. She received a warm reception, and the band began to play. She was superb, and her eyes never left me.

She sang 'Sunday morning up with the lark, I'm going to take a walk in the park. My, my, my, it's a wonderful day.' And it was. Her voice was fantastic, and she was singing for me. The next line of the song was: 'I know someone's waiting for me.' And I was. She looked straight at me with that lovely smile.

The crowd really enjoyed her singing and would not allow her to leave the stage until she sang some more. She reluctantly agreed to sing again, and then insisted that she was allowed to return to me.

The crowd roared their approval after she had finished, and shouted for more, but Lavender insisted that she would sing no more. She returned to our table, and I rose and greeted her. All eyes were on us as she sunk into my arms and we kissed.

My God, it was time to get out of there, so that we could have each other, alone and able to fulfil our deepest desires. We hugged and kissed some more and our host the Captain and Angie caught the mood. It was obvious that we wanted to be alone.

We paid our bill and headed for the exit. The band and crowd applauded Lavender as we left, and the band asked her to return and sing again. It had been a great night, but the best was still to come, at least for me. The Captain was also eager to be alone with Angie, and our car sped through the outskirts of Addis, and onto Debre Zeit.

Lavender and I curled up on the back seat, enjoying each other's caresses, and we soon arrived at my house. The guard was still awake, and raced to open the gate to allow us in. The Captain explained that he would return in about an hour, and we all agreed that it would give us enough time to be alone. We couldn't stay up too late, as I was due to return to work in the morning.

Lavender and I were hot for one another, and we began to strip as we entered my house. My maid kept a discreet distance, realising that we wanted to be left alone. We went into my bedroom and I helped Lavender to strip, savouring every moment as each garment was removed and placed in a neat pile so that it would not crease too much.

At last, her breasts were free for me to caress, and her dark nipples stood rigid as I took them into my mouth. We kissed and fondled each other, and once again, Lavender moaned, muted sounds of animal passion aroused.

My hands slipped down her back, and found the elastic of her panties, and I gently eased them down and exposed her wonderful womanhood. I kissed and caressed every part of her, the parts that I knew she would enjoy, and she writhed in front of me in a world of her own. Her body writhed with anticipation, and I could stand it no longer. I needed to be deep inside her, and my tool soon found its desire. I thrust deep inside her and she arched her back and writhed in the ecstasy of the moment, and our bodies were locked and we gyrated like wild animals. Our animal passions rose to the full as we screamed into the night. Our screams turned to soft animal groans as our passions began to be fulfilled. One again, we rose to a massive climax, and my house echoed to the screams of fulfilment. We both fell of the edge of the world, our bodies locked and covered in sweat.

We hugged and kissed each other, thanking each other for the passion that we had aroused, our eyes filled with tears of joy, and we did not want the moment to pass. Tomorrow must not ever come again. We wanted this moment to last for ever.

The calm returned slowly to our bodies and we lay there still, as one. We awoke to the hammering on the door and both realised that Lavender's sister and the Captain had returned, and we jumped up, trying to find our clothes, both in a bit of a panic. We shouted that we would not be long and we both started to laugh. We were like kids who had been caught out and it felt great.

We dressed as quickly as we could, but both of us looked a bit worse for wear.

It had after all been a very long day and night. But tomorrow was coming.

My maid had been awoken by the noise, and let Angie and the Captain into my house. Angie had a wicked, knowing grin on her face as she inspected Lavender and I.

My ever dutiful maid appeared with steaming coffee for us all.

Lavender and I disappeared into the bathroom to try to make ourselves more presentable, while Angie and the Captain drank their coffee. It was gone three in the morning, and I had to be at work in five hours, but I felt like a king.

Angie had agreed to take care of the arrangements regarding prolonging Lavender's stay, and so we wished each other goodnight, and Lavender left me to return home. She promised to come to our shop some time during the day, to let me know how her sister had got on with the deception. Lavender would be staying for at least two weeks, and the thought made me very happy. On that thought, I quickly fell asleep.

Chapter 20
The Officers' Mess

All too soon, my maid was knocking at my door, with hot coffee and breakfast.

After a quick cold bath and a shave, I was reasonably fit to face the world.

There was much work still to be done to ensure the success of the Imperial Ethiopian Air Force Trading Organisation, and it was my responsibility to ensure it did succeed.

As ever, I arrived ahead of Asgers. He was not the most punctual human being on earth. But when he did arrive, it was great to see his smiling face. He took one look at me.

'Mr Lupson, what happened to you?' he said – his now familiar quote. We both started to laugh. The festive season had obviously taken its toll on me. I didn't have to explain. Asgers knew that I had found a mate, and he was genuinely happy for me.

He had often urged me to "taste the local ladies", as he put it. But although I had enjoyed their company, I had not taken them to bed.

We laughed and talked about the Christmas holidays. He had really enjoyed the break with his family and they had all asked him to thank me for the generous presents that I had given them.

I told him of the great time I had shared with Lavender and her family, over the Christmas period, and Asgers beamed with delight at my happiness.

The rest of the staff arrived, and it was time to open for business.

After sharing greetings with them, and even more coffee, Asgers and I set off for the Air Force Base to ensure that all was well with our HQ service and the Airfield Café. We were delighted that everything looked great, and the café had improved in leaps and bounds. We were greeted like heroes as we entered the café, as the Air Force personnel really appreciated the very high standards that were being achieved. Asgers was a very proud man as the pilots and aircrew all greeted him. He chatted to the young air crew and you could actually see his chest expand as he accepted the compliments from them.

Asgers was a real character, and was loved and respected by all, even though he was a senior major. The customers now had a place to be proud of, and could enjoy an extended menu of Western dishes, as well as their local, highly spiced dishes. The transformation had been incredible, from a dark, dirty, unhygienic operation, to a smart café that wouldn't be out of place on a high street in the UK.

Asgers introduced me to one of his friends, a young fighter pilot who originated from the same province as Asgers, who was very proud of his young compatriot.

The fighter pilot had graduated with honours from the American training school in Texas, and was now an expert in flying F15 fighters.

As is the custom in Ethiopia, Asgers and the pilot held hands as we chatted. It always seemed strange to me, two grown men holding hands. It was only a sign of friendship, but to a Westerner, it looked odd. Asgers was telling me that the young, good looking pilot was married with a young family, and was a real "Top Gun". The pilot was a charming guy who spoke very good English with an American accent. He had been trained in the USA and obviously had picked up the American accent and ways. We chatted for quite a while, and then we tied up loose ends in the café, bid the pilots farewell, and returned to our shop.

When we arrived at the shop, I noticed that Angie's car was parked outside, and Lavender came dashing out to greet us. She looked fantastic. She grabbed my hand and gave me a peck on the cheek.

Asgers looked bemused and had his usual larger than life grin spread across his face from ear to ear. I formally introduced my close friend and colleague Major Asgedom Teshome to this lovely young lady.

The two of them became immediate friends, as Asgedom explained that he had never seen Derek looking so happy, and he knew that it was down to her. It was funny how we three all got on so well from the start. Asgers asked if I minded if he showed Lavender around our project, as he was obviously very proud of the set-up. I readily agreed, as I had a bit of admin to catch up on. Asgers and Lavender disappeared through the shop doors, laughing and chatting like old friends. Asgers was like a kid, excited at being in the company of such a beautiful girl, and being able to show off what we had achieved in such a short time.

Lavender's sister Angie appeared at my office door and came in, gave me a kiss, and popped her bum on my desk.

'This shop is super, Derek,' she said. 'It really is – stocking all the things we've been missing in Debre Zeit for such a long time.'

Her eyelids fluttered and she had a sly smile on her face.

'Derek, you know that Lavender has really taken to you.' Angie looked genuinely happy that we had found each other, and that her younger sister was in love with an Englishman.

We both knew deep down that the situation could not last forever. Nobody was entitled to be as happy as we were forever, but Lavender had that effect on people. Not only was she beautiful. She had a bubbly personality to match.

Angie said that Air India was satisfied with our ruse, and that the false doctor's note and the phone calls had been accepted by them. They insisted that Lavender should rest after her accident, and that she should only return when she was fit and able to do so.

It was great that we had been given more time together, but it was more than obvious that one day, Tomorrow would come, and Lavender would have to return to India. It was a day that I would hate.

We all put this to the back of our minds and agreed that we would enjoy today. Tomorrow would arrive all too soon, and I could not consider how I would cope, alone again.

Asgers and Lavender returned, still chatting and laughing. Asgers was telling Lavender how well we had done and how the project would grow into a very large concern. His chest expanded as Lavender told him how fantastic it all was.

We all enjoyed a cup of coffee and chatted for half an hour or so. All too soon, it was time for them to return home. It was also time for Asgers and I to do some real work.

I escorted Lavender to her car, gave her a quick kiss and a cuddle, and said I would see her later.

The day flew by as Asgers and I planned and agreed on replenishing the stock. There was quite a bit of admin to do, arranging supplies of local food.

Asgers had invited Lavender and I to his Officers Mess the coming Friday. It was going to be a very special occasion, as His Majesty had given two of his very best cows to the Mess for the celebrations. There would be lots of food, drink, and local entertainment, and Lavender was very excited at the thought, as was I. It was a chance to show the world how much we felt for each other.

Lavender's sister and her husband John had also been invited to the Mess celebrations by Angie's Ethiopian Captain boyfriend, so there was going to be quite a party of us. We were all looking forward to the occasion as it was the first time I would experience life in an Ethiopian Officers' Mess.

All the Ethiopian wives would be in National Dress, and would make it a spectacular sight. The rest of the week zoomed by, and I did manage to meet Lavender on most of the evenings, but we only managed to be alone together for a short time on one occasion.

Work kept both Asgedom and I very busy, but we made considerable progress, and the project was going exceptionally well. But I had noticed that Asgedom was becoming increasingly concerned about the state of the Nation, and he disappeared on a number of occasions to attend meetings at the main base.

All he would say on his return was that the situation was not looking good, and that there were black clouds looming. The political situation was very bad, and it appeared that the King was losing control, and that some of his Ministers were accused of being corrupt. I had seen evidence of this myself in my experiences in Assab, where even junior officials required bribes to function.

It was a very worrying time for Ethiopia. The Rebels in the North were continuing to flex their muscles, and combined with the drought, the country was fast becoming a total disaster area. It was very sad to see, as the people really did not deserve any additions to their suffering.

Life was hard enough, but things were about to get worse, much worse. Poor old Asgers, if he was worried, I should be too.

***

At last, Friday arrived, and we both managed to finish early, as we had to go home and prepare ourselves for the evening's celebrations.

I went home and my maid prepared my bath for me. I shaved, bathed, and managed a quick half hour snooze. I dressed in my best clothes, and even though I say it myself, I looked very smart. The loss of weight and lots of sunshine had helped, and I was young, fit and had lots of hair in those days. Asgers had commented that I could be a white Ethiopian, as many had the Italian strain in them. I felt great, and looked forward to the coming evening.

We were to gather at John and Angie's for drinks first, and Asgedom would meet us at the Mess at 2000hrs. I drove to John's house, and was greeted by their servants, offering drinks and snacks. John welcomed me and explained that the ladies would join us soon, as they were just finishing dressing.

It was a very pleasant, warm night, and the stars and moon shone brightly as we sat on the veranda, enjoying the cool night air. Laughter drifted through the house and the ladies appeared. Although all three ladies were immaculately dressed, Lavender was absolutely stunning. She wore a fantastic red and gold silk sari, and her hair and makeup took my breath away. I stood there, transfixed, as she glided towards me: total elegance, total beauty. She was magnificent.

She grabbed my arm and raised her lips to be kissed. Her smile said it all.

We all chatted excitedly, and Lavender never left my side. Whenever possible, she managed a quick cuddle when nobody appeared to be looking.

I would have been more than happy to have taken her off on our own, but unfortunately, I had to share her with the rest of the world. She looked knowingly into my eyes – those dark brown beautiful eyes read my mind and she giggled, knowing what I was thinking and planning.

I was miles away when there was a little cough beside me, and Lavender's mother stood there, also a picture of elegance. It was obvious where Lavender had got her looks and poise. Her mother must have been equally stunning in her youth. She smiled a knowing smile and kissed me on the cheek.

'What do you think of my lovely daughters?' she asked.

'Absolutely beautiful,' I replied.

She was very happy that her daughter was so happy, and her strangely blue eyes sparkled with delight.

It was time to go. Angie's Captain had arrived, also dressed in National Costume, and he looked dashing and elegant in his National attire, with riding breeches, a collarless shirt, and long flowing robes in immaculate hand-woven cotton, like a character from the Arabian Nights. He really looked every part a prince.

We set off for the Ethiopian officers' Mess, and as promised, dear old Asgers was waiting outside with his elegant wife to greet us. Asgers was similarly attired, in full National Dress, as was his wife. They both looked outstanding. Asgers' wife was dressed in pure white cotton, shaped like a sari. The edges of her robes were hand embroidered. She looked beautiful. Asgers was obviously a very proud man.

Asgers greeted us all with his broad grin, and he was clearly delighted that we were there as his guests. Lavender was breathtakingly beautiful, and the sparkle in Asgers' eyes as he saw that I was truly happy and in love, was a sight to behold.

There were hundreds of officers arriving, and it was going to be a spectacular night.

Everyone involved with the Imperial Ethiopian Air Force of officer status was there, including the whole of the Indian teaching population. They joined us as we were about to enter the mess. The young Indian girl, Geeta was amongst them. She looked beautiful in her sari. Our eyes met, and there was a hint of excitement as she noticed that I was in the party. She then noticed Lavender at my side, and her excitement turned to a touch of sadness in her eyes, and she turned her gaze to the ground. She maintained her smile and nodded as she walked by, into the Officers' Mess.

I'm not sure if anyone else had noticed what had happened between us, but there was something about Geeta that drew me to her. Even though I was with the most beautiful girl in the world, there was something hidden in Geeta's dark brown eyes that raised my curiosity.

Asgedom led the way to show us where we were to be seated, and as we passed through the inner door, we were handed a very sharp dagger wrapped in a serviette, which I thought was a bit strange, but we all walked to our table, and Asgers sorted out the seating arrangements. Fortunately for him, he sat Lavender and I together. I had the honour of Asgers' wife sitting on one side of me, and Lavender on the other.

Everyone was in very high spirits, and drinks were soon being served. As it was to be a traditional evening, the local brew of Tella was served to the men, and a strong local brew was also available for the women. Tella was a type of beer similar to old fashioned mead, containing honey. It was very sweet and quite strong.

Fortunately Coca Cola and other soft drinks were available, which most of the overseas guests preferred.

I surveyed the rest of the tables. I came to the conclusion that ours had the most elegant women on it. As I looked around, my eyes met with Geeta's, and she looked embarrassed and quickly looked away.

Asgedom was talking excitedly to Lavender, explaining the National Dress and other traditional customs. And Asgers' wife was filling in with the feminine aspects of Ethiopian life. How the men were to be looked after, and the duties of the wife.

The celebration in the Officers' Mess was fantastic, and one of the highlights of my tour of Ethiopia. There was a traditional Ethiopian folk band playing, and also a western rock band. They took turns to entertain us, and even played some Beatles songs.

The Officers' Mess had been built on the insistence of Haile Selassie as a thank you to the Imperial Ethiopian Air Force, his pride and joy.

The locally brewed Tella was beginning to take effect, and everyone was in a great mood. Hot savoury snacks were served and everyone was very relaxed and happy.

The Western band took over and Lavender and I joined in the dancing. She was so beautiful and elegant, and I could see that she was the main attraction on the dance floor. I was very proud to be holding this beautiful lady in my arms. It hurt just to look into those dark brown beautiful eyes. Life could not be better than this moment.

The food was announced, and there was a sudden rush to the buffet room. We allowed the rush to subside, and joined the queue. As we entered the room, there hung in front of us two dead cows, freshly slaughtered and dripping with blood. It was a pretty awful sight but it seemed normal to the Ethiopians. It then became apparent why we were given the sharp daggers on our arrival. You were supposed to cut any part of the cow that you fancied eating. The Ethiopian officers were attacking it with great enthusiasm. Blood dripped onto the trays beneath as they hacked away. The cows were a present from the King, and much enjoyed by the young officers.

The sight in front of us was even more bizarre as it was happening in a very smart, marble-lined Officers' Mess, with everyone dressed in their best clothing. I had forgotten the Ethiopians' tradition of eating raw meat, and we could not bring ourselves to copy their example. We politely refused the invitation.

We now knew what the daggers were for, and as we returned to the main hall with our traditionally cooked local curry, we were met by the sight of the young officers putting chunks of raw cow between their teeth and cutting it into edible pieces. They cut it into thin strips, put it into their mouths, and used the dagger to cut off the meat that still protruded. It was not a pretty sight, as excess blood ran from their mouths.

It was funny that we all pretended to ignore the sight. We were, after all, guests in their land. We ate our traditional food, and chatted, as though it was quite normal.

The young officers really got stuck into the raw meat. It was, after all, a present from their King, and was the best meat available, from the research farm run by John.

The beer was really taking effect on us all, and Asgers asked Lavender to dance, and his wife was whisked away by another senior Officer. I noticed that Geeta was on her own, and I decided to ask her to dance. She was very shy and in two minds as to whether she should accept, but a broad smile lit up her face and she decided to join me.

We danced and enjoyed the moment. It was too noisy to chat. But our eyes met on occasion, and we exchanged smiles. The music stopped and I thanked her for the dance and returned her to her table, where I was met by disapproving looks from her colleagues. What the hell – you only live once, and the beer was making me feel really great. Even the sight of blood running from the Ethiopian's gaping mouths didn't look so bad. I returned to Lavender, who was still engrossed with Asgers.

The African band started playing again. They had rough drums, and violin type instruments of different sizes and different tones. The music had a magical beat to it. This was Africa, after all. A woman from the troupe started singing, in a soft wailing voice, and Asgers translated it. It was an Ethiopian love song, beautiful even if we did not understand the words. I found Lavender, very close to me, and her knees were pressing against mine under the table. Her hand fell on my lap and began to massage my leg, ever so gently. It was a magical moment, and my hand soon found her leg in return.

The girl finished her song, and the beat was increased. Suddenly a troupe of dancers appeared on the floor, much to the delight of the Ethiopian Officers. The girls were doing the traditional shoulder and breast raising dance, and the audience went wild. Some of the young officers joined in the traditional dance, and they were amazing. Asgedom explained that it was also a traditional love dance, and the suggestive movements emulated African courtship rites. We all sat there, entranced by the magic of it all. The girls' lithe young bodies were amazingly agile, as they twisted and writhed in what appeared to be the nearest thing to a sex act I had ever seen in a dance, and that's saying something after Angie's antics at the ex-pat club.

One young officer was the best of them all, and it turned out to be Asgedom's best friend from the North.

'He is very experienced, Mr Lupson,' Asgers whispered in my ear, and laughed as he said it. The crowd was going absolutely wild and the women, although seated, all joined in the traditional shoulder shrugging swaying dance. The atmosphere was electric, and I felt Lavender, getting more and more excited beside me, and she leant forward and nibbled my ear. Nobody was looking in our direction, so I took advantage to have a quick kiss and a caress, much appreciated by the excited Lavender.

Chapter 21
My Last Night with Lavender

There followed many days of ecstasy and many nights of love making.

But the day when Lavender must leave me loomed nearer, and I dreaded it.

During those blissful days, thoughts about the growing unease in Ethiopia were pushed to the back of my mind and I was filled with love and excitement.

The day before Lavender's departure, John and Angie arranged for a farewell supper at their place, and all very close friends were invited. I arrived at their house, and I was greeted by Lavender. We hugged and kissed, not wanting to let go, not wanting other people near us, wanting to be alone. There was sadness in our hearts, as this was to be the last night that we would share together in Ethiopia. We were not sure if we could arrange to be alone together.

The rest of the guests arrived and we were forced to participate in the supper party. We were at least seated together and managed the odd squeeze of our hands under the table when nobody was looking.

The meal was superb, as was the company, but the thought of wasting precious moments hung heavily over both Lavender and myself. At last, the supper ended, and we all headed out onto the veranda. It was a perfect night and the stars were so close that you felt you could touch them. We sat around, drinking and enjoying the company, and eventually, the older ones bade farewell to Lavender and returned home. Only a few very close friends and family members remained, and at this point, Lavender and Angie decided to go off and make some fresh coffee. They were not gone long, and soon returned with coffee, and a glint of excitement in their eyes. I noticed this, but I didn't think the others did. Angie told us that she didn't feel tired, and it would be a shame if we didn't visit the top of the volcano and see the sights of the village and the palace from the top, on such a beautiful night.

I readily agreed that it would be an awful shame, and volunteered to take them to see the sights, hoping that the rest of the family would be too tired to join us. We were made to wrap up warm and promised to be careful on the drive up to the top. We bade goodnight to all, and promised not to be too late. All was in order because Angie would act as chaperone.

As soon as we were outside, Angie told me to drive to her Captain's Officers' Mess accommodation, and I thanked her for giving Lavender and myself a chance to be together. We drove off and parked outside the Officers' Mess. Lavender sat very close to me and as her sister went off to fetch her lover, Lavender buried herself in my arms, groping for me and I for her.

Angie returned from the Officers' Mess just in time to stop me from taking Lavender there and then. She said that we would indeed visit the top of the volcano, but she would travel in her Captain's car, and we were to follow. By this time, I was full of love and desire, and had great difficulty containing myself.

A car appeared from the shadows and Angie got inside. We set off, following the Captain's car. We travelled to the far end of the village of Debre Zeit and turned down the dusty track that led from the hills to the market. We had passed the volcano lake, and turned up another dirt track that wound its way up to the top of the volcano and would give us a spectacular panoramic view of the surrounding area. We drove with great care up the narrow, twisting track, and eventually arrived on the plateau. When the car in front stopped, we stopped too.

We got out of our cars and strolled around the sides of the plateau, taking in the magnificent view and atmosphere. It was truly a magnificent night. The moon was as large as I have ever seen, and although it was quite late, one could see for a considerable distance.

The stars sparkled in all their glory, and I felt Lavender, very close to me, squeezing my hand. No one spoke. We did not need words. It was the most beautiful, sad, emotional moment for us all. In the distance, we heard the laughter of the hyenas, and the grunts and howls of the other beasts of the night.

It was warm, and the smoke from dwindling charcoal fires rose from the village far below us. In the distance, the odd electric light shone. The rest of the landscape was shrouded in the light of the moon, and gave a sight that will be etched on my memory forever.

Lavender snuggled ever closer to me and I realised that she was shaking. I raised her face to mine, and saw in the moonlight the most magnificent, beautiful face I have ever seen. Tears were rolling down her face as she silently let herself give way to the beauty of the moment. We loved as we had never loved before, and this was to be our last night together for quite some time. Without a word, she pulled me towards the car, and brought out a blanket and laid it on the ground. Her eyes never left mine as we slowly lowered ourselves onto the blanket. We kissed and kissed in the most tender ways. Gone was the raw passion. Tenderness and love had replaced it, and we cuddled gently together under the magnificent night that God had provided for us.

Lavender was tender and loving, and she mewed as each touch of our bodies gave each other pleasure. Our bodies rose and fell in gently tenderness, and as the sea crashed into oblivion, our feelings for each other were expressed in intense tenderness and love. Tears still flowed from Lavender's beautiful eyes, and were caught by the ever-shining moon. Tears swelled in my eyes, although I did my best to hide them. We lay together, naked, under the skies. God's children, doing what he had shown us best, giving love to each other.

We slowly dressed and climbed into the car. Hardly a word had been spoken. Words were not necessary. Lavender's sister Angie and her Captain had taken themselves off, out of sight, and had presumably been likewise involved. We sat in my dear old Renault car, and held each other. Dawn would soon some, and the day I had feared would arrive.

***

The next day, John drove us to the main airport terminal at Addis Ababa. We saw the distinctive red and white colours of the Air India Airliner making its final approach to the airport. Lavender was snuggled up close to me in John's car, and all the family were crammed together in his station wagon, all coming to say farewell to the lovely Lavender. The night before still lingered, and although we put on brave faces, the hurt of having to say goodbye showed clearly on our faces.

As we walked into the Air Terminal, more tears welled in Lavender's eyes, and this set the rest of the family off. Being British, I kept a stiff upper lip, and managed to keep my feelings to myself.

The crew of the Air India Airline appeared and all dashed to welcome Lavender and asked how she felt. It was quite easy for her not to look too well, as the previous night's passion under the stars and the tears of the sad departure did not enhance Lavender's normally immaculate appearance. Her colleagues were full of sympathy and helped to carry her belongings. I had forgotten that Lavender was supposed to have been injured in the road accident, and up to that moment, so had she. Luckily, she was able to cover up, and act the part of an injured but recovering lady. As the tears flowed, we managed a little smile at the thought of our deception. Little did we realise that Lavender would be given an extra week off for convalescence on her return to India.

As last, she turned to me, and those big tear-filled brown eyes said it all. In just over three weeks, we had met and become lovers, enjoying each other to the full, a wonderful time that was now to end, at least for the time being. We hugged and kissed each other, vowing to meet each other in the not too distant future. She turned and walked to join her mother and colleagues, her shoulders slightly shaking as her tears flowed. I watched her go, and then wished that I had come to the airport in my own car. I just wanted to be alone, and not to have to act with a stiff upper lip.

We returned to Debre Zeit, having watched and waved at the departing Air India Aircraft. Angie invited me for tea, but I turned down the offer and I am sure that she understood that I needed to be alone.

I entered my empty house and again, I felt totally alone in the world. My maid appeared and made me a cup of tea. I thanked her and said that I was tired and I went to my room. I awoke to a gentle knocking on my door.

My maid was there with another cup of tea. The bath was poured, and my supper would be ready in half an hour…egg and chips, I suppose.

I wrote this in Ethiopia when I was at a very low ebb, feeling sorry for myself and very lonely, missing Lavender:

Midnight comes and slips away
O dear God, please roll on the day.
My thoughts and dreams are of you only.
The Night is long and o so lonely.

One o'clock strikes its mournful toll
And thoughts of you disturb my soul.
I wonder if you feel deep in your heart
The way I do now we are apart?

I toss and turn, the clock strikes two.
Without your love what can I do?
Your lovely eyes and dark brown hair,
In dreams of you I see them here.

The Night drags on and soon it's four.
I climb from my bed and pace the floor.
I hear you say please don't be afraid
My love is true and will never stray.

I close my eyes and feel you near
Caress your lips and shoulders bare.
My senses real and then I drift away
And light breaks through to welcome day.

Chapter 22
The Rebellion

Zola, the daughter of the Colonel who lived next door – the family fled to escape the rebellion.

The next few days passed in a blur of loneliness and hard work. I had to get Lavender out of my mind.

But tension had been mounting for a considerable time, and Asgers had become noticeably more agitated. He had told me that the situation was very bad, and something would happen very soon.

It was Asgers' turn to go into Addis for supplies and he clambered into my dear old Renault Four. He smiled and said his goodbyes. I returned to the stores and began checking off supplies. I had not been there long when a member of staff called Lizza screamed. I dashed from the stores. She was looking out of the window, wide-eyed and obviously very afraid. I dashed to her side.

Fifteen airmen, armed to the teeth with automatic rifles at the ready, were approaching our shop.

Without thinking, I opened the door and stepped outside. It was ridiculous that rebels were about to attack our Ethiopian NAAFI shop.

I put my hands up. Laughing my head off, I said:

'Okay, chaps. I surrender.'

The rebels stopped in their tracks, unsure of what to do. The last thing they expected was a stupid white Englishman to appear, waving his arms in the air.

The rebel leader came up to me, closely followed by the rest of the group.

'Shake my hand,' he said, and broke into a wide grin, as did the rest of the rebels. I shook his hand.

'We are going to search your building,' he said, so I led him into the shop.

They searched the premises and left within a few minutes. Obviously, they didn't find what they were looking for.

The shop staff stood, still wide-eyed, wondering what to do next. I thought I had better find out. I ran out of the building and shouted after the rebels.

'What are we supposed to do now?' I asked.

'Shut up the shop and go home,' came the reply.

I returned to the shop and got one of the girls to make a cup of tea. We all needed one.

One of the girls had spoken to one of the Air Force rebels and found out a little of what was going on. The rebels had taken over the Air Force Base at Debre Zeit and had gathered all of the Officers and senior ranks into a large hall on the base, until they decided what to do next. They had been unable to find all of the Officers, which is why they had searched the shop.

They were trying to decide on the fate of their prisoners and a number of the rebels were in favour of shooting them all.

As I drank my hot tea, it began to sink in – how lucky I'd been. The rebels could have decided to shoot me as a prelude to the commencement of the full rebellion. It would have made front page headlines in the world's press: British Ethiopian Air Force Advisor murdered at rebel-held Debre Zeit. It was quite worrying really.

I decided to take the advice of the rebels' leader and shut up shop and return home.

Asgedom was still in Addis with my car. I hadn't a clue where he'd be. I tried to use the telephone in the office, but the lines were dead. The rebels had taken over the whole of the village of Debre Zeit and the surrounding area, and we were cut off from the outside world. I locked up the shop, and told the staff to go home and not to return until they heard from me.

Having no car, I walked down the rough track and headed towards my home. On the way, I stopped at Asgedom's house and explained as best as I could what had happened. They didn't seem over worried, and I asked them that if and when he returned, to get in touch with me.

I then went around to Nicky and Dave's house and I found them at home. They had been sent home, and told to stay there until they were asked to return. The rebels had taken over the Air Force base that morning, in a very swift and efficient manner.

The rebellion had been very well organised, and no one, as far as Dave knew, had been harmed. It was rumoured that some of the officers were involved with the rebels and had cooperated to the full with the rebels. But the situation was very tense, as some of the hot-headed rebels wished to seek revenge on some of the officers. The Base Commander General was particularly disliked, and they wanted him dead.

I sat and talked with them for a while, and decided to go home. I promised them that I would return later that night and see if we could piece together what was happening and what to do next. We agreed to go onto the ex-pats club and have a meeting of all the members.

I met my maid at the gate of my house and she was obviously very worried about me. Next door, the men-folk had been rounded up. The servants told my maid what had happened. One of the Colonels, a hard man from the patch adjacent to mine, had received a visit from the rebels, and agreed to go with them. They took his Volkswagen and made him get into the back seat. Unbeknown to the rebels, the Colonel had a machine gun hidden under the back seat, and instead of going peacefully, he had shot the rebels dead. All this had happened twenty minutes before I had returned home. The Colonel then gathered his family together and drove off into the Bush.

No one ever heard of him or his family again. It is possible that he drove over one of Ethiopia's many borders, but he was certainly a wanted man by the rebels.

This was the first blood of the rebellion.

Outside, I heard occasional bursts of gunfire, and I wondered what was happening. But I couldn't do anything.

I had a meal of the inevitable egg and chips, and decided to go and have a snooze. The excitement of the day had worn me out. As soon as I had laid down on the bed, I was fast asleep.

I awoke to knocking on my door, and found the house in darkness. My maid whispered that Asgedom's son had arrived, and had a message that Asgers had returned home and wanted to see me.

It was quite dark by this time, and I decided to walk with him to Asgers' house. On the way, I would stop at Nicky and Dave's house and tell them that I might be a bit late for the meeting of ex-pats. When I arrived at their house, they insisted that they drove us to Asgers' house. It was dangerous to be out walking at this time, especially at night time. I eventually agreed, and we all set off for Asgers' house.

I couldn't see any lights on, but Asgers' son assured us that the family was at home. We knocked on the door and it was opened by Asgedom's wife. We quietly entered and found Asgers in the rear room, wide-eyed and excited. He quickly shook my hand and slapped me on the back, a wide grin spreading over his face.

'Mr Lupson, it is very dangerous times,' he said. I agreed, and asked him how he had managed to escape the road blocks and get home, as nearly all the rest of his colleagues were currently under armed guard.

He explained that he'd had a normal day in Addis, buying goods from the shops, and the old Renault Four was there to prove it, fully laden with goods. As he approached Debre Zeit, he had been stopped at the road block by armed rebels. After a lengthy conversation, they insisted that he left the car and joined the rest of the captives awaiting transportation back to the now rebel-held base at Debre Zeit.

Asgers had managed to persuade the rebels that the goods in the old Renault were destined for their own welfare shop, and that his first duty was to ensure that the goods were safe. Typical old Asgers.

'Mr Lupson,' he said, in a voice growing ever more excited. 'I asked the rebels to allow me to park my car at the side of the road in a friend's drive. As I drove to the side, I put my foot down and sped away.

I burst out laughing. Our old Renault car would not be capable of speeding away if it was totally empty and in full working order, let alone laden down as it was. The whole family joined in with the laughter. I could just imagine dear old Asgers' white knuckles, gripping the steering wheel as he sped away from the rebel road block, crouched determinedly below the wheel.

It was obvious that the rebels knew and liked loveable old Asgers and had made no attempt to stop him from making his heroic dash. It would have been quite easy for a reasonably fit man to have run faster than the Renault until it had built up steam.

Asgers' wife came in, bearing mugs of hot tea and some sweet-tasting thick liqueur, and we all sat down to discuss what the future held. Asgers was perturbed at the fact that his colleagues had been detained, but he felt sure that apart from the odd one or two who were not liked, the others would not be harmed.

It was time to attend our ex-pats club meeting and we said our farewells to Asgers' wife and went out to where my car was parked.

We decided to push my car out of Asgers' compound onto the road to avoid making any noise, in case someone was suspicious. It was pitch black outside, and we pushed the car onto the road, still fully laden. Nicky and Dave started their own car, and I started up the old Renault.

Obviously the thick, sweet liqueur had gone to my head, and without thinking, I went to toot my horn to say goodbye to Asgers and to tell Nicky and Dave that I was ready to set off.

I had forgotten that the horn got stuck occasionally, and this was to be one of those occasions. In the pitch-black night, I foolishly touched the horn and it stuck. The noise seemed impossibly loud. I thumped and fiddled with the button, and at last managed to get it unstuck after what seemed like ages.

Gunfire erupted from the direction of the palace some 800 yards away, and old Asgers and his family waved and dashed indoors. It was my turn to try to speed away from the rebels.

I looked back and saw what must have been tracer bullets, heading vaguely in my direction as the good old Renault built up steam and slowly escaped from the immediate danger.

**

My old Renault bumped and rumbled towards the ex-pat club, and its lights picked up the hideous red eyes of the hyenas as they scampered away in the darkness. When I arrived, the rest of the ex-pats were already there, and were glad that Dave and Nicky and I had managed to make it. The bar was open and it was obvious that a number of the members had been there a considerable time, as they were already well-oiled. We all sat around and discussed the day's events. We all decided to make the most of a bad, uncertain lot, and to meet every day and see how the situation progressed.

Chapter 23
A Dangerous Encounter

I ventured out to Asgedom's house once more.

I had spent the previous day visiting the ex-pats club, and discussing the little news that was available. The rebels still held the officers captive and the rebellion had made world headlines, although the situation was very uncertain.

I arrived at Asgedom's house and was let in at the side entrance by his son.

Asgedom appeared from the back room, and looked tired and strained. His wife greeted me, and Asgedom asked her to prepare some coffee. I told him what I had heard from the World Service, and we sat and discussed the possibilities. Asgedom was certain that none of his fellow officers would be harmed and that peace would return once the rebels were assured that the government would change its ways and take greater care of all of its people.

I thought at the time that this was a bit naïve, but I let Asgedom reassure himself.

I'm not sure whose suggestion it was, but I was soon agreeing to go to the Base and to try to find out what was going on. This decision nearly cost me my life. I drank my second cup of the strong, sweet, thick coffee, and set out in my trusty car for the Base.

I drove through the nearly deserted village of Debre Zeit, leading up to the Imperial Ethiopian Air Force Base, and turned down the major Tarmacked road that passed the main gate. As I approached the base, I saw the rebels, gathered in force at the main gates.

As I passed, they trained their rifles at me, and looked hostile. The only way to go home was to go back past the main gate. I drove for some six hundred yards or so, and slowly turned around, heading back to the village and safety. I drove steadily back towards the gate, and as I drew alongside, the rebels began shouting at me to stop, and a number of them left their comrades and raced towards me.

I stopped the car and waited. A couple of the NCOs came forward and one of them pushed his Armalite rifle through the car window and pushed the nozzle up my nostrils, forcing my head back at a painful angle..

There followed a torrent of questions.

'Who are you?'

'What do you want?'

'What are you doing here?'

'Why are you here?'

I tried to answer the questions and explain that I was here to run their welfare organisation. But it was difficult to speak with a rifle up my nose, and it was obvious that the man with the gun was not listening or not wanting to listen.

He was becoming more and more agitated, and it was obvious that he wanted to pull the trigger. The rebels started to argue about whether they should allow him to shoot me or not.

Thank God an NCO at the rear of the group pushed forwards and explained that I was indeed the man who had come to their country to run their own shop and cafes. I was a good man, who had worked hard and forced the General to improve their facilities. I had persuaded them to build the shop. I had taken over their filthy café and provided good food. I had given my own gas supply to the café, to keep the service going when the gas suppliers were on strike.

This NCO was virtually pleading for my life – and I was on his side.

At last, the rest of the group appeared to be listening to him, and the rifle was eased from my nose.

I was now able to speak more clearly and explain once again that I was only concerned that with the rebellion happening, I was unsure of what to do.

The Armalite rifle was removed from the car window.

'Go home, Mr Lupson,' the rebels' NCO said. 'Stay at home until you are told otherwise. Do not worry. Just stay at home.'

I thanked my saviour and drove off.

As I approached the outskirts of Debre Zeit, I began to realise how lucky I had been, and it was then that the fear caught up with me and I began to shake a bit. Throughout the whole ten or fifteen minutes, the situation had seemed unreal, like a dream that I was witnessing, as though it was nothing to do with me. I had been very close to death, and this would have brought home to the authorities that the rebels really meant what they said. I could see the headlines once more:

'NAAFI Ethiopian Advisor Shot Dead by Rebels'.

I had been very foolish, as the rebels were two days into the rebellion and were expecting some reaction from the King and his Government. The rebels were very much on edge and I had given them an ideal chance to bring their cause to the notice of the world. It's not until someone dies, especially a foreigner, that anyone really takes note in situations like this.

A couple of the rebels had died, but this was not even reported locally.

I returned to Asgedom's house and once again came the familiar Asgers cry:

'Mr Lupson, what has happened to you?'

The thick black coffee burned my throat, and I sat and told old Asgedom and his family what had happened. Old Asgedom's eyes became wider and wider, and he looked really worried about what had just happened. I could just imagine him trying to explain how I had been shot to old Norman Lee.

Asgers was scared enough of him under normal circumstances, but to have to explain the demise of old Luppers to Lee was unthinkable.

We all started to laugh, and the tension was eased.

The days seemed to pass, with rumour after rumour spreading throughout the ex-pat community. We heard that the rebels were about to shoot their captives, and more worryingly, that they had already shot their captives. Fortunately, the latter was proved untrue. Negotiations were going on with the various authorities and Paratroopers were being sent in to supervise the return to normality, within the next few days. Apparently, the Air Force Rebels had been persuaded that their claim for a better deal for their people and themselves would be heard, and they had agreed to release the prisoners.

It was good news, and although things were still extremely tense, it would ease the situation considerably.

The day arrived when the prisoners were to be released, but rumours were circulating that the rebels still wanted to kill some of the less popular senior officers. It was on that night that I drove out to the ex-pats club to find out the latest news.

As I left my compound, I saw in my headlights someone hiding in the shadow of the hedgerow. He recognised my car and waved me over urgently. I realised that it was the Aide de Camp to the General.

I stopped the car and called him over.

'What's up?' I asked.

The Lieutenant was dirty and dishevelled, having only been released from captivity hours earlier. He shook with fear and exhaustion.

'The General,' he mumbled. 'They are going to kill my General. I must warn him.'

It would have been extremely foolish of us to try to drive up to the General's house, especially if the rebels were intent on killing him.

I suggested that we drove to Texan John's house, which was situated next door to the General's, and try to make contact with the General from there. The Lieutenant agreed and off we set.

John welcomed us with open arms, offered us a drink, and called for Angie. She was having a bath but soon joined us. We explained what was happening and that the officers had been released unharmed, but that one of the rebel leaders had persuaded the hot-heads that they should kill the Base Commander General.

Angie expressed relief that all of the officers had been released, and of course, tactfully asked how the friend of the family, her pet Captain was. Had he been harmed? Was he well? She smiled brightly when she was informed that he was well, and had returned to his quarters. John said that he had been at home all day, and had not noticed any activity around the General's house. Nobody had called, and apart from the usual comings and goings of his servants, he had not noticed anything suspicious.

John, I and the Lieutenant decided to go and have a look, and crept over to the edge of his garden, which overlooked the General's house. By this time, darkness had fallen, and all was quiet. The General's house was in complete darkness and nobody was to be seen.

John called his own servants over and questioned them. They would know, as they were local, and all servants had an uncanny way of knowing exactly what was going on, not only in their own household, but in the surrounding households. They seemed reluctant to speak at first, but after being reassured by both the Lieutenant and John that their only concern was the safety of the General, they began to tell their story.

A messenger had arrived during the early afternoon to say that the General was about to be released. He had learned of the threat to kill him and had decided not to return to his home. His wife and family were to disguise themselves and gather as many of their possessions as possible, and meet them at a secret location, some five miles from Debre Zeit. This had been speedily arranged, and the wife and family had left.

We did not find out what happened to him and his family. I never heard from the General again.

The lieutenant was much relieved that his General had escaped death. He agreed to John's offer of a brandy, and then the Lieutenant said his goodbyes and slipped into the night. He declined my offer to drive him back to the Officer Accommodation. Although I met him on a number of occasions after this, the incident was never mentioned again. He obviously didn't want anyone to know that he was a supporter of the most hated General.

During the next few days, the situation gradually returned to a form of normality, although there was now considerable mistrust amongst the various forces of the King, and indeed amongst the various rank structures. The disliked Paratroopers were often seen on patrol in their open-backed Land Rovers, armed with heavy machine guns.

The situation had improved, and we decided to celebrate in great style at the ex-pat club on that very Saturday night.

***

Asgedom decided that it was now safe to leave his house and I went to his house to collect him. He had been in contact with his fellow officers who had all been held captive, and they had told him that they considered themselves very lucky to be alive.

One NCO, who was one of the leaders intent on killing all the officers, had actually gone into the hall where they were being held, fully armed, and had to be forcibly restrained by his fellow rebels from killing them there and then. Certainly, it was only the fact that a large number of the officers had risen through the ranks and were well liked and respected by most of the rebels that had saved their lives. The General and other less popular officers would be dealt with at a convenient time, and quite a number of them disappeared, never to be seen again. Most had escaped, but no one knew where they had gone.

Asgedom was full of himself, and related time and time again how he had escaped the road block and had gone into hiding inside his own house. It was such a small village that it was obvious that the rebels had known where he was hiding, but Asgers was a much-loved man and no one was about to drag him out of hiding or harm him in any way.

We sent messages to the staff that we were back in business, and the shop was once again open for our customers. It was a strange, tense time and everyone was on edge. We received a signal that a further shipment of goods was about to arrive at Assab, and once again, I was nominated to go and clear the goods. Asgers had obviously decided that I was now an expert at importing goods into Ethiopia.

Saturday night arrived, and we all gathered at the ex-pat club. Dear old Alfred and his trusty dog and all the others were there. Food was provided by "the marrieds", and we singles provided the booze. We all sat around in good cheer, feeling relieved that the situation was returning towards normal. Even the big fat one Jan Ruschin was in a good mood. He sat with his vast frame hanging over the edge of his stool. He was, as usual, worse for wear from booze, and he had his .22 pistol in his hand.

'I was ready for the rebels,' he said. 'I always carry my little friend everywhere I go.' He indicated the small, deadly pistol, which looked like a toy in his massive plump hands. We all ignored the stupid arse and got stuck into the food.

I suddenly remembered the letter I had received from Lavender. I'd wanted to bring it with me to show to Angie. I said I would return home to fetch it. I jumped into my trusty Renault car, turned on the headlights, and drove out of the ex-pat club's compound. Once again, my lights picked up the hideous eyes of the hyenas.

I drove to my house, hardly giving the guard time to open the gate. I was eager to return to the party and as I dashed up the steps to the kitchen entrance, I stepped on something strangely soft. I threw open the door, not thinking, and dashed past my maid to collect Lavender's letter. I left the door open, as I was in a hurry, and I dashed past. My maid went to close the door. By this time, I was in the living room. She let out a terrifying cry.

I spun around and dashed back to the kitchen. She just stood there, staring at the steps I had just dashed over. I had just trodden on one of Africa's most deadly snakes. My maid had just seen the end of it disappear into the darkness. I looked at her. Her eyes were wide with fright, and her face was drained.

The guard appeared and asked what was wrong. My maid explained in her native tongue that I had come rushing in and had trodden on a deadly snake which had been passing over my steps at the time. His eyes widened as he hurriedly came in, away from the danger. I quickly found a torch and with my guard armed with his spear, we went out to try and find the snake. Unfortunately, it had gone.

My maid was still in distress and it appeared that I had been very lucky. In my eagerness to get the letter and return to the party, I had not given the snake a chance to strike.

I returned to the party and told my tale. I was handed a very large brandy, which I downed with grateful thanks.

I took Angie to one side and showed her Lavender's latest letter.

The night was good fun, with all of us much relieved at the thought of normality returning, and the chance to proceed with our various projects. We drank, sang, and danced the night away, until I finally succumbed to the night and went home.

I collapsed into a drunken sleep, full of fitful dreams of Lavender, and of the darkness that now surrounded me. The excitement of the past few weeks had taken my mind off my loneliness, and now it returned with a vengeance.

I awoke to a hammering on my front door, and much loud conversation, including the voice of my maid.

'Mr Lupson is still asleep and doesn't wish to be disturbed!' she was shouting, at someone who was insisting on seeing me.

I became strangely angry at this intrusion in the middle of the night, and dragged on my trousers and staggered to the front door. I pushed the door open; about to shout *'what the bloody hell do you want?'* But the words stuck in my mouth.

It was broad daylight and the sun shone very brightly. Too bright for my liking, bearing in mind how we had been celebrating the night before.

There stood before me in all his glory, was the British Consulate. Dressed in formal regalia and outside my gate was a shining chauffeur-driven Range Rover.

'Doctor Livingstone, I presume,' uttered this immaculate man, dressed with the refinery of the Raj. I was lost for words, but I suggested that he came in.

I asked my maid to make some coffee, and asked if the Consulate would mind waiting while I made myself a little more presentable. I quickly shaved, splashed myself with lots of cold water, and began to feel better. What the bloody hell did this chap want anyway?

I introduced myself again properly, having got over the initial shock, and gratefully accepted the coffee produced by my maid.

'We have been worried about you, Mr Lupson,' said the Consulate. 'We did not even know that you were in the country. We have received a message from your HQ, expressing concern that they haven't heard from you for a few weeks, and with the current unrest and the fact that all the action has taken place here in Debre Zeit, your HQ has asked me to try to find you. Now, Mr Lupson, what exactly are you doing here?'

Typical of our HQ. Of course I hadn't been able to contact them. The phone lines hadn't been working. We had been cut off from the rest of the world for ages. How the hell did they expect me to contact them?

I explained in great detail to the Consulate my reason for being in Ethiopia, and expressed my concern that he was unaware of my presence. As it transpired, he was unaware that there were a number of ex-pats living in Debre Zeit. At this news, the Consulate looked even more worried.

'You have all been very lucky, Mr Lupson,' he said. I realised that anyway.

We talked for another half an hour or so, and then I explained that I had arrange to meet up with everyone for lunch at the ex-pats club, as customary on a Sunday, and that if he wished, I would take him to the club and he could meet most of the rest of the ex-pat community. He readily accepted my invitation and I got my old Renault and drove to the Club. The immaculate Range Rover followed.

The members of our club were just as surprised to meet such an exalted person on such an informal occasion, as I had been. We all sat around as he gave us a brief on the latest situation. The King was still in control and he had agreed to the rebels' demands that social changes should be made, giving a better deal to the poor and giving more freedom to all. The situation had stabilised and the

Paratroopers would police the area in cooperation with the Air Force rebels, to allow the situation to cool.

The Consulate seemed very concerned that his office was unaware of our group of ex-pats being in the country. He promised to take responsibility for us in the future. He explained in great detail the plan for evacuation, should the need arise. We must all travel to the residence of the British Ambassador, where we would come under his protection. Helicopters would then be used to ferry us out of Ethiopia. Presumably to Kenya. The plan, although well-meant, was daft. Here we were, situated South West of Addis Ababa and some fifty miles from the Ambassador's residence. It would mean that we would have to travel back into the most dangerous part of Ethiopia, should real trouble erupt, fifty miles into the heart of Addis, along presumably rebel-held roads. And so, if real trouble erupted, we had already planned to take the track roads south to the Kenyan border. We had all agreed that the main problems would be around Addis, and this was the definite place to avoid.

The Consulate and his driver were suitably wined and dined, and the day wore on, with all of us drinking gin and tonics, and talking, telling tales of the past. It was a very pleasant way to pass a Sunday. At last, the Consulate decided that it was time for him to depart, and he singled me out, to assure me that my HQ would be informed that I was alive and well. The consulate wobbled slightly as he made his way back to the immaculate Range Rover. He promised that we would hear from him and ensure that our interests were taken care of.

Chapter 24
Back to Assab

Once again it was time to set off to Assab to clear the bloody goods, and once again, old Asgers found an excuse not to accompany me there.

The old Renault bounced along the runway, to where the now familiar 119 sat ramped on the runway, looking even more battered than ever. Asgers' friend appeared at the door to the old aircraft, and they went through the ritual greeting of long-lost friends. The pilot was the same one as before, and his broad smile soon cheered me up as he helped me strap on my parachute.

I was again ushered into the navigator's seat and made comfortable. Again, I watched as each engine was fired up and coughed reluctantly into life. Pre-flight checks seemed to take ages, and it became increasingly hot. At last, all the engines seemed to be working, to the satisfaction of the pilot, and as the aircraft slowly moved forward, I waved farewell to Asgers and the lumbering aircraft gathered speed and bumped down the only runway in the world that had a slope on it, and took off, into the beautiful blue skies.

The old aircraft rose grudgingly over the cliffs and headed north, towards Assab. Once again, we passed over virtually the whole length of Ethiopia. We flew over many deserted villages with no sign of life. The ground had been burned darker by the never-ending sun. No rain had fallen again this year and the people of Ethiopia were dying in their thousands. The story was repeating itself again and again. I sat in the navigator's seat, transfixed by the sad, rugged beauty of it all, pitying the poor bastards below who were dying of hunger.

A tap on my shoulder roused me. A crew member had appeared with thick rough-cut sandwiches again, and hot coffee. He grinned as he passed me the refreshment and I nodded my thanks.

Once again, the old aircraft began to fall out of the sky as we made our final approach to Assab with its scorching hot burnt plains. Once again, the pilot fought to control the massive old heap of a plane, and managed to keep it straight down the runway. Even before we stopped, we could feel the intense heat, and when a member of the crew opened the door of the old 119, it was like opening an oven door. The heat was breath-taking.

We scrambled out of the hatch and quickly stripped off our flying kit.

My faithful Lieutenant, Charlie, was to hand with our transport. He welcomed us back to Assab.

***

I arrived at my hotel at the same time as a Chinese chap, who spoke only very broken English, as he tried to explain that he required a room, until he could find other accommodation.

I booked into my room, and had a shower. My Lieutenant would come and pick me up later, and we would go out on the town for a drink.

I had a short nap on my bed and then went through to the dining room for a meal. The Chinese chap was there, looking very lost, and trying to ask the waiter, who also spoke very limited English, what to eat. I took pity on the Chinese man and introduced myself, and asked if he required help. At least I could understand his broken English, and the waiter understood my English, so I ordered for the both of us. The poor Chinese chap was extremely grateful for my help. It was his first trip outside China and he had only arrived in Ethiopia the previous day.

He was a member of the Peace Corps, and had volunteered to come to Ethiopia to help build new docks in Assab. Until my previous visit to Assab, I had not realised that China had a Peace Corps. I had met the USA types before, and realised that they did a lot of overseas work. Rumour had it that the Peace Corps (of both the USA and China) were sponsored by their country's secret service, and that they used the Peace Corps to glean information about the various countries they worked in. It was only a rumour, but I can imagine that there was some truth in it.

The little Chinese chap was quite friendly and explained that he did not relish the thought of having to spend two years in Assab, working as an engineer to build the new docks. But he must not fail, either. It was a matter of honour and he must not let his friends or his parents down. He was considered a bit of a hero in the village he had left, going off to do good work for a poorer nation.

There was evidence that China had invested considerable funds and aid into Africa, and Ethiopia was to the fore. Obviously China saw Africa as a potential market for export, and was courting all the Third World countries for future trading rights. It was also keen on obtaining the mineral mining rights and it saw vast potential in the supply of all types of African ore.

It's funny, but no one seems to realise, both then and now, how China is slowly influencing Africa, and by sending its ever helpful young people to build African infrastructure, and by encouraging the Africans to send their students to China, the link is becoming stronger and stronger.

We ate together, and my escort, Charlie, arrived. I invited the Chinese chap to come with us but he declined, as he was too tired. I was also tired by now, but we went out for a drink anyway. The lieutenant didn't wish to discuss the troubles in the country, but agreed that it was far from over. Apart from the closure of the oil refinery and the lack of gas production, Assab had not been affected much by the troubles. The rebellion had been confined to Debre Zeit and Addis Ababa.

We entered a bar on the waterfront, full of lovely young ladies. We sat and drank cool beer. It was a very hot night, and we talked about the area surrounding Assab. A couple of the young bar girls joined us. They didn't speak or understand English, but we bought them drinks, anyway. The girls sat close to us and smiled as we talked.

Not far from where we sat were the Danakil Mountains, the home of the Danakil natives and the hottest place on Earth. The Danakil natives are very primitive warriors, who still hunt, and kill their enemies to prove that they are men. Danakil men use long, sharp knives, and once they have successfully killed their enemies, they use the knife to cut off his parts. They are then presented to the family of the girl he wishes to marry to prove to the world how brave the would-be groom is.

Charlie had told me this story the previous time I was in Assab, and I'd found it hard to believe, but the lieutenant assured me that it was true, and that if we had time during this trip, we would go up into the mountains and visit a village. I readily agreed, as I wanted a souvenir – a genuine Danakil knife. I had seen them on sale in the market in Addis, but a real one from a real Danakil village would be worth having.

We chatted on, and then I said that I really must get back to my hotel, as I was tired from the journey and the heat.

As we paid our bill, and rose to leave, the bar girls got ready to go with us. I was really tired and we took considerable effort to persuade the girls that I did not require their services that night, but that we would return some time again. The girls looked genuinely disappointed, but I suppose it was the money they wanted, more than myself. I gave them a few dollars for their time and they seemed to cheer up a bit. It was probably more than they would earn in a week anyway.

I bade Charlie goodnight, and went off to bed, having arranged for him to collect me at nine the following morning. I turned on the fan over my bed, and fell onto the mattress, covering myself with a sheet. I fell into a deep sleep.

I awoke at eight, showered, and went down for breakfast. It was a definite improvement on my last hotel in Assab, where the hygiene standards had been so bad that I'd nearly died of dysentery. This hotel had fresh watermelon, scrambled eggs, and fresh bread. The Chinese chap appeared and ordered the same as I had, in his broken English. He didn't seem any happier, as he had not slept too well. I told him that he should have joined us and had a couple of beers, as this would have helped him to sleep.

We chatted about what the day had in store for us. He was to be collected by the local port engineer to start work, ensuring that the docks were built to the correct specifications. I felt sorry for the chap. Having now spent some nine months trying to build a supermarket operation and a café, I realised the frustrations this poor chap would experience, made even worse by his poor standard of English. I wondered how he would survive.

Charlie turned up on time and we said our farewells to the Chinese man. We headed down to the port. We were in for the inevitable shock.

Yes, my ship had arrived. Yes the goods were on board. But with the troubles, everything was in chaos, and I would have to wait. In addition, the world had begun to respond to Ethiopia's sad state. The BBC had highlighted the fact that, although it had been happening for hundreds of years, and is still happening, millions of people were dying through lack of food and water.

I sat, listening to all this, and watching the chaos around me, when the fat, sweaty Head of Customs arrived.

'Still here, Mr Lupson?' he said. I hated that man, and he knew it.

I assured him that I was indeed still here and was determined as ever to process the importation of the Ethiopian Air Force goods without paying bribes.

He did not seem impressed.

He was quickly followed by an enraged German, who had also lost his temper. It turned out that the man was part of an aid group from Germany, who were trying to bring a water driller into the country to help to save the people. The rig was very expensive and had been donated by the German aid workers. But the fat bastard of a Customs Chief was insisting that he would not be allowed to import the rig unless the full Customs duties were paid.

The German Aid Worker was furious and started shouting abuse at the fat Customs Boss.

It was obvious that Charlie and I were not going to make any progress for the rest of the day so we decided to go and investigate the Danakil tribe.

Chapter 25

The Danakil Tribes

The Danakil Mountains: Inhospitable in more ways than one.

We set off for the Danakil Mountains in Charlie's open-top Military Jeep.

We left the Port of Assab, heading West. It was hot, very dusty and the track was rocky and rough.

After about an hour's drive, we came upon the Danakil Village. It was like something out of the Dark Ages.

Poorly constructed mud huts with grass roofs, no sanitation and no sign of a water supply. Chickens, goats and children were mixed in with the general muck surrounding their huts.

The smell was awful, and, as in most parts of this land, each child seemed to have its allocation of flies which crawled all over their faces, and they seemed to accept it.

Danakil mother and child

It may all look romantic in films but movies don't reflect the smell and poverty of the African villages.

We drove past the outskirts of the village and the Natives started to appear, all scantily dressed and armed with spears and their knives. They did not seem too happy at the appearance of a military jeep with a man in uniform and a strange looking white man. There was no sign of their womenfolk, who were obviously hiding in their huts.

Charlie pulled to a halt in the centre of the village and a large crowd of Natives surrounded us. I am not sure how Charlie managed to communicate with what appeared to be their leader, but he was babbling on to the Native's elder, and apparently negotiating for the purchase of one of their knives.

The trading was obviously not going well and the crowd looked quite menacing.

Charlie was looking very worried, and his feelings rubbed off on me too.

We decided that it was time to get the hell out of there.

I found a considerable amount of coins in my pockets and told Charlie to get in the Jeep and prepare to make a very quick getaway. I threw all the coins away from the jeep and it worked, as the natives all dashed to collect them and started fighting amongst themselves.

This gave us our chance to speed away.

Although they were very primitive, they obviously knew the value of money and fortunately the distraction enabled us to escape unharmed.

Traditional Danakil hut. The Afar people are nomadic and they mine salt from the parched Danakil depression.

I asked Charlie what had happened and why the Danakil natives had seemed so upset. He said that their leader was demanding about three times the amount that the knife was worth and Charlie had refused to pay such a large amount.

This had upset their leader, hence the hostile attitude. As I have said, they may have been very primitive but they knew how to trade and were not prepared to take no for an answer.

We were once again lucky to have escaped with our parts still attached to our bodies. I later found out that the practice of presenting male parts to their prospective brides was still practiced by the Danakil Tribes, known as the Afar people, although I wondered what they would have made of a white man's male parts.

We sped away from the hostile crowd and were relieved when the Port of Assab came into view.

The heat and strain of the day was taking its effect on both of us.

He delivered me safely at my hotel and we agreed to an early start the following day to commence the clearance of the latest delivery of our goods from NAAFI in the UK.

At least NAAFI HQ had taken my threat to resign seriously. The invoicing was now compiled in commodity groups and this would make our task a damn sight easier than the first time we had tried to import our stock.

***

I went to my room, had a quick shower and went through for dinner.

The poor old Chinese fellow was there and did not seem any happier with life.

I joined him, and once again he ordered the same as I, as he was unable to make the waiter understand what he wanted.

We discussed the day's events and he did not seem to understand my story of the Danakil visit, so I gave up, had a couple of beers and wished him a very good night.

I often wondered if he managed to survive the two year tour. It must have been Hell for him, not being able to understand the local language and the locals not understating his English.

I lay on my bed and thought of my Lavender. I missed her so much. Sleep thankfully came and put an end to my loneliness, at least for that night.

All too soon, morning came and I awoke from my fitful lonely sleep, showered and went through for breakfast.

It was still very early and thankfully there was no sign of the Chinese chap.

Charlie arrived on time and we set off for the battle with the Customs Officials.

They had at last realised that I was not one to be messed about and their attitude was now very different. They were actually being helpful, apart from the fat sweaty bastard.

'Still here, Mr Lupson?'

I smiled and assured him I was.

The day went well and we achieved a great deal in a short time, Charlie and I now knew what we were doing and the documentation went through very quickly without any bribes.

We still had to inspect the goods with the customs inspector but that would have to wait until another day.

Charlie and I walked through the docks to our transport and I counted in excess of three hundred sacks of grain donated from America's Aid programme, lying out in the open.

Sods Law, it had rained for the first time in months, and the sacks were damaged. Many had split open, and birds and rats were obviously enjoying this bonus.

It was a sad fact that most of the food aid was not getting to those that needed it. The corrupt officials were exporting vast amounts to the Sudan and making a lot of money.

Three hundred large sacks of grain could have eased the pain of many starving Ethiopians.

We also noticed drilling machinery, which could be used to find water, lying rusting on the docks. The Customs Officials had no interest in getting the grain and machinery to where it was needed in the central parts of this wonderful country.

No one seemed bothered. Only by bribing the corrupt officials would it be moved. It was a very sad state of affairs.

Those in authority got fatter on their corruption while many thousands were dying through starvation.

It had been thus for many years and the rebellion had tried to change it.

It would change soon, but not in a good way. The Marxist regime was becoming stronger and the King was becoming weaker.

It was not his fault entirely. He was a very old man and the country was really controlled by his corrupt officials.

All these thoughts passed through my head as we drove through the Port of Assab back to my hotel.

It had been a good day, and Charlie and I decided that we should go out to celebrate that night. We were both in a good mood and agreed that we had earned a night out on the town to celebrate. Charlie would pick me up at eight o'clock.

Charlie said that the following day was a celebration of the Burning Cross and he asked if I would like to be a guest at the ceremony.

I readily agreed. It transpired that part of the cross on which Jesus was crucified had apparently been sent to Ethiopia and this was celebrated once a year with large bonfires and much joy. It sounded interesting, and in any case, the final clearance of our goods would have to wait until the following day, as all would be celebrating the Burning Cross day as a sort of public holiday.

I had a quick shower and a snooze and went through for a meal. My body was obviously getting used to the poor standard of food hygiene, or perhaps it was the beer, but I felt very well. My Chinese friend was there and once again we tried to communicate. I again invited him to join Charlie and I, but he politely declined.

Charlie arrived on time and we set off for our night out.

Because of the holiday the following day, the town was buzzing.

Not only from the locals but from the crews of various ships that were visiting the Port of Assab.

We found a suitable bar and began enjoying the local music and beers.

We were soon joined by some very attractive bar girls and although they did not speak much English, they were good company. One girl with a superb figure attached herself to me. She was quite beautiful. Charlie translated as and when necessary.

The evening flew by and both Charlie and I decided that it was time for me to return to my Hotel, as the following day would be an interesting and exciting: the day of the Burning Cross. Charlie had arranged for us to be hosted by a local village official and I was to be an honoured guest as I was doing a special job for his Imperial Majesty.

The girls were extremely disappointed that we had decided not to take advantage of them. We had a last beer and set off for my hotel. Charlie arranged to pick me up at 11am, ready for the Burning Cross ceremony.

Chapter 26
The Burning Cross Ceremony

The Burning Cross Ceremony at Assab

Charlie arrived on time.

We had a cup of coffee and planned the day. We were both a little hungover from the night before.

I was to be one of the Guests of honour as I was a guest of his Imperial Majesty, or that was what Charlie had told them.

A local official was appointed to host us.

We drove to the outskirts of Assab, where hundreds of locals had gathered to start celebrating the ceremony of the Burning Cross which centred on a very large bonfire.

A local band played suitable music and there were many priests, all dressed in their finery. It was an amazing sight.

Food was being cooked on open fires and the local beer was readily available.

There was much excitement as the Priest lined up to lead the procession around the large bonfire.

Charlie and I were invited to join the procession and I was assured that it was a great honour to be allowed to do so.

The procession set off, to much joy, and we paraded around the fire to the chanting and singing of the Priests and surrounding town folk.

It was a great experience to be amongst true believers of Jesus. There are obviously many stories of what happened to the Cross on which Jesus was crucified but I believe that somehow part of it did actually arrive in Ethiopia.

The Priests and their people could have been straight out of the time when Jesus walked the Earth; true believers, dressed in long flowing robes. It was an amazing, emotional atmosphere.

After we had toured the fire a number of times, we joined our hosts for locally cooked food and Tella Beer.

We enjoyed the local music and chants from the Priests, with songs being sung by the local natives.

The day was an amazing experience and passed much too soon. Charlie and I thanked our host for the honour of being allowed to join the procession, and I returned to my hotel.

We still had business to do and Charlie agreed that he would contact HQ at Debre Zeit to see what the situation was with regard to getting our stock transported back to the Base.

We agreed that we would make an early start the following day.

Chapter 27
Death of a great fighter pilot

An F-15 Fighter Bomber in flight.

Charlie told me that the 119 Freighter plane was scheduled to arrive at Assab later that day to collect some more military arms.

If we could get the stock released and transported to the landing strip, they would take it back to Debre Zeit with me on board too.

It was extremely good news as I really wanted to get back to a cooler, more civilized part of Ethiopia.

We were going to be very busy if we were to complete the clearance and transportation of our goods to the airstrip in time.

I packed and checked out of the hotel in quick time and we set off to the Customs Office.

We were met by one of the more helpful Customs officials and we quickly explained that we needed to clear our goods, as transport from His Majesty's Air Force was on its way to collect it. He agreed to one of his staff making the necessary inspection of our goods, and once this was satisfactorily completed, the goods would be released.

We were lucky as the appointed Customs official was not really bothered and after a cursory check of the invoicing and a quick look at our stock and assurance that any duty would be paid on my word, he agreed to the release of the goods.

Charlie immediately got onto his base in Assab and told them to contact HQ Debre Zeit to inform them that the goods would be ready for collection by the 119. He also arranged for Air Force Transport to collect the goods and ship them to the airstrip.

It was amazing that we had achieved so much in such a short time.

Charlie and I went for a quick lunch and then set off for the Airstrip.

True to their word, the goods were released and shortly after our arrival, the stock arrived at the Airstrip together with a few cases of bombs and rockets, courtesy of the Americans.

It felt a bit odd that I was to travel in a lumbering old 119 freight plane loaded, not just with NAAFI Stock, but crates of bombs and rockets. We were to fly over territory that was being fought over by the Eritrean Forces. All it needed was for them to have a lucky shot and Lupson would be no more.

Charlie and I sat and waited for the 119 to appear and we soon spotted a glint on the horizon as the trusted old 119 lumbered towards us.

The pilot made a perfect landing which caused great clouds of dust to cover us.

The roar of the engines as the pilot put it into reverse thrust was deafening.

The old 119 taxied towards us and the loading doors were opened and our pilot appeared. He greeted Charlie and I, but did not seem his usual cheerful self.

I thought that perhaps the troubles at Debre Zeit had erupted again, and we asked him what the problem was.

He explained that a young fighter pilot had crashed on landing at Debre Zeit the previous day and had been killed. The F-15 fighter bomber was quite a small plane that landed in a similar way to Concord, with its nose in the air and coming in at quite an angle. Apparently the young pilot had not got his angle right and had been caught by a strong gust of wind which had flipped his plane onto its back.

As the plane hit the ground, it had caught fire and in spite of valiant attempts to rescue the poor lad, he had died in the fire.

The whole of the Imperial Ethiopian Air Force was in mourning for the loss of the pilot, who had been a popular guy.

I later found out that it was the good looking young Officer that I had met at the Officers' Mess party. He was the one who had joined in the traditional Ethiopian dancing and had entertained us all with his skill at the art.

He had left a wife and two small children.

It was why all of the Air Force lads were not their usual cheerful selves and were in a very sombre mood.

The plane's load master took charge of arranging our stock, and the rockets and bombs to be loaded properly onto his Aircraft. It was completed in a very short time, and soon the Aircraft was also refuelled and we were ready to depart.

Once again our pilot helped me into my parachute, making me feel very uncomfortable in the heat of the Red Sea Port of Assab.

I thanked my minder Charlie for all the help he had given me and for his great company. We had become good friends and both still felt lucky to have escaped alive from the Danakil mountains.

I said that I hoped that we would meet again soon but I was unsure as to when that would be, as my HQ was beginning to make noises that I should return to the UK.

I was once again shown to the navigator's seat and watched as the pilot did his usual pre-take-off checks.

Charlie stood at the side of the runway, as one by one, the old engines belched black smoke and reluctantly came to life.

I looked down towards Charlie and he saluted as we began to taxi, ready for take-off. I returned the salute and he smiled and waved farewell.

I often wondered what happened to him, as the fighting soon increased over Eritrea around the Northern part of Ethiopia.

The old 119 sped down the airstrip in clouds of dust and reluctantly rose into the blue skies.

We circled the Port of Assab and set course due South for Debre Zeit.

The death of the popular fighter pilot had obviously affected the whole crew and they were all in a subdued mood on the return journey.

After an hour, a crew member came through with hot coffee and the usual beef sandwiches.

We flew over the scorched barren lands of Northern Ethiopia.

Although it had rained a little at Assab, no rain had fallen where it was most needed.

Crops had failed, livestock had died and thousands were starving to death. It was an awful sight as we flew low over village after village with no sign of life.

A number of villagers had abandoned their homes and had tried to travel south in the hope of finding food and water.

Many perished on their journey.

***

It was getting late in the day and it was growing quite dark. The drone of the engines and the heat made me drowsy and I must have fallen asleep.

A change in the sound of the aircraft brought me back to life and I realised we were about to land at Debre Zeit.

The Pilot circled the airfield to make sure we were clear for our landing and once assured, he switched on his landing lights and prepared to land.

Once again we came in for a perfect landing and as we sped along the strange runway, the landing lights revealed the scorch marks, where the F15 had crashed the previous day.

The pilot turned the 119 and headed back to a suitable standing.

It was obviously very late and the aircraft would be secured for the night. Unloading would commence the following day.

Out of the darkness, Asgers appeared and it was great to see my dear friend.

We greeted each other as though we had not seen each other in weeks, and once again came the old refrain:

'Mr Lupson, what's happened to you?' We both laughed, but there was sadness in Asgers' eyes. We thanked my fantastic pilot and crew for their sterling work in collecting our goods in a very efficient way, and I promised to buy them a beer or two at their airfield café.

Asgers had my car nearby and I let him drive. On the way home, we talked about the sad events of the previous day and I could detect that Asgers was very upset. I suspect he had a tear in his eye.

I briefed him on what had happened in Assab and said we would go into more detail the following day.

We arrived at my compound and my guard sprang forward to open the gate. My trusty maid was there, ready with my hot bath, lots of coffee and of course my egg and chips.

Asgers had visited them when he had learned that I was on my way home and told them to ensure I was well looked after. He was a good friend and very caring.

I took full advantage of the bath, coffee and food and staggered off to bed. It had been a very long tiring day.

All too soon, my maid was knocking on my door. I awoke and had a quick shower and shave and went through for breakfast.

After lots of coffee, I felt ready to face the world again.

Asgers arrived and I invited him in for more coffee and to plan the day ahead.

We decided that the collection and delivery of our stock to our shop from the 119 was the priority. We drove to our office and contacted the Base to arrange for transport for the stock to be delivered to our shop.

Asgers was not his usual cheerful self and was obviously very upset at the death of his friend. He said that the funeral of the young fighter pilot was to be held in two days' time and I asked if it would be alright if I joined him to pay my respects. He readily agreed and I think he was glad that I had offered.

We sat and discussed my trip to Assab and awaited the arrival of our stock. It all arrived as promised and we spent the rest of the day unpacking the goods and pricing them.

I was delighted that while I was away, Asgers and the staff had maintained our very high standards in cleanliness and merchandising. My training had obviously been taken on board, and they were all very proud members of the Imperial Ethiopian Air Force Trading organisation.

I noticed that Asgers still wore his trusty pistol and it was obvious that although the situation had calmed, the troubles were far from over.

The Paratroopers were still patrolling menacingly around Debre Zeit, and the streets of Addis Ababa in their open-backed Land Rovers with mounted heavy machine guns.

They were not to be messed around with, and actually shot at a fellow ex-pat in Debre Zeit.

He was a French National who drove the same car as ours. Luckily, the bullet went through the door of the car and lodged in the driver's seat, missing him by some two inches.

I wondered if they had really meant to shoot us, as our cars were identical, and the incident had taken place at night.

After our day's toils, I went home and decided to visit the ex-pat club for an evening out with my friends.

I arrived and was given a warm welcome by all. They all appreciated having access to our shop and some good old English goods at reasonable prices.

The whole gang was there and this included the lovely Geeta, with her sparkling eyes and warm smile.

Although she was a shy person, she came over to me to hear what I had been up to in Assab.

I told them all of our lucky escape from the Danakil natives and the experience of the ceremony of the Burning Cross.

It was a very pleasant evening and Geeta never left my side. It was obvious that we were drawn to one another, and she was lovely company.

All the ex-pats who worked on the base had agreed to attend the young fighter pilot's funeral, and we agreed to meet up for it, two days later. It had been another long, hot day and I travelled home a very tired man.

The following day was taken up with clearing admin, and once again, there was a letter from my HQ asking when I thought the project would be safe to hand over to Asgers and for me to return to the UK.

I was delighted to get another letter from Lavender. She was working hard and travelling all over the world, but she was missing me.

I visited the Airstrip Café and HQ Tea Bar with Asgers, and once again I was delighted to see that standards had been maintained.

The Air Force personnel were delighted with what Asgers and I had achieved, and we received a very warm welcome.

They really were enjoying the fresh food and best quality beef. You could see that Asgers was a very proud man.

We returned to our office and I broached the subject of the current state of play with regard to the political situation and the position of his Imperial Majesty.

Asgers said that the situation was not good and that there were rumours that it was still the intention of the Marxist elements to depose the King and to take over the country.

Meanwhile, the fighting in the far North, in the province of Eritrea, was intensifying and not going well for the Ethiopian Forces.

The Eritreans were determined to gain their independence from the rest of Ethiopia. It would inevitably happen. It was surprising that the country had not fallen apart long before.

I feel that it was only the strength of King Haile Selassie in his younger days that had held the country together for so many years. But he was now an old tired man and his strength was fading fast. The Marxist plotters were slowly gaining ground and the world did not seem to notice that a coup was gradually happening. Those who tried to stop them were silenced or simply disappeared. Many were too scared to speak up.

Now that the King was a weak old man, the Marxist and corrupt officials were taking advantage of his lack of touch with the reality of the situation. Many of those who tried to oppose them in the coming months were denounced as traitors and got rid of.

Bearing in mind that Ethiopia comprised of some fourteen tribes all with their own dialects and traditions, with thousands of them dying from lack of food and clean water, it was inevitable that things would change, and sadly the Marxists would gain power without the rest of the world noticing or caring. It would be a sad ending to a great King, who was sadly past his prime.

It was a depressing situation and a worrying time for poor old Asgers and the rest of those who were loyal to their King.

The day soon passed, and Asgers and I agreed to keep our shop closed the following day as a mark of respect for the poor young pilot. In any case, most personnel would be attending his funeral.

The funeral would take place at a large church on the outskirts of Addis Ababa, and I agreed to collect Asgers at 9 o'clock the following morning.

I went to Asgers' house and he appeared in his full Number One uniform with full medals, looking very smart.

His wife would not be joining us as she had to look after their children.

We arrived at the church and were not surprised to find dozens of Air Force personnel there. The young pilot had been a very popular colleague of theirs. The church was full and overflowed outside. There was much chanting and burning of incense.

There were also many of the ex-pat community who worked at the base, all there to pay their respects.

Geeta appeared and joined Asgers and I. Asgers gave a knowing wink as he saw her coming to my side.

There were many priests in attendance, and a guard of young officers escorted the coffin into the church. The pilot's wife and family followed the coffin.

His wife was a beautiful, elegant lady, obviously heartbroken at the loss of her much-loved husband.

It was a very sad occasion, but an interesting sight to see how the service was conducted.

Being a Christian ceremony, it was similar to funerals in the UK apart from the long spells of praying and chanting.

The priests stood in their white flowing robes, supported by their sticks which were similar in shape to a shepherd's crook.

Asgers looked very sombre and was obviously very upset at the loss of his good friend.

After much chanting and prayers, the coffin was transported from the church, escorted by the Air Force Guard of Honour.

He would be buried with full military honours.

It was a very moving experience and all were sad at the loss of this young pilot, father and husband.

We left the service accompanied by Geeta. Asgers suggested that as we were close to Addis Ababa, we should go into town for lunch, and asked if Geeta would like to join us.

Geeta had arrived with her Indian colleagues, and she asked them if they minded if she joined us for lunch. They agreed, bearing in mind that Asgers would act as a chaperone.

Asgers was still very upset, but put a brave face on it in front of Geeta and I.

We went to a superb Italian restaurant in the centre of Addis. It was obvious that Asgers approved of Geeta, and they chatted like long-lost friends.

Asgers was becoming more relaxed, and we all enjoyed a superb Italian meal and each other's company.

We returned to Debre Zeit and I dropped Asgers off at his home, agreeing to meet at the shop the following day.

I invited Geeta to my house for afternoon tea, and assured her that my maid was at home and that all would be proper.

She laughed and said that she would be delighted to join me.

My trusty maid appeared and made us tea and a light snack.

Geeta and I spent time getting to know one another.

She told me that she had been born not far from the Mount Everest in the Himalayas. Her family was quite poor, but she had gone to a good school, sponsored by British Aid, followed by university.

She proved to be a good student and had managed to graduate with an honours degree.

She had met a young Russian engineer and had married him. All was well to start with, and then he started drinking heavily and became violent towards her. At this time she was teaching in a local school.

Geeta's husband was drinking more and more, and treating her very badly, often beating her for no apparent reason.

When she did not want to make love, he violently raped her, and this had occurred on a number of occasions.

Life became very difficult and fortunately some of her colleagues had decided that they would travel to Africa on an aid programme. They had learned that the Imperial Ethiopian Air Force urgently required teachers, and a group of them decided to take up a three year contract and asked if Geeta would like to join them.

The offer of a job in Africa was an excellent opportunity for her to escape from the abuse by her awful husband.

She had travelled to Ethiopia the previous year, about the same time as I had arrived, The Indian group knew that Geeta had had a very bad time and that's why they were very protective of her. It was strange how she poured her heart out to me and trusted me with her sad story.

As our relationship progressed, I was to find out why.

Time flew by and it was soon time for me to take her home, as we had arranged to meet the rest of the gang at the ex-pat club that night.

I drove her to her house and as she got out of the car, we embraced and kissed. She seemed a little unsure and flustered, but it was the beginning of a great friendship.

We agreed to meet in a couple of hours back at the ex-pat club. She went into her house and there was that lovely warm smile and wave. She was a beautiful, elegant young lady who'd had an awful start to her adult life, but she looked very happy for once.

The next day I received a letter from my HQ, informing me that I had just two months to tie up loose ends and return to the UK.

Apparently our Managing Director had another little job for me. It transpired that I was to be seconded to Cable and Wireless and sent to Ascension Island to take control of their retail operation. But that's another story.

I informed Asgers of the fact that we had very little time left and that the next two months would be very hectic.

Dear old Asgers was very upset, as he had hoped that I would stay for a lot longer.

We arranged a meeting with the Base Commander and went through a detailed programme of my departure.

It was arranged that Norman Lee and his successor from Kenya would visit Debre Zeit within the next six weeks, to arrange the formal completion of our projects and ensure that the Imperial Ethiopian Air Force Trading Organisation was on a sound footing for the future.

The next few days were very hectic, as I attended meetings with all concerned in the Trading Organisation, including the creditors, with whom I had personally promised that their bills would be paid by the Imperial Ethiopian Air Force.

All went well and things began to sort themselves out, so I decided that I needed to relax with my friends.

I visited our club and it was good to see that most of the ex-pats were there, including the lovely Geeta.

Word had spread that I would be leaving in the next two months, and everyone expressed sadness at the news.

Geeta came up to me and seemed very upset at the news. She was particularly upset, as the Indian community had arranged to return to India for an end of term holiday in six weeks' time and I would not be there on her return.

It was strange how close we had become in such a short time.

She was determined to make the most of our brief time together and invited me for a meal the following Sunday, which I readily accepted. I was getting tired of egg and chips by this time.

The next couple of days flew by. It was during this time that Asgers was giving me strange looks and enquiring as to my size. He was up to something, but I was too busy to take much notice.

***

Sunday quickly arrived and I set off for my lunch at Geeta's.

I managed to get a suitable bottle of wine and I was quite excited at the thought of spending some time alone with Geeta.

Geeta had prepared an excellent curry, which we both enjoyed with the bottle of wine. She had gone to a lot of trouble and she looked great.

We chatted as though we had known each other for ever and before we knew it, we were embraced in a passionate cuddle on her bed.

She had a magnificent body, slim and dark, with ample breasts. Our passion took hold of us, but although we both wanted each other, Geeta could not bring herself to make love to the full. The abuse by her husband had taken its toll, and she burst into tears, explaining her feelings.

I comforted her, and as tenderly as possible, I told her that I understood. It was frustrating for both of us but her experience of being beaten and raped had made her frigid and fearful. We lay together, caressing one another and it was a very tender experience.

Her tears subsided, and we held each other tight and fell asleep.

We awoke and said our goodnights. It had been a moving, loving experience and we realised how much we could mean to each other.

The next morning, I awoke to my maid knocking on the bedroom door with some hot coffee.

It began to dawn on me that I had an awful lot to do and that the next few weeks would fly by as I prepared to return to the UK.

Chapter 28
Lupson Leaves

An honorary Ethiopian: the reason why Asgers was asking me about my size. L-R Me, Norman's successor "George", Norman Lee and Asgedom.

Life became very hectic and time just flew by.

I attended meeting after meeting with various officials, and spent time going through the entire operation of the Ethiopian Air Force trading organisation with dear old Asgers to ensure he was up to speed with it all.

The situation in Ethiopia was getting worse, with the extreme Marxist element slowly and stealthily gaining ground. A coup was taking place and no one seemed to notice.

The outside world was occupied with other things and did not seem to care.

We were also fully occupied making plans for the arrival of Norman Lee and his successor, and for my departure back to the UK.

I was a bit concerned about Asgers as he kept asking about my size. Perhaps I was looking a bit thin.

We continued to work hard to ensure that every aspect of the business was fully understood by my dear friend Asgers.

Although life was very hectic, Geeta and I spent as much time as we could together and we developed a strong and tender relationship. I was so busy that I had not realised how much she thought of me. Looking back, I regret that I treated her so poorly, bearing in mind that she needed a lot of gentle loving care following the abuse she had suffered from her husband.

The day finally arrived when Geeta and her fellow compatriots were to fly off to India.

I picked her up from her house and she seemed to be very sad.

We set off for the airport and there were tears in her eyes as we drew nearer to Addis Ababa. She snuggled up to me in the car and began to sob.

We arrived at the airport and were met the rest of her companions and she tried to put on a brave face. It was then that she revealed that she had left her passport at home.

Luckily the flight to India was delayed by some two hours and this would give us enough time to return to her home and retrieve her passport.

It later transpired that she had done this deliberately as she did not want to leave me.

I had not realised how much our newly made friendship meant to her, as I had too much happening in my life trying to tie up loose ends with regard to the Imperial Ethiopian Air Force Trading Organisation.

It is a poor excuse but a true one.

We made it back in time for her flight, and once again, tears flowed as we were about to say goodbye.

She later sent me a letter saying that she really did not want to leave me and she had been waiting and hoping that I would ask her to stay.

I felt awful but my only excuse is that I had been rushed off my feet preparing for the visit of Norman and for my departure from Ethiopia.

It really was a busy difficult time and should Geeta ever read this, I am really sorry.

***

The day dawned when Norman Lee was due to arrive, and Asgers and I set off to collect him and his successor.

The airport was as chaotic as ever when Norman and his successor appeared, and this time they had to wait in the queue with everyone else.

Norman eventually emerged from the airport, as arrogant as ever, and showing off to his successor.

Asgers was once again a nervous wreck, as he really did not like Norman and felt intimidated by him.

No sooner had we said hello than Norman started asking question after question. I protected Asgers from the endless questioning, by explaining to Norman that everything was under control. Meetings had been arranged with all concerned with the project, including the local traders, and I would reveal everything in good time.

I gave Norman a rough outline of what we had planned and informed him that dear old Asgers had arranged for a formal farewell to me and Norman to be held at the Officers' Mess the day before Norman's departure. This pleased the vanity of this arrogant little man.

We drove back to Debre Zeit with a constant interrogation from Norman, to which I gave vague answers.

I felt sorry for Norman's successor, who seemed dazed by it all. I think he was beginning to realise that both Norman and I would soon be leaving Africa and as the sole remaining NAAFI person in charge, he would be left holding the can. Unfortunately, I can't remember Norman's successor's name, so I will call him George.

We arrived at the only reasonably decent hotel in Debre Zeit, and escorted Norman and George to their rooms.

Norman had hoped that I would put him up at my house but I could not stand the thought of it. Unfortunately, Norman insisted that I joined them for dinner. I had been hoping to excuse myself as I had already had enough of him, but I was stuck with him now. Whereas Asgers made his excuses and managed to escape, giving me a wink as he left.

I dutifully returned to their hotel for dinner and sat through another session of question after question.

I suggested that we should go to the ex-pat club to introduce George to the gang.

George thought this a good idea. I feel that he was also hoping to get a respite from Norman's constant questions.

We arrived at the club and fortunately quite a number of my friends were already there, including Nicky and Dave. But the club felt different, as Geeta and her Indian colleagues were not there.

The gang made Norman and George feel welcome, and we soon had them well oiled.

They told them how fantastic it was to have their own retail set up and how well Asgers and I had done.

Many drinks later, I managed to persuade Norman that it was time he and George returned to their hotel, as the following day would be very busy.

I returned home, very tired and not looking forward to the days ahead.

The following morning, I went to the hotel and joined Norman and George for a cup of coffee and told them about the day's plans.

We would visit the shop and café and tea bar and then return to the shop to go over the systems I had introduced.

Norman and George were very impressed with what we had achieved, and Norman was obviously trying to take some credit for it all.

We had arranged to meet the Base Commander and the Project Colonel and there followed a number of meetings during which Asgers and I received much praise for what we had achieved. Dear old Asgers' chest swelled with pride as the General heaped praise on his achievements.

There followed endless meetings over the next few days with visits to the Ethiopian Military HQ and to the suppliers.

All went exceptionally well and the only point of contention was that those responsible for arranging regular repayments to our NAAFI HQ in London were to say the least, slow in going about it.

While we were busy with our own problems behind the scenes, the political situation was very bad, with the Marxist elements gaining ground alarmingly.

Senior politicians and military men were disappearing without trace and nobody seemed to notice. The coup leaders were very clever in the very slow and quiet way they were taking over the country. The world, including us, didn't notice at the time, as we were trying to hand over our trading organisation to the Ethiopian Air Force Authorities.

The next few days flew by, and the day before the official farewell ceremony, Asgers arrived at my house bearing a strange looking parcel.

I opened it and found a complete Ethiopian National Dress which Asgers had secretly arranged to be made for me. I now knew why he kept asking me about my size.

It's fortunate that he insisted that I tried it on – we discovered that my legs were much bigger than he had estimated.

We measured my legs, and he disappeared with my breeches, saying that he would be back soon. True to his word, Asgers rapidly returned with the breeches and this time they fitted perfectly.

As he showed me how to dress properly, my maid appeared and was amazed at the sight of me dressed in full Ethiopian National Costume. We all had a good laugh.

Good old Asgers had pulled out all stops to ensure that Luper's farewell party would be one never to be forgotten.

The following morning we collected Norman and George from their hotel, and you can imagine their faces when I appeared in full National Dress.

It was great, and Asgers beamed with pride at what he had achieved in keeping my costume a secret until the very last moment.

We drove to the Officers' Mess and were met by the General and his entourage.

All of the Senior Officers were in attendance and the full mess staff were there to ensure we were well looked after.

It was then that our shop staff appeared, and most of them were in their best National Dress.

I felt very emotional at the effort that Asgers had put into the farewell party. The Commander in Chief of the Imperial Ethiopian Air Force was invited to make a speech. He spoke perfect English and praised the amazing achievements brought about by Mr Derek Lupson and his Major, Asgedom Teshome.

'Against a difficult time in the history of Ethiopia, they have managed to establish the Imperial Ethiopian Air Force Trading Organisation,' he continued. 'It is a measure of Mr Lupson's commitment to the project that he even donated his own gas supply from his home during the recent shortage. The support from the NAAFI organisation is much appreciated by His Majesty's Air Force, and I feel sure that the Organisation is now on a sound footing and will continue to progress. As a mark of our appreciation for all the work that Mr Lupson has done, I now wish to present him with a plaque from The Imperial Ethiopian Air Force.'

I was now made an honorary Ethiopian.

It was a very moving experience and I was delighted that Asgers was held in such high esteem by the Imperial Ethiopian Air Force that they had assembled the most senior officers in the Air Force, the General and the Commander in Chief, to attend the farewell ceremony and to thank all concerned for establishing the Trading Organisation.

There followed a marvellous lunch and for once, Norman had been silenced. He seemed a bit put out that Asgers and I had taken the limelight from him.

Our staff really enjoyed the occasion and we were all very emotional as we began to realise that we would soon be saying farewell.

The following day Asgers and I returned Norman and George to the airport and bade them both farewell. Norman seemed a changed man and treated Asgers with the respect he deserved. He even seemed to accept that I had done a good job against all odds and that Asgers and I had really achieved the near imposable.

Asgers and I said our farewells to Norman and George and watched with relief as their plane took off for their return to Kenya.

Asgers and I began to laugh: we had done it, and we were really proud of all that we had achieved. We decided to have a drink and then return to Debre Zeit to get really drunk. We had earned it.

On our return to Debre Zeit, we were stopped by a military road block and told that a curfew was in place and that we must go home and stay there. The situation must have really deteriorated.

We'd already had quite a few drinks at the airport and Asgers was having none of it and protested that we should be allowed to continue our celebrations.

We were promptly arrested and were escorted by armed guards to the Commander of the detachment. Another fine mess that dear old Asgers had gotten me into.

The Commander soon realised that we were well oiled, as Asgers tried to tell the story of what I had done for the People of Ethiopia.

He explained to the Commander that only the previous day Mr Lupson had been honoured by the General, and that in two days' time he was due to leave Ethiopia, having completed a marvellous job in establishing the Air Force Trading Organisation.

It was now only fair that we should be allowed to continue our celebrations to thank Mr Lupson for all his hard work.

Asgers and I could hardly stand straight as he told this emotional story, bringing tears to our eyes.

To my surprise, the Commander agreed and arranged for one of his men to escort us to one of the local bars. Asgers and I saluted the Commander and staggered off.

The bar owner was awakened and made to open his bar for his honoured guests. He greeted us like heroes of the nation, and arranged for some of his ladies to keep us company.

After many drinks, I vaguely remember being escorted home. I woke up many hours later with a terrible hangover. It must have been a hell of a night.

My trusty maid brought me endless cups of coffee, and I began to recover.

Some hours later, Asgers appeared and greeted me with the customary:

'Mr Lupson, what happened to you?'

We both laughed and laughed – we were brothers in arms.

The next day, I was due to depart this wonderful land and say goodbye to my new brother and the rest of the people whom I had grown to love.

I felt like hell after the previous night's exploits, but I forced myself to continue packing and tying up loose ends.

Having recovered, I thought I ought to go to the ex-pats club to say goodbye.

The club was full and everyone tried to buy me drinks, but I politely refused. Once I had related the story of the previous day, they all understood why.

They knew I was due to leave the following day, and to my surprise, they informed me that most of them would be at the airport to wave me off.

The next twenty-four hours would be very difficult, so I bade them all goodnight and returned home. My trusty maid served me coffee and a snack, and seemed very sad at the thought of me leaving the next day.

I completed my packing and went to bed.

All too soon, my maid was knocking at the door with a hot cup of coffee. This was the day I'd been dreading.

Asgers appeared in his best No.1 Uniform. He also looked very sad. He would escort me to the airport in our beat-up, trusty Renault Four Car, and we would stop at the shop so that I could say goodbye to the staff on the way.

He loaded my cases into the car and I turned to say goodbye to my lovely maid Alice, who was sobbing her heart out. I pressed a large wad of dollars into her hand and we hugged each other. I thanked her for her caring support and said that I could not have survived without her help. It was a very sad farewell.

It felt very strange to be leaving my home for the last time.

My armed guard was nowhere to be seen. He was probably lying drunk in some bar or other as I had given him a month's pay the previous night.

We drove off to our shop, and the staff assembled to say goodbye. The girls all had tears in their eyes. Nobody likes saying goodbye.

We managed to leave before I broke down too.

Asgers drove to the airport. We didn't speak very much. All that we had been through meant that we really understood how we felt, and words were not necessary.

We arrived at the airport and, true to their word, most of the ex-pats were there to see me off.

One-by-one, we hugged and said our farewells. The last in line was dear old sexy Angie, who had tears in her eyes.

We hugged, and once again for the last time, she pressed her whole body into mine.

Asgers took my luggage to the departure gate and we gave each other a "man hug".

It must have looked strange – an Ethiopian Major in full No.1 dress uniform, hugging a white man, but we were brothers.

I turned and waved goodbye to my friends and went through the departure gate. I turned one again and saw Asgers. He came to attention and saluted me,

I returned the salute and my eyes stung as the tears began to flow.

It was a very emotional time and people must have thought it strange but I did not care.

Getting my reward from the Head of the Airforce

The supermarket staff at my farewell party

The plaque presented to me from the Ethiopian Imperial Airforce in August 1974.

Chapter 29
Lavender in London

Me slightly older and wiser, on another international adventure.

I settled into my seat in the Jumbo Jet, and in no time, we were speeding down the rough runway and taking to the skies.

Lupson was leaving Ethiopia and it felt terrible.

It must have been late afternoon, as the sun began to set in the West and we followed the sunset for quite a long time.

It was a fitting end to my fantastic experience.

We were served with a meal and I was soon fast asleep. All too soon, the grey skies of London appeared. I had returned to my native land.

I was a different person now, having seen the plight of the Ethiopian nation at first hand.

We really do not appreciate how lucky we are.

Little things like turning on the tap and fresh water flowing, we take so much for granted.

***

I managed to have a few days back at dear old Doncaster, but life became very hectic, as I had to visit our London HQ on a number of occasions to de-brief and clear up loose ends of admin.

I then continued my training as an Area Manager, which entailed travelling to different establishments and returning to our training centre for various management courses.

I was at one of the NAAFI clubs, when the Manager called me to say that there was an urgent call for me from India.

I was amazed that whoever it was had actually tracked me down, because I had not been in the same place for more than a week since my return from Ethiopia.

The caller turned out to be a cousin of Lavender's, who explained that he worked for Indian Telecommunications, and had managed to find me through the NAAFI HQ.

He explained that Lavender had been transferred to London to work on the London to New York Flights.

She would be arriving in London in ten days' time and would love to meet me.

I could not believe it. I told him that I would be at the airport to meet her, and I thanked him for the great news. I was very excited at the thought that the lovely Lavender was coming back into my life.

At this time in my life, I had no permanent place to live, as the training entailed much travelling, but a very good friend of mine insisted that I use his home as a base. I contacted him and his wife and told them the good news. They immediately insisted that I should bring Lavender to their house to stay.

The next few days passed very quickly and it was soon time to go to the airport to meet Lavender.

The Air India Jumbo came into view and made a perfect landing. I dashed down to the arrivals area and waited in anticipation. All of a sudden, the doors opened and there she was – as beautiful as ever, surrounded by her colleagues.

She melted into my arms and we hugged and kissed, oblivious to her colleagues, who stood patiently by.

She explained that she had to go to the Hilton Hotel with her colleagues to book in and asked if I would come with her. I helped her with her luggage and off we went to her hotel. We had so many questions to ask one another, and it was fantastic to be with her once more. She really was beautiful and looked marvellous in her Air India sari/uniform. Everywhere she went, people stopped to admire her.

We went to her room and had a cuddle, and started to plan the way ahead.

She would be on the London New York Flight for up to three months, and this entailed some two flights a week. She would have time off during this period and I explained that my friends in Doncaster had invited her to come and stay, and she readily agreed.

We managed to clear the Air India admin and it was decided that she would share a flat in Hounslow with her colleagues and she would move there the following day. At last, we returned to her room and managed to be alone. We spent the night together making up for lost time. Over the next few weeks, we met as often as possible, but it was very difficult because she was travelling back and forth to New York, and I was all over the place training.

It all became too difficult, and we eventually agreed to part.

The last I heard of Lavender was that she had met a wealthy New Yorker and was enjoying life.

***

My life really took off, and I was destined to continue my life as a globe-trotter.

In my next assignment, I was seconded to Cable and Wireless to run their retail supply shops and stores on Ascension Island in the middle of the Atlantic.

Two years later, I commenced military training and was commissioned into the RAOC (Royal Army Ordnance Corps). I served with the Commandos in Norway for a few months, doing Winter Training.

I was then posted to Belize in Central America for two years. On my return, I spent another few months in Norway with the Commandos.

Following that, I was posted to Cyprus for three years, where I met a fantastic lady who became my wife on the completion of that tour!

We then moved to Germany, where I ran the flagship shops and shopping districts for the British Armed Forces. I was then promoted to Regional Manager and posted to Scotland as for three years.

Sadly, my opposite number in Northern Ireland resigned some four months into my tour and I was posted to Northern Ireland for three years instead. My wife and I experienced at first hand the difficulties of the Northern Island situation. It was the time of the Trick or Treat massacre by the Ulster Defence Association in a packed pub in Greysteel, County Londonderry in October 1993, and life was tough for everyone

On completing my three year tour, I was posted to Northern Germany, in charge of our trading in the north of the country.

I was diagnosed with a brain tumour at this time and life became quite difficult. Fortunately, my wife, who is a trained nurse, looked after me wonderfully during this time, and I made a good recovery.

***

Needless to say, I still remember Ethiopia and not a day goes by without my wondering what happened to those wonderful people.

Especially Asgers. I can still hear him saying, 'Mr Lupson, what happened to you?'

A lot has happened to me since then, but one day, I will return to the wonderful harsh land of Ethiopia and find out what happened to them all.

TOMMORROW…………..

Epilogue:
A Beginners' Guide to Ethiopia

Within weeks of me leaving Ethiopia in August 1974, His Imperial Majesty King Haile Selassie would be summoned by the rebel leaders and told he was to step down for the good of the country.

A few days later, a group of rebel leaders arrived at the King's Palace at Addis Ababa and summoned him. The king appeared in his full military dress and was told that it was time for him to go.

It was made clear that if he refused, a full scale coup would happen and many lives would be lost.

His Imperial Majesty, being very old and tired, reluctantly agreed that if it was for the good of his beloved Ethiopia, he would stand down.

I am not sure what happened, but I was led to believe that he was transferred to his favourite palace at Debre Zeit and following the withdrawal of his much needed care and medicine, he was allowed to die from "natural causes" in August 1975. However, it was rumoured that Haile Selassie had been murdered by the leader of the coup, Colonel Mengistu Haile Mariam.

There followed years of torment for the Ethiopian Nation with hundreds of thousands being murdered in the "Red Terror" or dying of famine under the ruthless Marxist regime known as the Derg, led by Colonel Mengistu. The world did not seem bothered about fate of this once great nation or about the disappearance of His Imperial Majesty King Haile Selassie, the last emperor of Ethiopia.

Giant Monoliths

Ethiopia is the site of some of humanity's earliest civilisations. The ancient settlement of Yeha in the Tigray region was established around 800BC, and the ruins of its temple are still standing.

Ethiopians claim that the Aksumite Kingdom was founded by Noah's Great-Grandson, around 500BC. The ancient city of Aksum, in the far north of modern Ethiopia, was the capital of a powerful empire that traded with ancient Greece, Egypt, Rome, Persia, Arabia and Persia, renowned for its metalwork, and also its impressive architecture. Aksum is famous for its giant monoliths known as Stelae, used as tombstones for local rulers. The toppled Great Stele in Aksum is 33 metres long, believed to be the largest single block of stone that humans have ever attempted to erect.

The Ark of the Covenant

According to Ethiopian tradition, the Ark of the Covenant containing the stone tablets inscribed with the Ten Commandments was brought to Ethiopia from Jerusalem in the First Century BC by Menelik, the son of King Solomon and the Queen of Sheba. The Ark is believed to be kept within the church of St Mary of Zion in Aksum. Every Ethiopian Orthodox Church has a replica of the Ark, known as the *tabot*, used in religious ceremonies and festivals.

The Orthodox Ethiopian Church claim that the Apostles themselves brought Christianity to Aksum, but there is no historical evidence of this.

However, St. Frumentius (known in Ethiopia as Abuna Selama) is credited with bringing Christianity to Ethiopia in the 4th Century.

As a boy, he was captured as a slave with his brother Edesius, and he was taken to the king of Aksum, where they both were given their freedom. The brothers converted the king's son Ezana to Christianity, and Abuna Selama became a bishop, built churches and began to convert the population to Christianity.

Around 43% of the modern population belong to the Ethiopian Orthodox Church, with 19% Protestant.

34% of the population is Muslim – Islam came to Ethiopia in ancient times, with the Prophet Mohammed sending his daughter to the village of Negash in Tigray in AD 615, to escape persecution in Arabia. Although violent religious wars were fought in Ethiopia in the Middle Ages, Christian and Muslim Ethiopians now live together peacefully.

Some of Ethiopia's most famous landmarks are its rock-hewn churches in Lalibela, carved out of solid rock in the 12th and 13th Centuries, under the Zagwe dynasty.

The Church at Lalibela: Carved out of solid rock

The Grand Mosque in Asmara, now part of Eritrea

An Ancient Dynasty?

The mysterious Zagwe dynasty produced some remarkable architecture, but it was overthrown in 1270 by Yakuno Amlak, who claimed to be a descendent of Menelik I, supposedly the son of the Queen of Sheba and King Solomon. The royal courts of medieval Ethiopia were nomadic, travelling through the empire and requiring up to 10,000 mules for transportation of their armies, courtiers, servants and everything else needed to keep the vast royal camp going. The peasants dreaded the arrival of the travelling court, as all the crops and resources of the area were consumed and exhausted by the rulers and their retinue.

In the 17th Century, Gonder was established as the first permanent capital of Ethiopia. For hundreds of years, impressive castles and palaces were built, but conspiracies, plotting, assassinations and civil wars resulted in Ethiopia disintegrating into rival fiefdoms, each with their own lords, and things remained like this until the mid-19th Century.

In 1855, Kassa Haylu, the son of a chief from western Ethiopia, gathered a large number of supporters by becoming a Robin Hood figure, stealing from the rich and giving to the poor. He gradually defeated the rival local princes, and crowned himself Emperor Tewodros in 1855. He proved himself a strong leader, as well as unifying the nation, but his success didn't last, and he was succeeded by Emperor Yohannes in 1871, who was confounded by the Italians arriving in Massawa in 1885, and was killed by a sniper's bullet in 1889.

Rival claimant to the throne, Menelik, made a bargain with the Italians by granting them the region to the north that is now Eritrea (including the capital Asmara, Massawa and Assab). Menelik founded Addis Ababa as the new capital, introducing telephones and electricity, and modern infrastructure such as banks, schools and hospitals, modernising the country until his death in 1913. He was succeeded by his grandson Iyasu, who continued with the reforms, but opposed the church by building mosques, and taking several Muslim wives. He was deposed in 1921for 'abjuring the Christian faith', and upsetting international relations.

Haile Selassie

Emperor Haile Selassie with his wife Empress Menen Awfar.

Menelik's daughter Zewditu was proclaimed empress in Iyasu's place, but she had a rival for the throne, Ras Tafari, the son of Menelik's cousin. A power-sharing agreement was reached, with Ras Tafari becoming the prince regent. In 1923, Ras Tafari secured Ethiopia's entry into the League of Nations, which helped the country to resist the European colonialism in surrounding countries.

In 1930, Ras Tafari was crowned, as Emperor Haile Selassie. The Emperor unified the whole country.

However, in 1935, the Mussolini-ruled Italians invaded Ethiopia. Haile Selassie fled Ethiopia and came to live in exile in Britain (in Bath). Meanwhile, the Ethiopian resistance grew, and Britain came to Ethiopia's defence with the outbreak of World War Two. The Emperor returned to Addis Ababa in May 1941, and in 1944, Ethiopia resumed its independence. At first, Ethiopia and Eritrea were joined in a federation sponsored by the United Nations, but Haile Selassie ended the federation in 1961and annexed Eritrea, and the war for Eritrean independence began. Eritrea finally gained independence in 1993.

In the 1940s and 50s, modernisation and reconstruction got underway in Ethiopia, but the pace of development was slow, with many parts of the country desperately poor and starving. In 1960, the emperor's own bodyguard staged a coup d'état, but it was suppressed by the armed forces. The students of Addis Ababa University also rebelled, but their rebellion was crushed by forces loyal to the emperor.

In 1973, the year I arrived in Ethiopia, tensions were beginning to grow again. The Derg (meaning committee) were undermining the power of Haile Selassie by exploiting the media , using footage of starving people from David Dimbleby's BBCTV report on the famine, with the images of banquets in palaces, just like the one that I attended in Massawa. Unrest grew, with the Air Force and the

Army mutinying, and strikes by workers and students in Addis Ababa. The elderly king was deposed and the Derg took over, led by Colonel Mengistu Haile Mariam.

The Red Terror

The Derg declared a socialist state in Ethiopia, and started nationalising farmland, industry and the infrastructure of the country. However, their new systems didn't work. Things were made worse by the continuing of fighting in Eritrea. Neighbouring Somalia invaded Ethiopia in 1977, but the Soviet Union backed Ethiopia and they managed to fight off the invasion.

The Derg collapsed in in-fighting and executions, and Mengistu sought to destroy any political opposition to his rule by proclaiming 'Death to counter revolutionaries'. Between 100,000 and 500,000 people were killed, with thousands more fleeing Ethiopia.

The Famine of 1984-1985

Between 400,000 and 1,000,000 people died in the terrible famine that was shown on our TV screens in 1984. The conditions that led to the famine were blamed on drought, but it was made much worse by the Derg government – rebellions and civil unrest were happening in many parts of the country, and the communal farms and resettlement of people established by the government failed.

The resistance to Mengistu's rule continued and united as the Ethiopian People's Revolutionary Democratic Front (the EPRDF), despite the military might of the Derg. Finally, Mengistu fled to Zimbabwe, and the EPRDF entered Addis Ababa.

Ethiopia began to move towards democracy.

Haile Selassie and Rastafarianism

Emperor Haile Selassie has a religion named after him, which needs a little explaining. In the 1920s, black political leader Marcus Garvey gathered popular support in Jamaica and the USA, and taught black people to empower themselves and to be proud of their race. He also believed that black people would one day be free of oppression in the lands where they were enslaved (known as Babylon) and would return to Africa (called Ethiopia) to live in freedom.

Marcus Garvey made a prophesy:

"Look to Africa where a black king shall be crowned, he shall be your Redeemer."

Shortly after this speech, Haile Selassie was crowned in 1930. Many of Marcus Garvey's followers saw this as the fulfilment of this prophesy, and they worshipped Haile Selassie as a figure of salvation and a living god, calling themselves Rastafarians, after Haile Selassie's birth name, Ras Tafari.

In 1966, Haile Selassie visited Jamaica to great enthusiasm. However, he did not regard himself as a living god, and was said to be a little embarrassed about it, although he didn't do much to dispel the Rastafarians' beliefs.

Some Rastafarians denied his death as 'lies of Babylon', an attempt to undermine the then rapidly growing Rastafarian movement, whereas others believe that his soul lives on.

Royal Remains

Crowds at Haile Selassie's funeral in 2000.

In 1992, following the failure of the Derg, Haile Selassie's remains were discovered, buried under a toilet in the Imperial Palace in Addis Ababa. His remains were transferred to the church of Ba'ata Mariam Geta.

The reburial of Haile Selassie's remains in Trinity Cathedral, Addis Ababa was agreed in 2000, where he would finally be laid to rest next to his wife and other members of the Ethiopian Imperial Family. The Ethiopian government refused to make the occasion a state funeral, accusing the late emperor of oppression and brutality during his 45 year rule.

However, it was still a proper burial ceremony, fit for a King, attended by thousands of people, including many dignitaries from around the world, dreadlocked Rastafarians (many of whom don't believe that Haile Selassie is really dead), elderly warriors from the days of the Emperor's reign and Ethiopian Orthodox Priests.

Further Reading and Information

I've only scratched the surface of Ethiopia's fascinating history in these pages.

Here are some recommended books and websites about Ethiopia:

Books:

A History of Ethiopia by Harold G Marcus – an eminently readable, concise history of the country.

The Emperor by Ryszard Kapuściński – fascinating interviews with ex-members of Haile Selassie's inner circle shortly after the coup.

The Lonely Planet Guide to Ethiopia, Djibouti & Somaliland – a practical guide to travel in Ethiopia, with insights into history, culture and its landscape.

Websites:

http://www.our-africa.org/ethiopia Films and information about Ethiopia made by children.

http://www.ethiopiantreasures.co.uk A wealth of information about Ethiopia.

http://www.lonelyplanet.com/ethiopia A guide to every aspect of Ethiopian life and culture.

Charities working in Ethiopia

Ethiopia is still one of the poorest nations in the world, although its economy is growing fast. The country faces many problems, such as one of the highest rates of maternal mortality in the world, and no state pensions or support for older people.

The following charities work with local communities in Ethiopia to transform the lives of ordinary people and to support the proud and determined people of Ethiopia.

http://ethiopiaid.org.uk

www.oxfam.org.uk/ethiopia

http://www.womenandchildrenfirst.org.uk

Printed in Great Britain
by Amazon